# The Upanishads

Shyam N. Shukla, Ph.D.

JAIN PUBLISHING COMPANY
Fremont, California

ISBN 0-87573-081-7

10 9 8 7 6 5 4 3 2 1

To

Adi Shankaracharya

The greatest teacher of the Vedanta

# CONTENTS

*Chhandogya Upanishad*

# FOREWORD

The Upanishads have been for thousands of years the most important source of Vedanta, the foremost mystical philosophical tradition of India. Kept secret for many centuries and taught only from guru to disciple, they became known to wider circles in the sixteenth century and now are available in translations in all the major languages of the world. There are several scholarly English translations of the Principal Upanishads available, such as the ones by R. H. Hume and S. Radhakrishnan, which are widely known. The present translation by Dr. Shyam N. Shukla stands out as being written by a practitioner of Upanishadic meditation and offering explanations for the general reader.

Dr. Shukla is by profession a structural engineer and is working presently at the Lawrence Livermore National Laboratory of the University of California. His background as a brahmin, who studied Sanskrit from childhood and who kept an active interest in the study of the *Bhagavadgita* and the Upanishads, qualifies him well for the stupendous task he has undertaken. He also serves as one of the Secretaries of the World Association of Vedic Studies, whose aim is to keep the Indian religious heritage alive throughout the world.

Readers of Dr. Shukla's *The Upanishads* will not only receive inspiration from the ancient text itself but will also be helped in their understanding by the Introduction and the comments of the translator. Since very few of the Indians now living in the West have a command of Sanskrit which would enable them to read their scriptures in the original, they will welcome such an authoritative translation into easily understandable English. I congratulate Dr. Shukla on his accomplishment and wish him success with this work.

Winnipeg, July 1, 1997

Klaus  Klostermaier
Professor and Chairman
Department of Religion
University of Manitoba

# INTRODUCTION

The principal objective of all the religions of the world is to make sure that their followers have a fulfilling life on this earth. If a person abides by certain laws of nature he would enjoy his life better here. If he leads a disciplined life he would be physically and emotionally stronger. With these basic principles in mind, the prophets or founders of the religions preached their messages. Their teachings, when written in the form of books, eventually became the scriptures of the religions. All the religions have one commonality. That is the concept of Heavens. If a person follows the dictates of religion he would be rewarded with a place in Heaven, where there is long-lasting peace and happiness. The Hindu religion did not have a prophet or a founder; however, it too has heaven and hell for good and evil people, respectively.

The Hindu sages did not feel content with the concept of Heaven as the ultimate goal. Like scientists they were very innovative people. They continued in their search for achieving freedom from the effect of time and space. They discovered that when a man identifies himself with his body, with all its limitations, then he is a tiny, weak and mortal creature in this vast universe. On the other hand, when he identifies himself with his inner self, the Atman, which is limitless, immortal and blissful, he achieves divinity in this very life. The Upanishads are collections of the teachings of the sages of ancient India, and they are unique gifts to this world. The Upanishadic teachings are not mere philosophical concepts but are realized facts experienced by our sages. Those teachings inspired when they were composed and they inspire even today, thousands of years later. They are as inspirational in America as they are in India. The Upanishads are beyond time and space.

### Veda and Vedanta

Each Veda *shakha* is divided into four parts, namely, the *Samhita*, the *Brahmana*, the *Aranyaka* , and the *Upanishad.* Since the Upanishads occur at the end of the Vedas they are called the Vedanta, which literally means "the end of the Vedas." The ultimate goal of the Vedas is contained in the Upanishads. Also because they are the end products of the Vedas, they are appropriately called the Vedanta. The part of a Veda where there are methods of rituals and sacrifices is the *Karmakanda*, and the part where the supreme knowledge of the Vedanta is dealt with is the *Jnanakanda*.

Western scholars have tried to establish the time when the Vedas and the Upanishads were written. The estimate ranges from 3000 B.C. to 1500 B.C. According to Bal Gangadhar Tilak the Vedas came into existence around 6000 B.C. However, according to one school of traditional Vedic scholars, the Vedas are considered *anadi* or without beginning. It is stated in the Vedas that they are vast and endless (*ananta vai Vedah*). They are also without human authorship (*apaurusheya*). What we have is a small portion of what God created as the Vedas. A portion of what was revealed to the *Rishis* is available to us today. Therefore, a Rishi who wrote down an Upanishad or a shakha of a Veda, is not its creator or *karta* but is its seer or *drishta*.

It was the sage Vyasa who organized the Vedas and wrote the *Bhagavadgita* and *Brahmasutra*, which made it possible for scholars to know how deep the philosophy of the Upanishads is. In the *Bhagavadgita* Vyasa put the essence of the Upanishads in the form of a conversation between Arjuna, the disciple, and Lord Krishna, the teacher. About 1200 years ago, when the Vedic knowledge was in danger of extinction, Adi Shankaracharya (788-820 A.D.) came as a teacher of the era (*yuga pravartaka*). He wrote commentaries to the *Bhagavadgita, Brahmasutra* and some principal Upanishads. Only then did the mystic knowledge of the Vedanta become easier to comprehend for others.

However, mere study of the Upanishads is not enough to fathom the depth of the philosophy or to achieve the supreme knowledge which is their main theme. In the *Chhandogya Upanishad* there is a story of Narada who approached Sanatkumara and said that he had studied all the scriptures and all the sciences and arts. He knew only the mantras but he had no knowledge of the Atman (*Mantravideva asmi na atmavid*). The Upanishads have to be studied at the feet of a *Brahmajnani* teacher (a teacher who has achieved Brahman). That is why it is called the Upanishad, which literally means "to sit near (with devotion)." It also means "secret teachings." When a student studies in a *Gurukul,* the mystic knowledge permeates into the student's mind by the subtle manner in which the teacher explains the subject, by merely observing his daily *sadhana* and his way of life. The teacher imparts the secret knowledge of Brahman only to those students who are spiritually ready for it. That is why the *Katha Upanishad* says:

"To many, mere hearing about that Self is not available, and many who can hear about It find it difficult to comprehend It. Wonderful is the expounder and also wonderful is the receiver of that knowledge. Wonderful indeed is he who understands It when taught by an adept preceptor." [*Katha Upanishad,* 1.2.7]

The Upanishads mention that the meditation on "Om" is the meditation on the Atman or Brahman which resides within a man. The *Chhandogya Upanishad* says that all the sacrifices prescribed in the Vedas cannot bring salvation. It is meditation on *Om* that leads one, step by step, to the highest object of the Upanishads, that is, the realization of Brahman.

### Do the Vedas and Vedanta Contradict Each Other?

Some people believe that the Vedas and Vedanta clash with each other. To prove their point they quote Lord Krishna. In the *Gita* Lord Krishna says:

"O Partha, those who follow the words of the Vedas literally and say that there is nothing other than this, are full of desire to dwell in Heaven, which leads to new birth as a result of their actions." (*Gita* 2.42-43)

Also,

"O Arjuna, the Vedas deal with the three gunas (*satva, raja and tama*). You should transcend these three gunas." (*Gita* 2.45)

These verses give an impression that Lord Krishna encourages us to follow the teachings of the Upanishads directly, and ignore the rituals prescribed in the Vedas. The traditional *Vedantis* (scholars of the Vedanta) tell us that jumping to the study of the Upanishads directly, without preliminary preparation of purifying the mind and body does not help a student to realize Atman. The mind and body are disciplined by the *yajnas* and worship prescribed in the Vedas. Only after undergoing that discipline are we qualified to take up the study of the Upanishads. When the mind is purified by yajnas, then the world around us ceases to be real. Then all the actions we perform become yajnas and we are no more separate from Brahman. Then we are ready to merge in Him. That is why Adi Shankaracharya tells us in his book, *Sopana Panchaka*, that first we must study and recite the Vedas, perform the prescribed rituals, be guided by the *Mahavakyas*, meditate on them constantly, and then only try to reach Brahman. (We will discuss the Mahavakyas in a later paragraph). The fact that the seers of the Upanishads quoted hymns from the Vedas in support of their teachings shows that they were not against the Vedas.

The reason why Lord Krishna says the above about the Vedas has to be understood in the context of the *Mahabharata* period. During those days a majority of the people performed yajnas as a means to achieve worldly and heavenly pleasures. They behaved as if that was the ultimate teaching of the Vedas. They almost ignored the teachings of the Upanishads, that realization of Brahman is the ultimate goal in their lives. Lord Krishna has chastised those people in the *Gita*. He rebuked those who took the *Karma* path and did not go beyond it to adopt the *Jnana* path in their lives. He would have certainly taken to task those also who would directly go to study the Upanishads without performing the Vedic Karmas.

Even in the time of Shankaracharya many great scholars specialized only in the Karma path of the Vedas. Mandana Mishra, a famous Vedic scholar of Varanasi, was a staunch follower of *Purva Mimamsa* (scholarly analysis of the *Karmakanda* of the Vedas) before he became a disciple of Shankaracharya. After he entered *Sannyasa Ashrama* and became Sureshvaracharya he shifted from *karma* to the *jnana* path. He wrote the *Varttika* (explanation) of the Shankara Bhashya on the *Brahmasutra*.

### The Principal Upanishads

It is believed that there are about two hundred Upanishads. However, only one hundred and eighty-eight have been preserved. The principal Upanishads are those which Adi Shankaracharya selected to comment upon. They are ten in number and are traditionally studied in a certain order. The following *shloka* (Sanskrit verse) enumerates the principal Upanishads in that order:

*Isha Kena Katha Prashna Munda Mandukya Taittiri
Aitareyam cha Chhandogyam Brihadaranyakam Dasha*

"Isha, Kena, Katha, Prashna, Mundaka, Mandukya, Taittiriya,
Aitareya, Chhandogya and Brihadaranyaka are the ten (principal)
Upanishads."

Shankaracharya also commented on an eleventh Upanishad,
the *Shvetashvatara.* In his commentary on the *Brahmasutra* he has
made references to four more Upanishads. They are: *Kaushitaki,
Jabala, Mahanarayana,* and *Paingala.* Here is a brief description
of the ten principal Upanishads.

***Ishavasya Upanishad:*** Usually the Upanishads appear at the
end of an Aranyaka. As an exception this Upanishad appears in the
Samhita portion of the *Shukla Yajurveda.* The very opening verse of
this Upanishad contains the central theme of all the Upanishads. It
says that Ishvara or God pervades the whole universe and we
should realize Him by offering the fruits of all our actions to Him.
Offering the fruits of action to Brahman is *Karmayoga* in a nutshell.
This is the first time that the principle of Karmayoga is introduced in
the Upanishads. Only in the *Gita* do we see its more elaborate form.

***Kena Upanishad:*** It is also called *Talavakara Upanishad* because it occurs in the *Talavakara Brahmana* of the Jaimini Shakha
of the *Sama Veda.* This Upanishad teaches through an allegorical
story, that all our powers are derived from the *Mahashakti,* the
Supreme God or the *Paramatma.* The Paramatma is without beginning or end.

***Katha Upanishad:*** The *Katha Upanishad* occurs in the Katha
Shakha of the *Krishna Yajurveda.* This Upanishad became very
popular for its fascinating story of young Nachiketa going to Yama,
the God of Death, and asking him to teach him about what happens
to the soul after one's death. Yama then tells him about the true
nature of the soul or the *Atman.* It defines Atman as divine, without
birth and death, indestructible, etc.

***Prashna Upanishad:*** This belongs to the *Atharva Veda.* As
the name implies (*prashna* means question), this answers six

questions on: how creation began; who are the devas; how does life become connected to the body; what is the truth about the states of waking, sleep, and dreaming; why should one worship Omkara; and what is the relationship between *Purusha* and *Jiva.*

**Mundaka Upanishad:** This Upanishad, too, is from the *Atharva Veda.* "Mundaka" means shaven head. Its teachings are meant for the *Sannyasis* or monks who are free from worldly attachment. It talks of *Akshara Brahman* which is free from destruction. It classifies the knowledge into *para*, higher, and *apara*, lower. The knowledge of Atman is para and all other knowledge is apara.

**Mandukya Upanishad:** This is the third Upanishad from the *Atharva Veda.* "Manduka" means a frog. This Upanishad shows the way to pass the three stages of waking, dream, and dreamless sleep, and reach the fourth stage of *Turiya* in one leap. Turiya is the stage of pure consciousness which reveals the Atman.

**Taittiriya Upanishad:** This is the most widely studied Upanishad. Its first part, *Shikshavalli*, teaches the self-control involved in Brahmacharya, the order in which the Vedas should be studied, the worship of Pranava, etc. The precepts such as, "speak the truth," "follow the dharma," "treat mother, father and teacher as divinities," appear in this part. Its second part, *Anandavalli*, describes how there is an ascending order of bliss, starting from that of a human being and culminating in Brahmananda. *Bhriguvalli*, the third part, is what Varuna taught to his son, Bhrigu.

**Aitareya Upanishad:** This Upanishad occurs in the *Rigveda.* It talks about how a Jiva (soul) takes birth again and again according to sin and merit, and how liberation from birth and death is possible only through the realization of the true nature of the Atman. The Upanishad proclaims that thought (*Prajna*) itself is Brahman.

**Chhandogya Upanishad:** The last two Upanishads, namely, the *Chhandogya* and the *Brihadaranyaka*, are large in size. The *Chhandogya Upanishad* appears in the *Chhandogya Brahmana* of the *Sama Veda.* "Chhandogya" means one who sings the "sama gana" (the singing of the *Sama Veda* hymns, which are the source of Indian classical music, praising all the gods). This Upanishad introduces us to devout truth-seekers like Satyakama, Shvetaketu and Narada, and learned spiritual teachers like Aruni, Sanatkumara and Prajapati. The Upanishad teaches that there is no difference between the Atman within a person and Brahman. It tells us how, starting from purity of food and going up to purity of mind and soul, we reach a stage when we get rid of all bonds and achieve Atmananda (bliss).

***Brihadaranyaka Upanishad*:** "Brihad" means large, and "Aranyaka" means forest. As its name suggests this is the largest of all the Upanishads, and it is a forest of spiritual inspiration and thoughts. Usually the Upanishads appear at the end of an Aranyaka, as mentioned earlier. The entire Aranyaka of the *Shukla Yajurveda* forms the *Brihadaranyaka Upanishad*. (The Samhita of the *Shukla Yajus* contains the *Isha Upanishad*). We learn of two Kshatriya kings, namely, Ajatashatru and Janaka, who were well versed in the Vedantic philosophy. Then there is an interesting anecdote and philosophical dialogue of Sage Yajnavalkya and his learned wife Maitreyi. Yajnavalkya says that the nature of the Atman is love and happiness. The Upanishad expounds the central theme of all the Upanishads, that man is divine and that this whole universe is Brahman.

## The Four *Mahavakyas*

There are four *Mahavakyas*, or "great statements," in the Upanishads. An Upanishad from each of the four Vedas proclaims boldly the ultimate conclusion of its philosophy, in the form of a Mahavakya. The *Aitareya Upanishad* of the *Rigveda* proclaims, *Prajnanam Brahma*—"Brahman is pure consciousness." The *Brihadaranyaka Upanishad* of the *Shukla Yajurveda* says, *Aham Brahmasmi*—"I am Brahman." The Mahavakya of the *Chhandogya Upanishad* of the *Samaveda* is, *Tat Tvamasi*—"You are That." Here "That" means Brahman, according to the language of the Upanishads. Finally, the *Mandukya Upanishad* of the *Atharvaveda* proclaims as a Mahavakya, *Ayamatma Brahma*—"This Atman is Brahman."

This kind of bold proclamation, that a human being has the Atman (the soul) within him or her which is none other than the Supreme Brahman Himself, is unparalleled in the history of religions anywhere other than in the Vedas.

## Peace Invocation

The mind, if full of lust, cannot grasp the depth of spiritual philosophy. The peace invocations in the Upanishads are meant to purify and calm the minds of the pupil and the preceptor of the Brahmavidya. The refreshed and peaceful mind is then equiped to impart or receive the deep spiritual philosophy which is to be discussed ahead. That is why each Upanishad starts with a peace invocation.

## The Concept of *Brahman* in the Upanishads

It is very difficult to describe Brahman or the Supreme God in words. That is why it is said: *Ekam Sat, vipra bahudha vadanti,* or, "Truth is one, the wise speak of It in different ways." Devotees usually heap many highest human qualities on God to describe Him. Even then they are unable to describe Him adequately, and end up making Him human-like. The Rishis finally gave up human-like descriptions of Brahman and described Him by saying, "Not this, not this." In the Upanishads Brahman is compared to a spider, and His creation with the spider's cobweb, which comes out of it. The whole universe comes out of Brahman, who resides in the center of it. The Atman residing within the body is Brahman too. The *Taittiriya Upanishad* says, "Brahman is That from which these beings are born, That by which they live when born, and That into which they enter on passing away." There is a subtle difference between God (Ishvara) and Brahman. Ishvara is God when viewed through human eyes, in relation to the universe. It is then *Saguna* (with form) Brahman. When Brahman is God as He is and viewed independently, He is Brahman, or *Nirguna* Brahman, or God without form. Some sages believed that the best way of indicating Brahman is by silence.

## Conclusion

The Upanishads form the *Jnanakanda,* or the portion dealing with the supreme knowledge, of the Vedas. They contain the ultimate messages of the Vedas. They tell us that a human being is not only made up of a body which is subject to old age, decay and death, but also of Atman within it, which is divine, eternal and blissful. A person can realize the Atman by meditating on Om, the symbol of the Supreme God, and can become immortal and blissful in this very life.

****

# GLOSSARY

| | |
|---|---|
| Acharya | A teacher, guru |
| Adhidaivata | Related to the gods |
| Adhvaryu | The priest performing yajna |
| Adhyatma | Related to Atman, related to the body |
| Aditya | The sun, son of Aditi (daughter of Daksha, one of the Prajapatis) |
| Advaita | Non-dual |
| Agni | Fire |
| Agnidhriya | The southern fire (Dakshinagni) |
| Ahavaniya | A kind of fire maintained by performers of yajna |
| Akasha | The sky |
| Akshara | That which does not perish or change |
| Ananda | Bliss |
| Anandamaya | Made of bliss |
| Annamaya | Made of food |
| Anvaharya | A fire maintained by performers of yajna |
| Aparavidya | Knowledge or science related to other things than that of Brahman |

| | |
|---|---|
| Aranyaka | Forest |
| Aryama | One of the twelve Adityas |
| Ashrama | Residence of a Rishi for spiritual practice |
| Ashvamedha-yajna | Horse-sacrifice |
| Ashvin | The two Ashvin brothers were the physicians of the gods |
| *Atharvaveda* | The Veda containing mantras to ward off yajna evil and hardship |
| Atman | The divine and infinite Self within a person |
| Brahma | One of the trinity of gods (Brahma, Vishnu and Mahesh), and the creator of the universe |
| Brahma (priest) | The superintending priest |
| Brahmacharya | Seeking Brahman by leading a celibate life |
| Brahmajnana | Knowledge of Brahman |
| Brahman | The Supreme Being |
| Brahmana | One who is a seeker of Brahman, the caste of priests |
| *Brahmasutra* | The aphoristic text on Vedanta written by Vyasa |
| Brahmavidya | The knowledge which leads to the recognition of Brahman |
| Brihaspati | The preceptor of the gods |
| Buddhi | Intellect |

| | |
|---|---|
| Charvaka | An agnostic philosopher of ancient India. |
| Chhanda | Meter or rythmic pattern of a musical song |
| Dakshinagni | The southern fire (maintained in the south end of the house) |
| Dama | Self-restraint |
| Dvaita | Dual |
| Gandharva | The divine singers in the court of Indra |
| Garhapatya | A fire maintained by a householder |
| Garuda | A divine bird used by Lord Vishnu for his transportation |
| Gayatri | The most sacred Vedic mantra |
| *Gita* | Also called *Bhagavadgita*, which is sermons by Lord Krishna to Arjuna in the *Mahabharata* war |
| Gotra | Lineage, family name |
| Gunas | Every one has a combination of three kinds of gunas or traits, namely, *satvik, rajasik* and *tamasik*. Satvik is of the highest (saintly) quality, rajasik is of the medium (kingly) quality, and tamasik is of the lowest (undesirable) quality |
| Gurukul | House of a preceptor where a disciple stays to get education |
| Hiranyagarbha | Prajapati or Brahma, when he identifies himself with the sum total of subtle bodies in the universe |

| | |
|---|---|
| Hotri | The presiding or invoking priest in the yajna |
| Hridayakasha | Imaginary cavity in the chest where the Atman resides |
| Indra | The king of the gods |
| Ishana | Lord Shiva; one of the Rudras; the north-east direction |
| Jagati | A Vedic mantra chanted in the Soma yajna |
| Jiva/Jivatman | The finite self of a man |
| Jnana | The supreme knowledge of Brahman |
| Jnanakanda | The part of a Veda dealing with the knowledge of Brahman |
| Jnanayoga | The yoga of knowledge about Brahman |
| Karma | Action or work done by us which shapes our fate |
| Karmakanda | The part of a Veda where there are methods of rituals and sacrifices |
| Karmayoga | The yoga of action, which teaches that we should do necessary work skillfully but without attachment to it or its result |
| Kosha | Sheath |
| Kshatriya | A caste of kings and warriors, next to Brahmana |
| Kusha | A kind of grass used during worship of deities |

| | |
|---|---|
| Madhu-vidya | Brahma-vidya, knowledge to achieve Brahman |
| *Mahabharata* | An epic of which the *Gita* forms a part. It describes the war between two sets of cousins, the Kauravas and Pandavas |
| Mahat | The cosmic mind |
| Mahavakyas | The great declarations or utterances of the Vedas |
| Manomaya | Made of mind |
| Mantra | Sacred syllables or words which are very potent |
| *Manusmriti* | The code of conduct written by King Manu |
| Maya | The creation of Brahman; illusion |
| Mimamsa | Scholarly analysis of the Karmakanda portion of the Vedas |
| Mitra | One of the twelve Adityas |
| Muni | A man of knowledge |
| Nirguna | Unmanifested form, without "gunas" |
| Om | The syllable which represents Brahman/ Atman, also called Pranava |
| Panchamahabhuta | The five elements, which our body is made of, namely, earth, water, air, fire and ether |
| Paramatman | The Supreme Being |
| Paravidya | The supreme knowledge about Brahman/ Atman |

| | |
|---|---|
| Parjanya | The god of rain |
| Pipal | A sacred large tree like a banyan tree |
| Pitri | Father, forefather, mane |
| Prajapati | The Creator, who attains this status after being purified by Vedic knowledge in his past life |
| Prajnana | Knowledge |
| Prakriti | Nature |
| Prana | The vital energy, breath. (According to ancient Indians there are five Pranas or breaths in different parts of the body, namely, Prana in the respiratory system, Apana in the bladder and colon, Samana in the digestive system, Udana in the vocal system, and Vyana in blood circulation and nerve currents.) |
| Pranamaya | Made of Prana |
| Pranava | See "Om" |
| Pranayama | Control of breath |
| Prastotri | The priest who chants the Prastava part of the Saman |
| Pratihartri | The priest who chants the Pratihara Saman |
| Purusha | A person; Brahman |
| Pusha | The god of the earth |
| Pushan | One who nourishes |

| | |
|---|---|
| Rajasuya-yajna | The yajna performed by kings to win more kingdoms |
| Rayi | The moon; food |
| *Rigveda* | The oldest Veda, containing verses of prayers |
| Rik (Rig) | Hymn |
| Rudra | Lord Shiva |
| Sadhaka | One who does practices for spiritual achievement |
| Sadhana | Practice for spiritual achievement |
| Saguna | Manifested form |
| Saman | The melodious mantras from the *Samaveda* |
| *Samaveda* | The Veda in which the hymns of the *Rigveda* are set in melodious songs. This Veda is also the source of the Indian classical music |
| Samhita | The portion of a Veda which has prayers |
| Sannyasa | Renunciation |
| Sannyasi(n) | One who has renounced the world |
| Shakha | A branch of a Veda |
| Shantipatha | Peace invocation |
| Shiksha | Education, teachings |
| Shudra | A caste consisting of service class people |

| | |
|---|---|
| Somayaga | A yajna performed every quarter, in which a drink of Soma juice was taken |
| Stoma | Hymn |
| Stotra | Verses of praise |
| Sushumna | A hollow canal running along the spinal cord |
| Taijas | Luminous, brilliant |
| Tapa | Penance |
| Trishtubha | A potent Vedic mantra chanted in the Somayaga |
| Turiya | The state of self-realization |
| Udgatri | The priest who chants the Udgitha Saman mantras |
| Udgitha | Saman mantras |
| Uma | The goddess Parvati, wife of Lord Shiva |
| Upanishad | Sacred teachings about Brahman, in the last part (Jnanakanda) of the Vedas |
| Vaishvanara | Universal Person |
| Vaishya | A caste of businessmen and landowners |
| Valli | A vine |
| Varna | Color; caste based on nature of work |
| Varttika | Explanation |
| Varuna | The god of water; one of the twelve Adityas |

| | |
|---|---|
| Vasus | A class of gods |
| Vayu | Air, wind |
| Veda | The ancient Hindu scripture containing knowledge of Brahman |
| Vedanta | The last portion of the Vedas, where the Upanishads occur |
| Vijnana | The knowledge about the Supreme Being; intellect |
| Vijnanamaya | Made of knowledge |
| Vishvadeva | A class of gods |
| Vishvajit | A kind of yajna (sacrifice) which is performed to achieve heavenly rewards |
| Vyahriti | The mantra containing the names of the seven mystical worlds: Bhuh, Bhuvah, Svah, Mahah, Janah, Tapah and Satyam |
| Yajna | Sacrifice, performance of Vedic rituals described in the Karmakanda of the Vedas to achieve some worldly rewards |
| *Yajurveda* | The Veda containing mantras to perform yajnas |
| Yaksha | A venerable being, a race superior to humans |
| Yama | The god of death; some qualities of a yogi which include truthfulness, nonviolence, non-stealing, etc. |
| Yoga | Union with Brahman with steady control of the sense organs |

Yogi(n)            One who unites with Brahman

Yuga-pravartaka    A person of an era who shows a new path to
                   the people

# *Ishavasya Upanishad*

## Introduction

The *Ishavasya* or *Isha Upanishad* derives its name from the opening words of its first mantra (verse), "Ishavasyamidam sarvam . . ." (All the things in this universe are enveloped by the Lord . . .). Traditionally this is the first Upanishad which is taught to a student of Vedanta, perhaps because of its deep spiritual content. This Upanishad has a peace invocation, like all other Upanishads, followed by eighteen verses. Some of the verses, particularly the ninth through fourteenth, are very difficult to translate, because literal translation makes hardly any sense. Therefore, the interpretations of distinguished commentators, like Acharya Shankara, have been used in deciphering the true meaning of the verses.

This is the only Upanishad which forms part of a "Samhita." It is actually the last chapter of *Shukla-Yajurveda Samhita.* Generally, the Upanishads occur in the Aranyaka portion of the Vedas.

The Upanishad can be divided into four themes or parts. The first part consists of the first three mantras, which tell us that the God pervades everything in this universe, and therefore, everything here belongs to Him. We should try to live with whatever is necessary to sustain life and not try to collect wealth. This, of course, is the required code of conduct for the sannyasins (monks). For the householders the second mantra has this advice: "Do your works but do not get attached to them or their fruits." This is what is the central idea of "karma-yoga" in the *Bhagavadgita.* Then it says: "Doing something against your conscience is like killing your inner self." Mantras (verses) four through eight make the second part of the Upanishad. Here an attempt has been made to describe the nature of the Atman. It also describes the state of self-realization. Then, mantras nine through thirteen make the third part, where there is a reconciliation of some contradictions. The Upanishad tries to say in some mystical terms that those who are contented with the theoretical knowledge of God are ignorant. Those who perform only rituals and never strive to know their real significance are somewhat superior. Only those who are striving to unite with the Atman are wise people. The fourth part is made by mantras fourteen through eighteen. It has a prayer by a dying devotee to the Lord. There is a belief that whatever a person has in mind at the time of his death, he attains it. Therefore, the devotee wishes to merge with Brahman. It has become a tradition that the prayers in the last four mantras to the sun and fire are repeated by the relatives of a dying person.

### Peace Invocation

The peace invocation states the central theme of all the Upanishads: The visible universe is full (infinite) and has come out of the invisible Brahman, which is also full (infinite). Even though the universe is of an infinite extension it came out of Brahman, which still remains infinite. Om. Peace, Peace, Peace.

(This is what the mathematical science tells us too, that an infinite entity remains infinite even though we take an infinity out of it. The peace invocation underscores two characteristics of Brahman, namely, that Brahman, the creator of this universe, is ever of infinite dimensions, and that everything in this universe came out of Him, just like a cobweb comes out of a spider.)

***

Everything in this ephemeral world belongs to the Lord, because the whole universe came out of Him. He pervades everything in the universe. Therefore, enjoy the world by renouncing materialistic desires. Do not crave for any kind of possessions. [1]

(This first mantra [verse] sounds like a corollary of the peace invocation. It, of course, is the path of knowledge or "jnana-yoga" suitable for sannyasins or monks.)

Enjoy this life for a hundred years, but only by performing actions. In addition, do not be attached to your actions. [2]

(This mantra talks about an alternative path, the path of action or "karma-yoga," which is more suitable for a householder. In the scriptures this is the earliest mention of "action-without-attachment." Later, it was further expanded by Lord Krishna in the *Bhagavadgita*, or *Gita*, and was called "karma-yoga." Lord Krishna says in the *Gita*, too, that He has shown two paths to achieve divinity, namely, jnana-yoga [yoga of knowledge] for intellectuals and karma-yoga [yoga of action] for active ones [*Gita* 3.3].)

People who are ignorant and devoid of knowledge of the Atman go to the joyless worlds covered with blinding darkness, after their death. [3]

(See *Brihadaranyaka Upanishad* 4.4.11)

The same Atman dwells in every being. It is unmoving and yet It is faster than the mind. Since It is faster than the mind, It is naturally beyond the reach of the senses. Ever steady It travels, faster than anything that moves. Because of Its presence, the air carries the water (in the form of clouds) and sustains the activities of living beings. [4]

That Atman moves and It moves not. It is far and yet It is near. It is within all beings and It is also outside of them. [5]

(It may be mentioned here that it is very difficult to describe the nature of the Atman. Language fails to articulate It. The seer who realizes the Atman merely gives hints or suggestions about Its nature.)

He is a wise man who sees all beings in his own Self and his Self in all beings. He has hatred for none. What delusion and what sorrow could there be for that wise man who perceives all beings as his own Self, thus realizing unity of existence? [6, 7]

The Atman is self-sufficient, is everywhere, without a body, without blemish, radiant, pure, knowing all, seeing all and encompassing all. He has duly assigned their respective duties to the Prajapatis. [8]

In the mantras nine through eleven, the term "vidya" means the knowledge of Atman, the changeless reality; and the term "avidya" refers to the knowledge of the changeful universe, which we laboriously build up from our childhood.

Those who are devoted to "avidya" eventually enter into blinding darkness. But those who are engaged in mere theoretical

knowledge of the Atman, without trying to realize It, enter into even greater darkness. [9]
   (See *Brihadaranyaka Upanishad* 4.4.10)

"Vidya" or knowledge brings quite a different result than "avidya" (pure rituals) or ignorance. However, he who understands vidya and avidya, both together, attains immortality through vidya after having conquered death by avidya. [10, 11]
   (It may be mentioned here that "avidya" is also all other physical sciences which, when mastered, can help a person manipulate the laws of nature in the interest of a richer and fuller life. This way, death of the physical body can be avoided for a longer time to achieve a richer spiritual life.)

   In the mantras twelve through fourteen, the term "sambhuti" stands for "pure Being," that is "Brahman," and "asambhuti" is used for "Prakriti" (nature) or "Maya" or the non-intelligent first cause of the universe in the state of equilibrium, before the creation.

   Those who worship the asambhuti enter into blind darkness (because the worship of the materialistic world leads one away from spiritual enlightenment). Into even greater darkness do they enter who delight in sambhuti or Brahman. [12]
   (The second part of the mantra sounds unbelievably inconsistent, just like the second part of the ninth mantra. But what is meant here is that the pursuit of Brahman is fraught with dangers. The path of negation or "nivritti" and the path of inaction, as the path of sannyasa may be misinterpreted, may lead one not to fulfillment of life but to negation of life.)

   Each of these paths brings a definite result based on limited and inadequate views of reality. However, one who knows both sambhuti (Brahman) and "vinasha" (the perishable world), both together, overcomes death through the knowledge of the world, and achieves immortality through the knowledge of Brahman. [13, 14]

   The last four mantras, fifteen through eighteen, are the prayers of a seeker of Brahman, who is nearing the end of his life. The sun who nourishes the world, is the source of light and energy for the whole solar system, and represents Brahman in the Vedic literature. That is why the Gayatri mantra, which is the prayer of Brahman, sounds like the prayer of the Sun god. Therefore, the dying seeker of Brahman, as if addressing the sun, says:

O Sun, like a shining golden lid you have, as it were, covered the entrance of the Truth (Brahman) within you. Please remove it so that I, a devotee of Brahman, may see Him. [15]

O offspring of Prajapati, O lonely courser of the heavens, O supporter and controller of all, contract your rays, withdraw your brightness, so that I may see your most auspicious form. [16]

That Person who dwells within you, I am indeed He. My breath is about to merge in the cosmic energy and my mortal body is about to be reduced to ashes. At this juncture, Om! O mind, remember my good deeds only. [17]

(It is believed that whatever thoughts enter the mind of a dying person, his future life is shaped accordingly, to some extent. That is why it is emphasized that one should dwell on good thoughts and particularly fix one's mind on God.)

The last verse is prayer to Agni, the fire god. The dying devotee offers prayers to the burning fire:

O Agni, lead us by the good path so that we may enjoy the fruits of the good deeds we have done. Destroy all the deceitful sins in us. We salute you with words again and again. [18]

*****

# Kena Upanishad

## Introduction

Like the *Isha Upanishad,* the *Kena Upanishad* also derives its name from the very first word (*kena*) of the opening verse. "Kena" in Sanskrit means "by whom." In the first verse a curious student asks his teacher some questions. One of the questions he asks is, "By whom is the mind directed to think?" The Upanishad forms part of the *Talavakara-Brahmana* of the Jaimini Shakha (branch) of the *Samaveda.* That is why it is also called the *Talavakara Upanishad.*

The Upanishad has a "shantipatha" or peace invocation followed by thirty-four mantras divided into four chapters.

The mantras of the first two chapters are in verses and the remaining are in prose form. The central idea of this Upanishad is that Brahman is verily the source of all vital energies in this universe. The Upanishad, in its first and second chapters, tells us that speech and mind cannot comprehend Brahman. Then in the third chapter, with the help of an allegorical story, the Upanishad emphasizes the same theme. In the story Agni, the god of speech, and Vayu, the god of skin (touch) both failed to recognize Brahman who appeared as a *yaksha,* a venerable person. When Agni and Vayu returned baffled, not recognizing Brahman, Indra representing the Jiva or self, tries to identify the yaksha. But the yaksha disappears from the scene. Finally, Uma appears and tells Indra that the yaksha was none other than Brahman Himself. This signifies that Brahman and Jiva (the finite self of a man) are not two separate identities but are one and the same. This sense of unity comes through knowledge, represented by the grace of Uma.

## Peace Invocation

Om. May my limbs, speech, Prana, sight, hearing and all the sense organs be strong. Everything is Brahman revealed in the

Upanishads. May I never deny Brahman and may Brahman never deny me. Let there be no rejection of Brahman by me and may Brahman never reject me. May all the virtues spoken of in the Upanishads reside in me, who is devoted to the Atman. Om. Peace, Peace, Peace.

(The seeker of Brahman knows that he can achieve Brahman with sound mind only, and that sound mind needs a sound body. Therefore, he prays for strong body and sense organs. Then he prays for his greatest desire, that his mind may always be devoted to Brahman and that Brahman may never reject him.)

***

## Chapter 1

In the first mantra of the first chapter the student asks the teacher: "Directed by whom does the mind think, impelled by whom does Prana, or vital force, function, and willed by which god does speech utter, eyes see and the ears hear?" [1.1]

The student has valid questions and wants to find out what controls our sense organs. Is it the body, is it nature or is it some god? The teacher replies in the second mantra:

It is the Atman, the Self, which is the ear of the ear, mind of the mind, speech of the speech, life of life and eye of the eye. Therefore, wise men, after separating the Self from these sense organs and by renouncing the world, become immortal. [1.2]

It is implied here that the sense organs work as long as the Jiva or Atman is in the body. After death, when the Atman leaves the body, the sense organs don't function. The Atman, however, is beyond description. The teacher continues in the third mantra:

The Atman cannot be seen by the eyes, cannot be described by speech and is beyond all imaginations of the mind. We do not know It and, therefore, we do not know how to teach about the Atman. [1.3]

The teacher has realized the Atman, yet he is finding it difficult to tell the student what It is like. What humility! He does not hesitate to confess to the student that he does not know exactly how to teach him about the Atman. He further says in the fourth mantra:

Even the ancient teachers have said that the Atman is beyond all the known and the unknown. [1.4]

After having expressed the inability of describing the Atman the teacher talks about It in an indirect way:

What speech cannot reveal but what reveals the speech, what mind does not comprehend but what comprehends the mind, what eyes fail to see but what sees the activities of the eyes, what hearing fails to hear but what hears the hearing, what smell does not reveal but what reveals the smell, know that alone as Brahman and not what people worship as an object. [1.5]

In the Upanishads there is the concept of the unity of Atman and Brahman. So while talking about the Atman the teacher is now talking about Brahman and yet there is no change of the subject, because they are one and the same.

What mind cannot comprehend, but what comprehends the mind, know that alone as Brahman and not what people worship as an object. [1.6]

What sight cannot see but what sees the sight, know that alone as Brahman and not what people worship as an object. [1.7]

What hearing cannot hear but what hears the hearing, know that alone as Brahman and not what people worship as an object. [1.8]

What smell cannot reveal but what reveals the smell, know that alone as Brahman and not what people worship as an object. [1.9]

(The teacher says ". . . know that alone as Brahman and not what people worship as an object." On this, Swami Ranganathananda says, in his commentary [*The Message of the Upanishads*, Bombay: Bharatiya Vidya Bhavan, p. 216], "These verses also stress the need to go beyond all idolatry in order to be able to worship God in spirit and in truth. Vedanta treats as idolatry not only the worship of sticks and stones, which Semitic monotheism condemns as heathen superstition, but also the Semitic monotheistic personal God.")

## Chapter 2

The teacher continues his lecture to the student. He says, in the first mantra of this second chapter:

If you think you have known Brahman well enough, then you know little indeed. The form of Brahman that you see as conditioned in the human beings and in the celestial beings is but a trifle (because Brahman is infinite and beyond sight, hearing and description). Therefore, you should still further inquire about Brahman. [2.1]

The disciple reflected on what the teacher told him about Brahman and replied: I think I have understood Brahman. I don't think I know It well nor do I think that I don't know It. Anyone amongst my fellow students who really understands Brahman can only say thus about It. (The knowledge of Brahman is not the knowledge of things objective. Brahman is the eternal subject.) [2.2]

The Upanishad itself clarifies the student's statement, in this mantra thus: He knows Brahman who conceives It not, and he knows It not who conceives It. To the person of true knowledge It remains the unknown, while to the ignorant It is the known. [2.3]

The essence of what the disciple says in the third mantra is this:

A concept of Brahman is not Brahman. Therefore, when a person thinks that he/she knows Brahman, only the concept of Brahman has been formed in his/her mind. He/she does not know Brahman truly. On the other hand, when one truly knows It, one realizes that one cannot know It through one's sense organs or mind.

Brahman is known through knowledge and awareness. By the Atman one obtains strength and vigor and through Its knowledge, immortality. [2.4]

If one realizes Brahman in this life, then one has seen the truth. But for one who has not realized It, life is in vain. The wise ones, having realized Brahman in all beings, after departing this world, become immortal. [2.5]

## Chapter 3

In this chapter the Upanishad fortifies the above concept about Brahman through an allegorical story:

Brahman achieved victory for the gods in a war with the demons. The gods became elated. [3.1]

They thought that the victory was won by them only (without any help from Brahman). Brahman perceived their vanity and appeared before them as a yaksha, a venerable person. They were wondering who that yaksha was. [3.2]

They said to Agni (fire god), "O Omniscient One, please find out who this yaksha is."
"Yes," he said. [3.3]

He hastened to Brahman. Brahman asked him who he was. Agni said he was fire god Agni, the omniscient. [3.4]

Brahman asked, what power he had. Agni said he could burn everything there was on the earth. [3.5]

Brahman placed a straw before him and asked him to burn it. He tried to ignite it with all his strength but in vain. Then he returned to the other gods and said he could not find out who that person was. [3.6]

Then the gods said to Vayu, the wind god, "O Vayu, please find out who this Spirit is."
"Yes," said Vayu. [3.7]

He went to Brahman, who asked him, "Who are you?"
He said, "I am Vayu and am also known as Matarishva (courser of the sky)." Vayu did not lag behind Agni in self praise. [3.8]

Brahman asked, "What power do you possess, you of such fame?"
"I can blow away everything whatsoever there is on this earth," said Vayu. [3.9]

Brahman placed a straw for him and asked him to blow it away. Vayu approached it with all his speed but was unable to blow it away. Then he returned back to the gods and confessed that he was unable to ascertain who the Spirit was. [3.10]

The gods then decided to ask their leader Indra. They said, "O Maghava (the strong one), please find out who this yaksha is."
"Yes," said Indra and hastened to Brahman. But Brahman disappeared from his view. [3.11]

Indra was baffled, but to his astonishment he saw Uma, the daughter of the snow clad mountain, Himalaya, at the very part of the sky where Brahman was a moment ago. He approached beautiful Uma and asked her who the yaksha was. [3.12]

## Chapter 4

In this last and fourth chapter, Uma tells the gods that the yaksha was none other than Brahman, who won victory for them against the demons.

Uma said that It was Brahman indeed whose victory had elated the gods. [4.1]

The three gods, Fire, Air and Indra did excel other gods for they approached Brahman nearest and were first to know the yaksha as Brahman. [4.2]

Indra excelled other gods because he approached Brahman closest. He was also the first to know Him as Brahman. [4.3]

In Its divine context this is the teaching regarding Brahman: Brahman's appearance is momentary like a flash of lightning and like the wink of an eye (because eyes cannot see It; It can only be experienced). Only as a result of intense spiritual experience Brahman gives a momentary glimpse of Itself. [4.4]

In the context of Adhyatma or Its aspect as manifested in man, the teaching of Brahman is: The mind tries to reach Brahman and it always remembers Brahman and imagines It as near. (Though the mind cannot reveal Brahman, it has a constant desire to know It.) [4.5]

Brahman is adored by all creatures, because It is the innermost Self of all beings. [4.6]

The teacher said to his disciple, "As you requested me to teach you the Upanishad, I have revealed the Upanishad to you. I have taught you the Brahmi Upanishad, the secret knowledge about Brahman." [4.7]

*Tapa* (austerities or concentration of the energies of the mind), *dama* (self-restraint), and *karma* (action) form the support of the secret knowledge of the Upanishad. The Vedas are its limbs, and truth its abode. (The Upanishad emphasizes the need for good moral character for the seeker of Brahman). [4.8]

Anyone who realizes the knowledge of Brahman to be thus, having destroyed sins, is firmly established in the blissful and boundless Brahman. [4.9]

*****

# Katha Upanishad

## Introduction

The *Katha Upanishad* is so named because it forms part of the Brahmana belonging to the Katha Shakha of the *Krishna Yajurveda*. In this Upanishad Nachiketa, a young son of sage Uddalaka, goes to Yama, the god of death, who imparts the supreme knowledge of Atman to him.

Professor Max Muller tells us that this Upanishad "has been frequently quoted by English, French and German writers as one of the most perfect specimens of the mystic philosophy and poetry of the ancient Hindus." (Max Muller, *The Upanishads*, Pt. II, New York: Dover Publications, p.xxi.)

As the story goes, a *rishi* (sage) named Uddalaka performed the *Vishvajit* yajna with a desire to get heavenly rewards. It may be mentioned here that Uddalaka is referred to by two other names in the Upanishad. He is introduced as Vajashravas in the beginning. Vajashravas literally means son of Vajashrava, which in turn means one who gained fame by giving away food grains. On one occasion Nachiketa uses "Gautama" as his father's name. Perhaps that was his *gotra* or family name. Yama uses the name Auddaliki Aruni for Uddalaka. Auddaliki is the same as Uddalaka, as Acharya Shankara tells us, and Aruni means son of Aruna. In other words Uddalaka was the son of Aruna who had gained fame by giving away food grains to Brahmanas and other needy people.

In the Vishvajit yajna, the performer of the yajna gives away all his possessions to priests. Uddalaka had a young son who was still merely a boy. He was full of devotion and faith. When the cows were brought as the last sacrificial gifts, Nachiketa was very upset that his father was giving away those cows who were old, weak and had stopped giving milk or calves. He thought that a person who gives away such cows will certainly go to an unhappy world after this life. Perhaps his father had set aside young and healthy cows for Nachiketa. He wanted to awaken his father's conscience and asked him with sarcasm, "Father, to whom will you give me?" His father first ignored him, but when Nachiketa repeated the same question for the third time he could not control his anger and shouted, "I give you to Death!"

Soon after uttering those words Uddalaka realized that by virtue of his *tapa* (austerity) and *yajna* (sacrifice) he had achieved such powers that whatever he said would come to be true. He knew that his son would die soon in front of him, all due to his uncontrollable rage. He started repenting and crying. Nachiketa asked him to calm down and not to feel sorry for him, because one who is born is sure to die. He also reminded him of his ancestors who neither swerved from truth nor took their words back.

Nachiketa went to Yama, the god of death, but the latter was not home. Nachiketa waited for him for three days and three nights there, without any food. When Yama returned back, someone told him that a Brahmana boy had been waiting for him for three days without any food. He was also reminded that a Brahmana guest is like fire, who if not pacified, would burn not only his household but all his fruits of good deeds, his offspring and his cattle to ashes. Thereupon, Yama hurried to fetch a jug of water for Nachiketa to wash his feet (as the custom was in India in old days), bowed to him with respect and said, "O Brahmana, you have stayed at my house for three nights without any food. I am aware of the consequences of all this. I would like to make up with you by awarding you three boons."

Nachiketa said, "O Death, may my father be pacified and may I go back to him alive. This is my first boon." "So be it," said Yama. "Ask for the second boon," he continued.

Nachiketa said, "I have heard that in Heaven there is no fear, disease, old age or death. O Yama, you know the method of that fire (sacrifice) which leads to Heaven. Please teach me that sacrifice, as my second boon."

Yama taught him that sacrifice. When Nachiketa repeated the method in exact detail, Yama was pleased with him. He said that since he was such a good student he would name that sacrifice as Nachiketa-Agni after him, from that day. He asked Nachiketa to ask for the third boon.

Nachiketa said, "There is a doubt about what happens to a person after he dies. Some say he still exists while others say he does not exist. Teach me about this secret. This is my third boon."

(At one time, in ancient India, there was a group of people who were agnostics and didn't believe in life after death. One such group was called Charvakas. They said, "Live a happy life. Even borrow money to buy *ghee* [clarified butter]. How can this body come back when it is turned into ash after death?" Maybe Nachiketa was referring to such people when he said, ". . . while others say he does not exist.") Who knows better than Yama, the god of death, as to exactly what happens on the other side of the screen of death? He is also an Atmajnani or a knower of the Atman. However, Yama realized that what Nachiketa was asking was to teach him the secret knowledge of the Atman. He thought he was too immature and young for that supreme and deep knowledge. On this, Shri Shankaracharya comments that perhaps Yama thought he was merely curious like a boy who wanted to examine a crow's teeth (*kak-danta-pariksha*).

Yama asked him not to seek that knowledge because it was too difficult for him to understand. Instead he was willing to give him a long life, a huge kingdom with many horses, elephants, enormous wealth, and beautiful women who would entertain him with their music, song and dance. He could also choose sons and grandsons with long life. But Nachiketa refused to take these worldly boons. He said there was no comparison between the supreme knowledge of life-after-death, of which even gods have no knowledge, and short lived worldly pleasure. He thought there was no better teacher of the knowledge of the Self than the god of death himself.

Yama eventually yielded, when he realized that Nachiketa was a qualified student for the knowledge of the Atman. He praised him for his determination to learn the supreme knowledge and for not being swerved by ephemeral worldly objects. He finally taught him the knowledge of the Self.

The story of Nachiketa and Yama as disciple and teacher must have been popular amongst the writers of the Vedic literature. They together form a perfect pair of a disciple and a preceptor. We find that their story has been used in three other places before it appeared in the *Katha Upanishad*. At least the first two of the stories given below seem to be precursors of the story in the *Katha Upanishad*. The third one is from the *Mahabharata*, but is quoted as an ancient story.

For the very first time the story appears in the *Rigveda*. There, in the 135th Sukta of the tenth Mandala, there is mention of a boy who goes to Yama's heaven, as desired by his father, and learns some secret knowledge of a transcendental nature from him. The boy's name is not mentioned in this story. But this seems to be the embryonic form of the story of Nachiketa.

Next, the story occurs in a more developed form in the *Taittiriya Brahmana*. This is similar to the story in the *Katha Upanishad*, except that the third boon is not for the knowledge of the Self but for the knowledge of conquering death. Yama teaches him about the sacrifice again, by which he conquers death. It is a kind of repetition of the second boon. It seems that by that time the Upanishadic philosophy had not been developed. The story goes thus:

Vajashravas was desirous of heavenly rewards and therefore, performed yajna, in which he gave all his belongings. He had a son named Nachiketa who was a young boy. When the cows were brought as the last item of the sacrificial gift, Nachiketa was overcome by faith and asked his father, "Father, to whom will you give me away?" When he repeated the question twice and thrice his father got angry and said, "I give you to Death."

Then Nachiketa heard an unknown voice from the sky which said, "Your father has uttered that he has given you to death. Now you have to go to Yama, the god of death. When you reach there, Yama will be away from his home. You should wait for him for three days and three nights without taking any food. When he asks you, 'Boy, how many nights have you been here?' then say, 'Three nights.' When he asks, 'What did you eat the first night?' say, 'Your offspring.' When he asks, 'What did you eat the second night?' say, 'Your cattle.' When he asks about the third night say, 'Your good works.'"

So, when Nachiketa reached Yama's home he found that he was not home. He stayed there for three days without any food. When Yama came back on the fourth day, he asked him those same questions. Nachiketa answered in the same way as instructed by the unknown voice. Then Yama saluted him with respect and said, "O revered Brahmana, ask for a boon."

Nachiketa said, "Please grant that I may return back to my father alive."

Yama said, "So be it. Ask for another boon."

Nachiketa replied, "Please provide me with the knowledge to protect the fruits of my good deeds." Then Yama taught him the secret of a sacrifice and called it "Nachiketa Agni."

"Please tell me how to conquer death," said Nachiketa. Yama explained to him the Nachiketa Agni again, through which he conquered death.

It seems that later this story was modified for the *Katha Upanishad.*

The story of Nachiketa, in the *Mahabharata*, is somewhat different and runs thus:

When the grandsire, Bhishma, was on his death bed, Yudhishthira went to see him. Bhishma instructed him on many religious subjects. On the importance of giving away cows to Brahmanas he told him a story. He said, "There is an old story on this. There was a rishi whose name was Auddaliki. He had a young son named Nachiketa. One day Auddaliki went for a bath in the river before performing a yajna. When he came back to his *ashrama* he realized that he had forgotten to bring back with him the flowers, *kusha* grass and some utensils from the river. He asked Nachiketa to fetch them from the river. When Nachiketa reached there he could not find them. Perhaps they were swept away by the river current. When he returned back without them, his father was furious and in a rage shouted, 'To death you go.' Nachiketa asked his father to calm down. However, because of his father's curse he died. His father started crying after his son's death. Nachiketa's dead body remained lying there for two days. Suddenly, on the third day, Nachiketa was alive. His father was very happy to see him. He asked, 'My dear son, I am so happy that you came back alive from the clutches of the death. You look stronger and more handsome. Do tell me what happened there in Yama's heaven.' Nachiketa said, 'The world of Yama is all golden. All the houses there are made of gold. There are rivers flowing with milk and butter. When I asked Yama, for whom are those rivers, he told me that they are for those good people who give away cows to Brahmanas. He taught me some superior knowledge, showed me around some beautiful worlds and made my body strong.'"

The *Katha Upanishad* has two chapters, each divided into three cantos or sections. The first canto of the first chapter introduces Nachiketa and tells under what circumstances he goes to Yama and asks for three boons. Nachiketa is then tested by Yama to see if he is a suitable candidate for Atmavidya (the supreme knowledge of self). In the second canto of the first chapter Yama praises Nachiketa for his steadfastness to achieve Brahmavidya. Nachiketa then asks about the symbol of Brahman, and Yama tells him that it is Om. Yama also tells him about the nature of the Atman, which is never born, never dies, is changeless and eternal. In the third canto there is a beautiful allegory of the Atman as the master of the chariot, the body as the chariot, the intellect as the charioteer, the mind as the reins, the sense organs as the horses and the green grass in the fields next to the road as the sense-objects. Only a person with restrained mind can have his senses controlled and attain the ultimate goal, the Atman. Since the path of jnana-yoga is difficult to walk on, one should approach a preceptor, who is well versed in the knowledge of Brahman.

In the first canto of the second chapter Yama describes again the nature of Atman, which is also the cause of cognition and perception of the sense-objects. Yama speaks about all the supernatural attributes of Atman, which is of the size of a thumb while residing in the cavity of one's heart. In the second canto Yama talks about what happens to the Jivatman after the death of the body. He says a person is born as different species of creatures and plants according to his karma and knowledge. However, Atman is not affected by the external impurities and remains untainted. In the third canto Yama compares the creation with a *Pipal* tree and its roots with Brahman, who supports the creation from above. The Atman cannot be seen with the eyes, cannot be described by speech, but is revealed by intuition. After being instructed by Yama on the supreme knowledge and the process of yoga, Nachiketa became free from all impurities and attained Brahman.

### Peace Invocation

Om! May Brahman protect us both, the preceptor and the disciple. May He nourish us both. May both of us acquire energy through the study of the Upanishad. May this study illumine us both. May we never hate each other. Om. Peace, Peace, Peace.

(Imparting knowledge is like lighting one lamp with another lamp. The teacher enlightens his disciple with the knowledge of Brahman that he already has. This is a great endeavor not only for the student but also for the teacher. The teacher wishes that the study of the Upanishad is completed without any worry of security, food or shelter for both of them. Each time he enlightens a student with the supreme knowledge he feels more energized and illumined. He also prays that the teacher and the student maintain love and respect for each other, otherwise the study may remain incomplete. And above all, they pray for peace during the study and for the rest of their lives.)

\*\*\*

## CHAPTER 1

### Section 1.1

Vajashravas, desirous of heavenly rewards, gave all his possessions at the Vishvajit sacrifice that he performed, to the priests. He had a son named Nachiketa. [1.1.1]

Nachiketa was merely a boy. When the cows were brought in, as final sacrificial gifts, he felt very ashamed and thought: [1.1.2]

The person who gives such cows, which have stopped giving milk and calves, and which are so old that they cannot even eat grass or drink water, will surely go to the unpleasant worlds after this life. [1.1.3]

He said to his father, "Father, to whom will you give me?" He repeated thus twice and thrice. Then the father angrily replied, "To Death I give you." [1.1.4]

Nachiketa thought that amongst his father's many disciples he was the first in some skills, and was the middlemost in some other skills. But he had never been the worst. He was wondering why he was being given away to death. Of what use was he to Yama? [1.1.5]

When he saw his father repenting for his utterances he told him, "Remember how the ancients behaved and how even the

present day sages never swerve from the path of truth. Also remember that like corn a mortal ripens and falls, and like corn he is
born again." [1.1.6]

Nachiketa went to Yama's house but he was not there. So
Nachiketa waited for him for three days without food. When Yama
came back he was told by somebody in his household: "Like fire, a
Brahmana guest enters the house. Therefore, good hosts greet him
with respect. O son of Vivasvata, quickly bring water to wash his
feet." [1.1.7]

(The *Taittiriya Upanishad* says, "Worship your guest as a deity." And
*Manusmriti* says, "When a guest arrives at your residence, offer him
*padyam* [water to wash his feet], *asanam* [a seat], worhip him with
*arghyam* [consisting of rice, flowers and durva grass], satisfy him with food
and then offer him some gift.")

Yama was further advised thus: A foolish person, in whose
house a Brahmana stays without a meal, finds all his hopes and
expectations, the fruit of association with good people, the merit of
sweet speech, the sacred and good deeds, and all his children and
cattle destroyed. [1.1.8]

Yama came to Nachiketa and said, "O venerable Brahmana,
you have stayed in my house as my guest for three nights without
any food. On that account, choose three boons from me. May all be
well with me." [1.1.9]

Nachiketa then said, "O Yama, as the first of the three boons,
I choose that my father Gautama be cheerful and free from anxiety,
his anger be pacified and that he may recognize me when you send
me back to him alive." [1.1.10]

Yama said, "By my command, your father Auddaliki Aruni will
recognize you, will love you just like before, will be free from anger
and will sleep peacefully at night, when he sees you released from
the jaws of death." [1.1.11]

Nachiketa then said, "In heaven there is no fear of any kind,
not even of old age or death. There, one is far from hunger, thirst or
sorrow. All one does in that heaven is just rejoice. [1.1.12]

"O Death, you know that sacrifice which leads to heaven. Teach it to me because I am full of faith. Achieving that heaven people attain immortality. I choose the knowledge of this sacrifice as my second boon." [1.1.13]

Yama replied, "O Nachiketa, I surely know that sacrifice, by which one attains heaven, very well. I will teach it to you in such a way that you will learn it thoroughly. You should consider that sacrifice as the support of the world and as a secret knowledge of the learned, hidden in the Vedas." [1.1.14]

Yama then explained to him that sacrifice which is the source of the world. He told him how many and what kind of bricks are required for the altar and how to light the sacrificial fire. Nachiketa, when asked, repeated the whole process exactly as he was taught. Yama was satisfied and said: [1.1.15]

"Nachiketa, I am pleased with you. I will give you an additional boon. This sacrifice will be named after you from today and will be called Nachiketa Agni. Please also accept this garland of different colors. (The last sentence may mean that Yama taught him some other secret knowledge which gives many good results.) [1.1.16]

"A person who performs this Nachiketa sacrifice three times has united himself with the three instructions (by the mother, the father, and the preceptor), and has done the threefold duties (study of the Vedas, performance of the Vedic rituals, and giving alms), and he overcomes the recurrence of birth and death. Having learned and realized the worshipful, omniscient and resplendent Fire, born of Brahman, he attains the supreme peace. [1.1.17]

"A wise person who, having known the three details of the sacrifice (what kind of bricks are required for the altar, how many bricks, and how to light the fire), performs the Nachiketa-sacrifice three times, enjoys heaven free from grief, after destroying the bondage of death even before his death. [1.1.18]

"O Nachiketa, this is your fire which leads to heaven and which you have chosen as your second boon. People will call this fire after your name only. Now choose your third boon." [1.1.19]

Nachiketa said, "When a man dies there is this big contro-
versy: Some say he still exists, while some others say that he does
not exist. I would like to clear my doubt with your teaching on the
subject. This is my third boon." [1.1.20]

Yama replied, "On this subject even the gods seem to be confused since long ago. This is a very difficult subject to comprehend.
Therefore, O Nachiketa, choose some other boon. Do not insist on
this. Please release me from this obligation." [1.1.21]

To this Nachiketa said, "O Death, you yourself mentioned that
this subject is too difficult to understand and that even the gods had
doubts about it. But I know that there is no other teacher of this
subject as good as you are. Therefore, I consider no other boon
equal to this." [1.1.22]

Death said, "Nachiketa, choose sons and grandsons who shall
live a hundred years. Choose herds of cattle, elephants, horses and
a huge amount of gold. Choose a vast territory on earth. You yourself live for as many years as you desire. [1.1.23]

"Ask for any other boon that you think is equal to this, such as
wealth and long life. Nachiketa, be a king of a vast land. I shall
make you the enjoyer of all kinds of pleasures. [1.1.24]

"According to your choice you may ask for all those pleasures
which are difficult to get in this mortal world. Ask for beautiful
ladies with chariots and their musical instruments to entertain you. I
will give you all those. But, Nachiketa, please do not ask me again
anything about death." [1.1.25]

Now it was Nachiketa's turn to reply. He said, "O Death, the
things you have enumerated are most transient. They wear out the
strength of all the sense organs of mortal man. Also, the human life
span is so short! Therefore, please keep your kingdom, horses, elephants and dancing and singing women with yourself. [1.1.26]

"Man is never satisfied with whatever wealth he has. Moreover, now that I have met you, I shall surely get whatever wealth and long life I want (by virtue of the Nachiketa sacrifice). Therefore, I would like to choose only that boon. [1.1.27]

"Having approached the ageless and immortal ones (like you), and knowing that more worthy boons can be received from them, what man living on the earth down there, subject to aging and death, would like to enjoy a long life, after scrutinizing the pleasures of dancing and singing girls. [1.1.28]

"O Death, tell me about that supreme subject of life-after-death, about which they have this doubt. Nachiketa shall not choose any other boon than this which is so mysterious." [1.1.29]

## Section 1.2

Yama was very pleased with Nachiketa after seeing a strong determination in him to learn the *Atmavidya*. He then considered him to be a qualified student of the secret knowledge. Acharya Shankara tells us (in his *Vivekachudamani*, verses 18.19) that there are four kinds of disciplines required in a person, to be qualified to learn the supreme knowledge. First is the discrimination between the eternal and the ephemeral; second is renunciation of enjoyment of the fruits of one's actions in this world and in heaven; third is the sixfold virtues, namely, *shama* (calmness of mind), *dama* (control of the sense organs), *uparati* (the in-drawn state of mind), *titiksha* (calm endurance of the pairs of opposites like pleasure-pain, hot-cold, etc.), *shraddha* (faith in truth), and *samadhana* (inward concentration); and fourth is a strong desire for *moksha* (liberation). Yama now says to Nachiketa:

"There are two choices for a person, namely, *shreya,* the good, and *preya,* the pleasant. They both have different end results. They both bind man in their own way. The good befalls him who follows the *shreya*, and he who chooses the *preya* misses his goal. [1.2.1]

"Both *shreya* and *preya* approach man simultaneously. The wise man examining the two well, verily prefers *shreya* which brings spiritual welfare, to *preya* which is pleasant to the sense organs. The foolish man, on the other hand, chooses *preya* through love for gain and attachment. [1.2.2]

"O Nachiketa, after due deliberation you renounced all those attractive and pleasant objects of desire, which were easily available to you. You refused to go through that path of wealth where many people drown. [1.2.3]

"Ignorance and knowledge are two opposite things. They lead to different ends. Nachiketa, I consider you an aspirant of knowledge because the prospect of so much pleasure could not influence you. [1.2.4]

"Fools, dwelling in the very midst of ignorance, yet vainly considering themselves as wise and learned, go round and round stumbling hither and thither, like the blind guided by the blind. (See *Mundaka Upanishad* 1.2.9.) [1.2.5]

"The truth of the hereafter never dawns on the childish person who is inattentive and is delusioned by wealth. Thinking that there is nothing beyond this world experienced by his sense organs, he falls into my (death's) clutches time and again. [1.2.6]

"To many, mere hearing about that Self is not available, and many who can hear about It find it difficult to comprehend It. Wonderful is the expounder and also wonderful is the receiver of that knowledge. Wonderful indeed is he who understands It when taught by an adept preceptor. [1.2.7]

(The *Gita* also talks about the knowledge of Atman in similar terms. See *Gita* 2.29.)

"This Atman can never be comprehended if taught by a teacher who has not realized It himself, even if one ponders upon It deeply. On the other hand, It is easily understood when taught by a teacher who has realized his unity with It. Atman is subtler than the subtlest and beyond logic. [1.2.8]

"This spiritual understanding that you have cannot be attained through logical reasoning. It surely leads to sound knowledge of the Atman, when imparted by someone competent. O Nachiketa, you are of true resolve indeed. I wish there were more inquirers like you! [1.2.9]

"I am aware of the fact that all wealth is transient, and that the eternal can never be attained through the transient. Yet I performed the Nachiketa sacrifice, a transient object, to achieve Yamahood, which is also transient (though eternal in the eyes of short-lived human beings). [1.2.10]

(Yama is praising Nachiketa and telling him that though Nachiketa has the knowledge of the Nachiketa-sacrifice, he is not desirous of using it, unlike Yama. Nachiketa's goal is the knowledge of the Atman, which is far superior.)

"O Nachiketa, being intelligent and brave, you have rejected the highest reach of desire, the support of the universe (that is Hiranyagarbha or Brahma), the endless fruit of all sacred rites, and the other shore of fearlessness, after having examined them patiently. [1.2.11]

(Through Nachiketa-Agni Nachiketa could achieve even Brahma's position but he chose instead knowledge of the Atman. Yama chose to be god of death through it.)

"The wise man gets rid of both joy and sorrow when he realizes the Atman, by meditating on that ancient effulgent One. He (the Atman) is difficult to be seen, profound, hidden in experience, established in the cavity of the heart, and residing in the body. [1.2.12]

"After hearing the reality of the Self (that I am going to talk about), grasping it fully, after separating it from body and mind, and attaining this subtle knowledge, the mortal rejoices, for he has attained that which is the cause of delight. I consider that the mansion of Atman is wide open for Nachiketa." [1.2.13]

Nachiketa said, "If you are pleased with me and consider me fit for it, tell me about that Truth which you see as independent of virtue or *dharma* (scriptural duties and their fruits), independent of vice (*adharma*), which is beyond cause and effect, and is independent of the past and the present." [1.2.14]

Yama said, "I will tell you briefly of that goal which all the Vedas propound with one voice, which all the *tapas* (penance) speak of, and desiring which people practice brahmacharya. It is *Om*. [1.2.15]

"This syllable, *Om*, indeed is Brahman. This syllable indeed is the highest. Having known this syllable, one gets whatever one desires. [1.2.16]

"Om is the best support. This support is the supreme. Knowing this support one is glorified in the world of Brahman. [1.2.17]

"The intelligent Self is neither born nor does It die. It did not originate from anything nor did anything originate from It. This Self is unborn, eternal, undecaying, and ancient. It is not killed when the body is killed. [1.2.18]
(The nature of the Atman mentioned here is also found in the *Gita*, 2.20, with the same words rearranged in a different order. The words of the next mantra, which continue to describe the nature of the Atman, are also rearranged in the *Gita*, 2.19.)

"If the killer thinks that he is killing the Atman, and if the killed thinks that his Atman is killed, both of them are ignorant. Atman neither kills nor is killed. [1.2.19]

"The Atman is smaller than the atom and is greater than the greatest (cosmos). It is ever present in the heart of every creature. One who is free from desires realizes the glory of the Atman through purity of mind and sense organs, and becomes free from grief. [1.2.20]

"The Atman, while sitting still, can travel far; while lying down, can go everywhere. Who, other than myself, can know that the Atman is joyful and joyless. [1.2.21]

"Having known the bodiless, all-pervading Atman who dwells in all impermanent bodies, the wise do not grieve. [1.2.22]

"This Atman cannot be attained by the study of the scriptures, nor by intelligence, nor by much hearing. It is attained by him to whom It chooses to reveal Its own true form. [1.2.23]

"Nobody who has not given up evil conduct, who is not self-restrained, who is not meditative, nor one who is not pacified in mind can attain this Atman, even if he is intelligent. [1.2.24]

"Otherwise, how can an ignorant one, without proper qualifications as mentioned above, know where the Atman is? In the unity of the Atman merge all the distinctions of Brahmana and Kshatriya, and in whose contemplation even death has no significance." [1.2.25]

## Section 1.3

Yama continued his discourse:

"There are two—the *jiva* or the finite self of man, and the Atman or Brahman, the infinite Self—who dwell within the body, in the supreme cavity of the intelligence, enjoying the fruits of karma or deeds. The knowers of Brahman, as well as the householders who have performed the Nachiketa sacrifice three times, know them as shade and light. [1.3.1]

(According to the Vedantic literature the highest truth, Brahman or Atman, is within us. Our intelligence is like a cave where jiva and Brahman reside. Brahman is light and jiva its shadow. Only the jiva enjoys the fruits of our karma. Brahman or Atman is only the witness, watching it. However, this mantra refers to Brahman also enjoying the fruits. According to Shankaracharya this should be taken as just a figure of speech. Since Brahman is supposed to reside in us along with our jiva, it is said to be sharing the fruits of karma, because of its association with the jiva.)

"We are capable of performing the Nachiketa sacrifice which is a bridge to heaven for the sacrificers. We are also capable of knowing the supreme Brahman which is sought by those who want to reach the shore of fearlessness. [1.3.2]

"In life's journey consider the Atman as the master, the body as the chariot, the intellect as the charioteer, and the mind as the reins. [1.3.3]

"In this journey consider the sense organs as the horses and the sense objects as the road. The wise call Him (the Atman) the enjoyer when He is united with the body, mind and senses. [1.3.4]

(When the mind and senses are under control, the sense objects do not divert the mind during the journey of the man towards perfection. The Atman is ever pure, perfect and free. Yet He is said to be making the journey and enjoying the fruits of action. According to the Vedanta when the Atman is united with the body, mind and senses, or in other words, when the mind and senses are projected on the Atman, He is referred to as the individual soul or jiva. The same Atman lives in all individuals but in each individual the jiva or soul is unique.)

"He whose mind is undisciplined and is devoid of right understanding, his senses become uncontrolled like the wicked horses of a charioteer. [1.3.5]

"But he who is always of restrained mind with right understanding, his senses are under control like the good horses of a charioteer. [1.3.6]

"And he who is devoid of proper understanding, with no control over his mind and always impure, never attains that goal but gets into the cycle of births and deaths. [1.3.7]

"But he who is intelligent, ever pure and with mind controlled, reaches that goal whence there is no return to birth again. [1.3.8]

"The man who has intelligence as his charioteer and a disciplined mind as the reins, surely reaches the end of his journey, that supreme abode of Vishnu (the all-pervading Atman). [1.3.9]

"The objects (the panchamahabhutas or five elements, namely, earth, water, fire, air and ether, out of which have come all the objects and senses) are subtler than the senses, the mind is subtler than the objects, the intellect is subtler than the mind, and the great soul or Hiranyagarbha (Brahma, the Creator) is subtler than the intellect. [1.3.10]

(Senses, pancha-mahabhutas, mind, intellect and Hiranyagarbha form a hierarchy such that each is superior to its predecessor.

Hiranyagarbha is the aggregate cosmic intellect and, therefore, is superior to the intellect of an individual.)

"Unmanifested Prakriti (nature or primal matter) is superior to the great soul (Hiranyagarbha), and Purusha or Atman is superior to Prakriti. Nothing is superior to the Atman. That is the supreme goal. [1.3.11]
(Hiranyagarbha or Brahma is the first offspring of Prakriti, primal matter.)

"This Atman is hidden in all beings and does not reveal Itself to everybody. It is realized by only the seers of the subtle, through their sharp intellect. [1.3.12]

"The wise should merge speech in the mind, the mind in the intellect, the intellect in the great self (Hiranyagarbha), and the great self in the Atman. [1.3.13]
(Here Yama is talking about the step by step procedure for self realization. Speech actually represents all the sense organs here. As the first step, all the activities of the sense organs must be stopped and consciousness must be focused on mind. Then consciousness should be withdrawn from mind and further drawn inward towards intellect, or *buddhi*, the higher discriminating faculty of the mind. Next, the consciousness should be withdrawn even from intellect and should be made as clear as that of the great soul, Brahma the creator, who represents the aggregate intellect of the whole universe. Then only the cosmic existence of life will be understood. Then it becomes clear that this world is but a mirage, a *Maya*. Finally, the wise realize their true nature, the blissful Atman who is within all. This is the process of jnanayoga [yoga of knowledge].)

"O mankind, arise, awake and, having approached great teachers of the supreme knowledge, realize that Atman. The path of jnanayoga is difficult indeed; it is like walking on the sharp edge of a razor. [1.3.14]

"Atman is soundless, touchless, formless, imperishable, eternal, without taste or smell, without beginning or end, eternal and immutable. It is even above and beyond Mahat, Brahma the creator. Having realized Him one is emancipated from the bondage of birth and death. [1.3.15]

"The wise person who hears this story of Nachiketa, as told by Yama, and relates it to others is glorified in the world of Brahman. [1.3.16]

"He who repeats this story of profound mystery, with great faith, in the assembly of seekers of spiritual wisdom or at the time of religious rites for the deceased, obtains infinite rewards." [1.3.17]

(There has been a tradition in India to encourage the reader of a scripture to read it as many times as possible, and to relate it to others. The repeated study rekindles the knowledge and also helps the reader penetrate into the spiritual depth more every time. The last two mantras (verses) of this Section emphasize that if the reader does this he will be well rewarded.)

## CHAPTER 2

### Section 2.1

Yama continues his teaching:

"It seems that the self-existent Lord has made the sense organs, including the mind, with a defect. No wonder a man thinks of only outward objects and does not think of the Self within. A rare discriminating man, desirous of immortality, turns his eyes inward to see the indwelling Atman. [2.1.1]

"The ignorant pursue external pleasures. That results in their fall into the widespread clutches of the cycle of births and deaths. But the wise, knowing what is eternal and immortal (that is, the Atman), do not crave for the impermanent things in this world." [2.1.2]

In the following mantras (verses) Yama tries to define the undefinable Atman in many different ways:

"That by which we know form, taste, smell, sound, touch and sexual pleasure is this very Atman. What else is there unknown to Him? This indeed is that Atman you have wanted to know. [2.1.3]

"Wise men who realize that great, all-pervading Atman, through which they perceive all objects in dream as well as in the waking state, do not grieve. [2.1.4]

"He who knows the Atman as the enjoyer of the fruits of action, sustainer of life, the lord of the past and the future, and as very near (within this body), gets rid of all fear. This is that Atman you inquired about. [2.1.5]

"He existed before the creation of the universe, even before the primordial five elements, and He exists in the hearts of all beings. This is that Atman you inquired about. [2.1.6]

"Aditi, the mother of all the gods, who takes birth as Hiranyagarbha (Brahma) through *Prana* (cosmic energy), dwells in the hearts of all beings, and is found amidst the primordial elements. That is the Atman whom you are inquiring about. [2.1.7]
(In simple words, when our mind becomes pure through pranayama and meditation, then we are closer to that pure consciousness, the Atman.)

"The sacrificial fire hidden in two fire sticks (*aranis* to produce fire for *yajna*; as also the fire lodged in the hearts of yogis) is well protected, just as much as the fetus by a pregnant mother. That fire is adored every day by the awakened men (yogis) and by those who perform yajna. That fire is the Atman you have inquired about. [2.1.8]

"That from which the sun rises and into which it merges again, That in which all the gods (cosmic energies) are established, That which no one transcends, That is the Atman about which you have inquired. [2.1.9]

"Whatever is here is there and whatever is there is here likewise. (In other words this manifested universe is the same as Brahman, just as the ocean and the wave are the same materially.) One who sees differently goes from death to death. [2.1.10]

"By pure mind alone can it be understood that there is no difference between Brahman and the manifested universe. One who sees differently goes from death to death. [2.1.11]

"The Purusha (Atman) with the size of a thumb resides within the body. He is the ruler of the past and the future. Knowing Him one fears no more. That is the Atman you inquired about. [2.1.12]

"The Purusha, who is of the size of a thumb, is like a light without smoke. He remains the same today and tomorrow. That is the Atman you inquired about. [2.1.13]

"As the rain water falling on a high peak gets dispersed down the hill, similarly, one who perceives them differently (sees the Atman in them as different) sees them in their separate forms. [2.1.14]

"O Gautama, as pure water poured on pure water becomes the same, so also becomes the Atman of a *muni* (a man of knowledge) who knows the unity of the Atman." [2.1.15]

### Section 2.2

Yama continues:

"The Atman, Who is without birth and is of bright intelligence lives in the body, which is like a city of eleven gates. Having meditated upon Him and realized Him, one grieves no more. One becomes liberated from all bonds of ignorance and is free from the cycle of births and deaths. That is the Atman you inquired about. [2.2.1]

(The body is compared with a city of eleven gates because it has seven openings in the head, the navel, the two lower ones, and one is assumed at the top of the head. Here, the Upanishad hints that "the kingdom of God is within us," as Jesus said. This comparison of the Atman as a dweller of a city, which is the body, with nine rather than eleven gates, also occurs in the *Gita*, 5.13.)

"Atman is the swan dwelling in heaven (in the form of the sun), the air filling space, the fire burning in the sacrificial altar, the holy guest in the house. He is in man, in the gods, in the sacrifice, and in the sky. He is born in water, on earth, in the yajna (sacrifice), and on the mountains. He is the true; He is the great. [2.2.2]

(The Upanishad is trying to say that the Atman is omnipresent.)

"Atman sends *Prana* (the vital energy of the upper parts of the body) upwards and *Apana* (the vital energy of the lower parts of the body) downwards. All the gods, that is, all the sense organs, worship the adorable one (Atman) seated in the middle. [2.2.3]

(In the Vedic period it was believed that the physical functions of the body are carried on by five vital energies, namely, *Prana, Apana, Samana, Udana* and *Vyana*. Prana works in the respiratory system, Apana in the bladder and colon, Samana in the digestive system, Udana in the vocal system and Vyana in the blood circulation and nerve currents.)

"After departing the body what else remains of Him, of that owner of the body, who dwells in it? (No trace of the Atman remains in the body, which falls after Its departure.) That is the Atman you inquired about. [2.2.4]

"No mortal ever lives on *Prana* or *Apana*. Mortals live by something else (that is, Atman), on which these two depend. [2.2.5]

"O Gautama, now I shall tell you again of the mysterious eternal Brahman, and also what happens to the soul after meeting death. [2.2.6]

"Some souls enter the womb to have a body, while others go to the plants, according to their action and according to their knowledge. [2.2.7]

"That Atman remains awake and goes on creating desirable things, even while the senses are asleep. (Because He is the witness during all the three states, namely, waking, dreaming and dreamless deep sleep.) He is pure, He is Brahman, and is also called immortal. He is the support of all the worlds. None can transcend Him. That is the Atman you inquired about. [2.2.8]

"Just as fire, though one, after having entered the world (after getting ignited) assumes different forms according to the shapes of the objects it burns, similarly, Atman inside all beings, though one, appears in different forms according to the different bodies It enters. Yet It exists beyond them. [2.2.9]

"As air, though one, having entered this world assumes different shapes according to different objects it occupies, so the one Self of all beings appears in various forms according to different objects through which It manifests. And yet It exists beyond them. [2.2.10]

"As the Sun, the eye of the whole world, is not contaminated by impurities of the eyes of creatures, so the one Self of all beings is never affected by the miseries of the world. [2.2.11]

"Eternal peace belongs to those wise men who realize the Supreme Controller of all, the inner Self of all beings who makes His one form manifold, as existing within themselves, and to no others. [2.2.12]

"The eternal among the non-eternals, the intelligence among the intelligent, who, though one, fulfills the desires of many. Those wise men who perceive Him as existing within themselves, to them belongs eternal peace, and to no others. [2.2.13]

"The sages perceive that indescribable supreme joy as 'This is That.' How can I know That? Does It shine in Its own light or does It shine in reflection? [2.2.14]

"In the Atman the sun does not shine, nor the moon and the stars, nor does this lightning shine there, much less this fire. When That shines, everything shines after That. By Its light all this manifested universe is lighted." [2.2.15]

### Section 2.3

Yama continues his discourse further:

"This is the beginningless *Pipal* tree that has its roots above and its branches spread below. That (which is its roots above) is pure, that is Brahman and that is called immortal. On that are fixed all the worlds. None transcends that. That is the Atman you inquired about. [2.3.1]

(Here the creation, whose root is Brahman from whom the whole universe came down, is compared with a pipal tree. Cf. *Gita* 15.1-3.)

"All this universe that exists, emerges and moves because there is the supreme Brahman which is a great terror like an uplifted thunderbolt. Those who know this become immortal. [2.3.2]

"For fear of Him the fire burns, the sun shines, and *Indra*, *Vayu* (air) and *Mrityu* (death) perform their respective functions. (Here, "for fear of Him the fire burns," etc., actually means the fire, etc., obtained their respective natures from Brahman only.) [2.3.3]

"If one is able to realize Brahman in this very world before the fall of this body, one becomes free from the bondage of the world. Otherwise one has to take birth again in this world of manifestation. [2.3.4]

"Brahman is realized in one's self as one sees oneself in a mirror, in the *pitriloka* (world of manes) as in a dream, in the world of *gandharvas* (celestial singers) as reflected in water, and in the world of Brahma as light and shade. [2.3.5]

(Yama is trying to emphasize to Nachiketa that Brahman is perceived differently in different worlds. The ultimate aim is, however, to realize Him in whatever world we are residing in. Why and how we should know Him is answered below.)

"The wise do not grieve having known that the sense organs are created differently and have their rising and setting, unlike the Atman which is changeless. [2.3.6]

"Superior to the sense organs is the mind, superior to the mind is the intellect, superior to the intellect is *mahat* (the cosmic mind), and superior to mahat is the unmanifested nature. [2.3.7]

"Even superior to the unmanifested nature is the Atman, who is all-pervading and without worldly attributes. Knowing Him a man becomes freed and attains immortality. [2.3.8]

(These last two verses, 7 and 8, are a modified version of verses 10 and 11 in Section 1.3.)

"His form is beyond the range of vision. None can see Him with the eyes. He is revealed in the heart by the intellect, which controls the mind. Those who know this become immortal. [2.3.9]

"When the five senses of knowledge come to rest, together with the mind, and when the intellect too does not function, that is called the supreme state. [2.3.10]

"The sages consider that state, the steady control of the sense organs, as yoga. The yogi must then be vigilant, for yoga can be acquired and lost. [2.3.11]

(These last two verses describe the state of one's senses, mind and intellect when one is in meditation. Once this state has been achieved the yogi has to maintain it carefully, because the mind can play tricks and the control of the senses can be lost easily.)

"The Atman cannot be reached by speech, by eyes or even by mind. How can It be realized otherwise than from those who say that It exists (who have realized It themselves). [2.3.12]

"Between the two views about the Atman, namely, that It exists and It does not exist, the Atman can be realized only as existing. When one realizes Its existence Its true nature is revealed to that one. [2.3.13]

"When all the desires that dwell in the heart are destroyed, then the mortal becomes immortal and attains Brahman even in this very life. [2.3.14]

"When in this very life all the knots of the heart are destroyed, then a mortal becomes immortal. This much alone is the teaching of all the Upanishads. [2.3.15]

"Out of one hundred and one nerves of the heart only one (the *sushumna nadi* of the yogins) extends towards the crown of the head. Going out by it at death, one attains immortality, but going through others leads to different forms of rebirth. [2.3.16]

"The Purusha, the indwelling Self, of the size of a thumb, is ever seated in the hearts of men. One should separate Him, with perseverance, from one's body like a stalk from the Munja grass. One should know Him as pure and immortal. Yes, one should know Him as pure and immortal." [2.3.17]

Nachiketa, having been so taught by Death in this knowledge and in the whole process of yoga, became free from all impurities and death, and attained Brahman. Anyone else who becomes a knower thus, like Nachiketa, of the indwelling Self, attains Brahman too. [2.3.18]

*****

# Prashna Upanishad

## Introduction

Traditionally this Upanishad is the fourth in order to be studied by a student of the Vedanta. It belongs to the Pippalada Shakha of the *Atharvaveda*.

Prashna means question, and as the name implies, this Upanishad is made up of questions and answers. Six students, who are seekers of the truth, each ask sage Pippalada philosophical questions, one at a time. The sage gives an appropriate deep philosophical answer to each question.

The six students are: (1) Kabandhi Katyayana (descendent of Katya); (2) Bhargava Vaidarbhi (a scion of Bhrigu, born in Vidarbha); (3) Kausalya Ashvalayana (son of Ashvala); (4) Sauryayani Gargya (grandson of Surya, born in the family of Garga); (5) Satyakama Shaibya (son of Shibi); and (6) Sukesha Bharadvaja (son of Bharadvaja).

In the Vedic tradition the students approached Pippalada with sacrificial fuel in their hands, as a present to the teacher, and wanted to ask questions. The sage advised them to stay for a year with him practicing tapa (self control), brahmacharya (celibacy) and faith and then ask the questions.

At the end of the year Kabandhi Katyayana asked about the source of all beings. The sage said that the Lord of creation, Brahma, desirous of progeny, created a pair of a male and a female. Prana (energy) and Rayi (matter), which are the two fundamental principles of creation, indeed form that pair. Then the sage talked about various expressions and functions of Prana and Rayi. He then talked about two paths, the material and the spiritual, by which a person's soul travels after death according to his karma and knowledge. Next he diverged from the main topic and talked about different subdivisions of time, namely, year, season, month and day, which are but the working of Prana and Rayi (Energy and Matter) only, and that through these divisions they control life. Then the

41

sage gives a very simple answer to the question, that it is the seed from which all creatures are born. The sage perhaps knew that the questioner was aware of the simple biological answer, and therefore he interjected the Vedantic philosophy of Energy and Matter as the origin of life. Through this philosophy he is trying to say that life is beginningless.

The second question was asked by Bhargava Vaidarbhi. He wanted to know which are the deities (constituents of the body) that sustain life and which amongst them is the most important one. To this the sage replied that ether, air, fire, water, earth, speech, mind, eye, ear and Prana are the deities that support life. According to the Vedanta and the Sankhya philosophy the first five are the five elements (*panchamahabhuta*) which are the constituents of the physical body. The next four impart intelligence to a living body. The body cannot stay alive without Prana, the last one, even for a moment. That is why it is the most important amongst all these deities. Prana is divided into five kinds, as we will see as the answer to the third question.

Kausalya Ashvalayana asked the third question. He wanted to know where the Prana comes from into the body and how it divides itself. Pippalada answered that the Atman is the source of the Prana. Prana is like the shadow of the Atman. It divides itself into five kinds of energies for proper functioning of the body, namely, Prana, Apana, Samana, Vyana and Udana. Prana controls breathing through the mouth and nostrils. Apana is responsible for excretion and generation. Samana assimilates food equally in the digestive system. Vyana is responsible for the circulation of the blood through the arteries and veins. Udana carries the soul after death to different worlds, good or bad, according to the karma of the soul.

Sauryayani Gargya asked the fourth question. His question was: When a person sleeps, which organs go to sleep and which ones keep awake? Furthermore, which organ sees dreams and which one enjoys the happiness of dreamless sleep? To this Pippalada replied that all the senses become dormant in the mind during sleep. However, the five energies or Pranas remain active. It is the mind which creates dreams during sleep, based on what it experienced in the waking state. When the mind is overcome by some kind of power, of *tamasic* (lethargic) nature, the jiva enjoys a dreamless, deep and blissful sleep.

The fifth question, about Om, was asked by Satyakama Shaibya. He asked, "When a person meditates upon Om until his death, what world does he attain?" The sage replied that Om is made of three syllables, namely, A, U and M. When a person concentrates only on the first syllable, A, he returns back to this mortal world, but attains greatness in life. When he concentrates on two syllables, A and U, he attains the world of the moon and enjoys its grandeur for a long time before coming to this world again. When a person concentrates on Om with all its three syllables he attains the world of Brahma, on his way to *moksha.*

Sukesha Bharadvaja asked the sixth and last question. He asked, "Where does the Purusha (Atman or Brahman) live?" Pippalada said the Purusha lives right inside this body. He is the creator of this universe. There is nothing higher than that.

## Peace Invocation

Om! O gods, may our ears hear auspicious words. May we, who are good in worship, see auspicious things with our eyes. May we, who sing your praise, live our allotted span of life in perfect health and strength.

May Indra of ancient fame confer success in our study of the Upanishad. May all-knowing Pusha, god of the earth, confer prosperity on us. May Garuda, the destroyer of evil, be well disposed toward us. May Brihaspati ensure our welfare in the study of this scripture. Om. Peace, Peace, Peace.

## FIRST QUESTION

Om, salutation to the Supreme Lord, who is ever attracting all toward Him, the highest reality.

Sukesha Bharadvaja, Satyakama Shaibya, Sauryayani Gargya, Kausalya Ashvalayana, Bhargava Vaidarbhi and Kabandhi Katyayana, all devoted to Brahman, engaged in realizing Brahman and in search of the Supreme Brahman, approached the venerable Pippalada. They had sacrificial fuel in their hands, as a present to the teacher. They thought he would answer all their questions about Brahman. [1.1]

To them the Rishi said, "Stay here for another year with tapa (penance), brahmacharya (celibacy) and faith. Then you may ask your questions. If I know the answers I will certainly explain everything to you." [1.2]

Then Kabandhi Katyayana approached him and asked, "Reverend Sir, from what are all creatures born?" [1.3]

To him Pippalada replied, "The creator, Brahma, when he desired progeny, performed austerity in the form of meditation. He then created a couple, Rayi (matter) and Prana (energy). He thought these two would produce creatures of many kinds for him." [1.4]

The sun and moon are indeed energy and matter respectively. All these, with and without form, are matter indeed. But ordinarily that which has form is matter. [1.5]
(According to Vedic notion the moon provides nourishment to all vegetation and the sun is the source of energy for their growth.)

After the sun rises in the east it spreads its energy in all the directions, namely, north, south, east, west, zenith, nadir and the intermediate space, through its rays. [1.6]

The sun, which is of universal form and is universal life, rises as Prana, which is also fire. It has been praised thus: [1.7]

The sun is of universal form, full of rays, omniscient, basis of all life, the single light of all, and the great radiator of heat. It rises with a thousand rays, exists in a hundred forms and is the life of all creatures. [1.8]

The year is Prajapati, the lord of creatures. It has two paths, namely, the southern path and the northern path. Performing Vedic rites and doing charitable works, thinking them works of supreme value, leads people to the southern path of the year. Those people desiring offspring attain the world of the moon and later return back to earth in another birth. This path of the manes, leading to the world of the moon, is matter (the sun being energy). [1.9]
(In this passage "year," meaning Time, is said to be Prajapati because it controls everything. The year has two parts according to two solstices.

The southern solstice is compared to the duties of a good householder who performs good deeds and brings up progeny, as prescribed by the scriptures. He attains Chandraloka, or heaven, after his death, due to his good karma, but is still subject to rebirth. The next passage talks about what is the northern path and what happens to the person who follows that path.)

Those who seek the Atman by tapa, brahmacharya, faith and knowledge attain the world of Aditya (the sun). This is the northern path—a path of immortals—free from fear, the supreme resort and the source of all energy. There is no return from there. The ignorant are unable to tread this path. Here is a verse pertaining to this: [1.10]

Some say that the sun is the father, has five feet (five seasons, counting Hemanta and Shishira as one) and twelve limbs (twelve months), and gives rain from the upper half of the sky. Some others say that the omniscient one is placed on a chariot of seven wheels and six spokes. [1.11]

(This verse is taken from the *Rigveda*. Seven wheels or seven horses represent the seven colors in a ray of the sun, and six spokes are the six seasons it brings.)

The month too is Prajapati. Its dark fortnight is matter and the bright fortnight is energy. Therefore, some Rishis perform their sacrifices in the bright fortnight. The others perform it in the dark fortnight. [1.12]

(A month too is divided into the dark and bright periods just as the year is, according to two solstices. In the next passage we will see that a day is also divided into day and night. Each unit of time plays a part in creation and dissolution with energy and matter inherent in it.)

Day and night are Prajapati, with day as Prana and night as Rayi. Those who indulge in passion during the day waste away Prana, but those who indulge at night are as good as those who practice brahmacharya. [1.13]

Food indeed is Prajapati. From that is produced the seed (semen). From the seed all the creatures are born. [1.14]

(This is the simple answer to the first question.)

Therefore, those who observe the rule of Prajapati (rule of progeny) produce sons and daughters. But those who observe tapa, brahmacharya and truthfulness attain Brahmaloka. [1.15]

The pure world of Brahma belongs to them only who are not tainted by deceit, falsehood or maya (cunningness). [1.16]

### SECOND QUESTION

Next, Bhargava of Vidarbha asked of Pippalada, "Holy Sir, how many deities (elements, powers or organs) sustain a creature? How many of them express their power and which amongst them is the most important?" [2.1]

Pippalada replied to him, "Ether, air, fire, water, earth, the organ of speech, mind, eye and ear are the deities that support a creature. They exhibit their power and declare, 'We hold together this body and support it.'" [2.2]

Then Prana, an important supporter of the body, said, "Do not be deluded. I alone support it by dividing myself into five parts." But the other deities did not seem to believe his words. (The five parts of Prana are: Prana, Apana, Samana, Udana and Vyana.) [2.3]

Out of indignation, Prana appeared to rise up from the body. As he ascended, all the others ascended immediately. When he remained quiet all the others settled down. Just as when the queen bee flies away all the other bees follow her, and with her they all settle down, so did the speech, mind, eye, ear, etc. Being satisfied they all started praising Prana. [2.4]

It is Prana in the form of fire, it is Prana in the form of the sun, it is Prana in the form of a cloud, it is Prana in the form of Indra, it is Prana in the form of the wind, and it is Prana in the form of the earth that supports the body. That bright one is indeed also matter, subtle, gross and immortal. [2.5]

The Vedas, namely, *Rik*, *Yajus* and *Sama*, as well as yajna (sacrifice), Kshatriyas and Brahmanas are fixed on Prana, just as the spokes of a wheel are fixed at its hub. [2.6]

O Prana, it is you who move about in the womb as the Lord of creation (a finite principle of creation), and it is you who are born later. It is you who resides in the body for whom these creatures carry their offerings with the senses. (The senses—eyes, ears, etc.— use their sense-objects to help Prana so that it can support life.) [2.7]

You carry oblations to the gods as fire. You are the first food-offering to the Pitris (manes). To every sense-organ you give its function. [2.8]

O Prana, you are the Creator, you are the Supporter and you are the Destroyer. You move in the sky like the sun, the Lord of all luminaries. [2.9]

O Prana, when you pour down rain these creatures of yours are delighted, hoping that food will be produced to their satisfaction. [2.10]

O Prana, you are purity itself, you are fire, the enjoyer of offerings, and you are the master of all that exists. We, the sense-organs, offer food to you, the father of all. [2.11]

Please calm that power of yours that dwells in speech, in the ear, in the eye and in the mind. Please do not rise up. [2.12]

Whatever exists in the three worlds is all under the control of Prana. O Prana, protect us as a mother protects her children. Give us splendor and intelligence. [2.13]

### THIRD QUESTION

Kausalya Ashvalayana asked the next question. He asked, "Sir, where is the Prana born from? How does it come into the body? How does it stay in the body after dividing itself into five parts? How does it depart? How does it hold together the body and the Atman?" [3.1]

Pippalada replied, "You have asked difficult questions. You are a knower of Brahman. Therefore, I will answer your questions. [3.2]

"This Prana is born of the Atman. Just like the shadow of a man, Prana is inseparable from the Atman. At birth Prana enters the body to fulfill the desires of the mind, from the past birth. [3.3]

"Just as a king appoints officials to rule different parts of his kingdom, so does Prana engage the other four Pranas, which are parts of itself, to perform different functions. [3.4]

"Prana itself dwells in the eye, ear, mouth, and nose. Apana, the second Prana, controls the organs of excretion and generation. Samana dwells in the navel and governs digestion and assimilation of food. Because of that only, the seven organs function. (The seven organs are: two eyes, two ears, two nostrils and the mouth.) [3.5]

"The Atman dwells in the heart. From the heart originate one hundred and one main nerves. Each of these nerves has a hundred branch nerves. Each branch nerve has smaller branches, which are seventy-two thousand in number. Vyana, the fourth Prana, moves in all these nerves. [3.6]

"Through one of these nerves called the *Sushumna Nadi*, in the center of the spine, Udana, the fifth Prana, leads the virtuous man at the moment of death upwards to a higher birth, the sinful man downwards to a lower birth, and the man both virtuous and sinful to rebirth in the world of men. [3.7]

(After talking about the individual Prana, Pippalada next talks about the universal Prana in the following verse.)

"The sun indeed is the universal Prana. It rises to help the Prana dwelling in the eye of man, so that he can see. The force in the earth (perhaps the gravity) maintains the Apana in man. The ether in the inter-space is the Samana and air is Vyana. [3.8]

"The fire is the universal Udana. Therefore, he whose body heat is gone out, dies. Thereafter his senses are absorbed in mind and he is born again. [3.9]

"Together with whatever are the thoughts at the moment of death a person unites with Prana. Prana, in association with Udana, leads him to the world he merits. [3.10]

"The progeny of the man who knows Prana, as described above, never perishes. He becomes immortal. Here is the following verse about it: [3.11]

"One who knows the origin of Prana, how it enters the body, how it lives there after dividing itself fivefold, and what its inner workings are, surely attains immortality. He attains immortality without fail." [3.12]

## FOURTH QUESTION

The first three questions dealt with more mundane subjects, namely, the birth and sustenance of the body. This fourth and the subsequent two questions deal with higher knowledge, that is, the nature of the Purusha, that calm, immutable and unchanging Truth.

Sauryayani Gargya asked the next question thus: "Reverend Sir, what is it that sleeps in a man when his body sleeps, what is it that keeps awake, and what is it that dreams? What is it again that enjoys happiness and with whom are all the sense-organs united?" [4.1]

To him Pippalada replied, "O Gargya, as all the rays of the setting sun become united with the orb of the sun, to radiate from it again when it rises, similarly all the senses merge into the mind when a man sleeps. That is why he does not hear, see, smell, taste, touch, speak, enjoy or move. [4.2]

"Only the Pranas remain awake in this city of the body. The Apana is like the Garhapatya fire, the Vyana is like the Anvaharyapachana fire and the Prana is like the Ahavaniya fire. [4.3]
(The three kinds of fires mentioned here are used in the Agnihotra sacrifice. The first fire is kept burning on an altar and is used as a source of all the other fires. The second fire is placed at the southern end of the house and is used to offer oblations to dead forefathers. The third fire is

used to offer oblations to the gods. The Upanishad is comparing the functions of the three Pranas in the body with those of the three fires in a household.)

"The Samana is the priest in the sacrifice, because it balances inhalation and exhalation which are like the two oblations of an Agnihotra sacrifice. The mind indeed is the sacrificer. The desired fruit is the Udana, which leads the sacrificer every day to Brahman. [4.4]

(It is the Udana which leads a soul to Brahmaloka. Unlike the other two states, namely, waking and dreaming, dreamless deep sleep is compared here to Turiya or the Samadhi state. The Upanishad says here that the Udana takes the mind, the sacrificer, every day in deep sleep to a state which is very near to Brahman.)

"In the dream state the mind enjoys those experiences that it did in the waking state. It sees things, hears sounds and visits places again and again in the dream as if it is really seeing, hearing and visiting them. It creates them all which are seen and unseen, heard and unheard, perceived and unperceived, real and unreal. [4.5]

"When the mind is overpowered by deep sleep it does not dream any more. Then it enjoys the calm repose in the body itself. [4.6]

"O handsome one, just as the birds fly to the tree that provides lodging, in this state of deep sleep all the sense-organs, mind and Prana rest in the Jivatman. [4.7]

"Earth, water, fire, air and ether along with their respective subtle elements, the eyes and what can be seen, the ears and what can be heard, the smell and what can be smelled, the taste and what can be tasted, the touch and what can be touched, the organ of speech and what can be spoken, the hands and what can be taken, the organ of generation and its object of enjoyment, the organ of excretion and what can be excreted, the feet and the path trodden, the mind and its thoughts, the intellect and what can be comprehended, ego and the object of egoism, the memory and its objects, the light and what can be lit up, the Prana and what can be sustained—all these rest in the Atman during deep sleep. [4.8]

"This Self is the seer, feeler, hearer, smeller, taster, thinker, knower, doer and the intelligent Purusha. He is established in the supreme immutable Atman. [4.9]

"He who realizes that shadowless, bodiless, colorless, pure, immutable one attains the Omniscient. About that there is the following shloka (verse): [4.10]

"O handsome man, he who knows the imperishable Atman in which rest the mind, the senses and the Pranas, surely becomes omniscient, and realizing himself as the Atman feels himself as existing in all." [4.11]

## FIFTH QUESTION

Next Satyakama Shaibya asked Pippalada, "Holy Sir, which world does a man attain who concentrates upon Om until his death?" [5.1]

To him Pippalada replied, "O Satyakama, Om is the unmanifested supreme Brahman as well as the manifested Brahman. Therefore, the wise man who meditates on Om achieves either of the two. [5.2]

(The manifested Brahman is the "saguna" form of god, namely, Vishnu, Rama, Krishna, etc.)

"Even if he meditates upon one syllable (A) of Om (made up of A, U and M) he comes back to this world very soon after his death. He is enlightened by it and attains greatness in life, being endowed with austerity, continence and faith. [5.3]

("Even one syllable" actually means with little knowledge of the real meaning of Om.)

"If he meditates on two syllables of Om (A and U), that is, with somewhat greater knowledge of its meaning, upon his death he will ascend to the world of the moon. After having enjoyed its pleasures he comes back again to the earth in a new birth. [5.4]

"If a person meditates on Om with the full knowledge that it is one with Brahman, upon his death he will be united with the effulgent sun. He will be freed from all sins just as a snake is freed from its slough. He is then taken by Sama hymns to the world of Brahma. There he sees the supreme Brahman which resides in the heart. There are two verses on this which mean: [5.5]

"When each of the syllables of Om is meditated upon separately a man is reborn as a mortal, but when all the three syllables are united and meditated upon, one truly meditates upon Brahman. Then in all the three states, namely, waking, dreaming and deep sleep, his consciousness of Brahman or Atman remains unwavering. [5.6]

"This world is attained by the *Rik* hymns, the world of the moon is attained by the *Yajus* hymns, and the wise know that the world of Brahma is attained by the *Sama* hymns. The sages attain all that, which is peaceful, undecaying, immortal, free from all fear and supreme, by means of Om." [5.7]

### SIXTH QUESTION

The last question was asked by Sukesha Bharadvaja. He asked, "Venerable Sir, Hiranyanabha, the prince of Kosala, came to me and asked me whether I knew the Purusha who has sixteen limbs. I told him that I did not know him and that if I knew, I would have told him about him certainly. I also told him that one who lies perishes with all his roots. Then he got into his chariot and went away. Therefore, now I ask you to tell me where that Purusha dwells." [6.1]

To him he said: "My dear fellow, that Purusha dwells here in this very body. From him the sixteen limbs originate. [6.2]

"He, the Purusha, reflected: 'As a result of whose departure will I too depart and with whose stay will I stay in this body?' [6.3]

"He created Prana, from Prana he created intellect, ether, air, fire, water, earth, the senses, the mind and food. From food he created vigor, self-control, the Vedas, yajnas, the worlds and name. (These are the sixteen limbs he has or the sixteen parts of the universe.) [6.4]

"Just as the rivers, after reaching the ocean, lose their names and form by merging into it, so also the sixteen limbs of the Purusha disappear in Him. There is a verse about it: [6.5]

"The sixteen parts of the universe rest on Him like the spokes on the hub of a chariot wheel. Know that Self (Purusha), and death will not hurt you." [6.6]

The sage finally said to them: "What I have told you is all that can be said about the Atman, the supreme Brahman. There is nothing higher than that." [6.7]

They worshipped him and said: "You are our father. You have taken us across to the other shore beyond ignorance. We bow down to all the great seers. Obeisance to the great seers." [6.8]

*****

# Mundaka Upanishad

## Introduction

The *Mundaka Upanishad* belongs to the Shaunakiya shakha of the *Atharvaveda*. Its content was originally taught by Brahma, the lord of creation, to his eldest son Atharvan. Through the succession of teachers it was revealed to Shaunaka, as we see in the beginning of the first section of the first chapter.

The word "mundaka" means a person with shaven head, or a sannyasin (monk). Even each chapter of the Upanishad is called mundaka. It was so named perhaps because the Upanishad was intended for the sannyasins, who keep their heads shaven, emphasizing sannyasa as the only means of realizing the eternal Brahman. The other explanation given is that the supreme wisdom revealed in the Upanishad removes the veil of ignorance from one's mind, showing Brahman, just as the razor clearly shows the skin of the head after removing the hair. The Upanishad has three chapters (mundakas) with two sections in each.

The Upanishad starts with a declaration that the knowledge of Brahman is the basis of all the sciences (*Brahma-vidyam sarva-vidya-pratishtham*). Shaunaka asked of Angiras a question: "What is that knowledge, knowing which everything in this world is known?" Angiras first tells him that there are two kinds of knowledge, the higher and the lower. Study of any subject including the study of the four Vedas is lower knowledge. Only the knowledge of the eternal and imperishable Brahman is the higher knowledge. It is Brahman who brought forth the material cause of this whole universe out of Himself and made all this universe at his sheer will. This is the topic of the first section of the first chapter. In the second section the merits of the yajna (sacrifice) and works of charity, as prescribed in the Vedas, are first praised. The Upanishad tells us that they surely are the means of purifying one's inner self. Also one enjoys heavenly pleasures after death, as fruits of those good works. Then it points out that those good works have their own flaws. They are only temporary, and the enjoyer of the fruits eventually falls back to the cycle of births and deaths, after enjoying the fruits. Therefore, if one wants to merge with the imperishable and immortal Brahman, one should live the life of a mendicant in the forest with austerity and purity, under a knowledgeable teacher of Brahman.

In the second chapter, the first section describes in beautiful verses how the all-pervading Brahman brought forth all these worlds, and on them these mountains, oceans, rivers, plants and creatures. Then it concludes by saying that the supreme Brahman Itself is all that, the sacrificial works and knowledge. He is in our heart and knowing Him breaks the shackles of ignorance in this very life. The second section describes how, by meditating on Him with the help of His sound symbol Om, one can achieve Him. Brahman is again described as all-knowing, all-pervading, illuminating the whole universe, and yet seated within one's heart. It concludes by declaring, "All this universe indeed is the supreme Brahman."

The first section of the third chapter starts with the well known allegory of "two birds of golden plumes" seated on the same tree. One of them is the individual self (Jivatman) and the other is the Supreme Self (Paramatman). The former identifies itself with the body, mind and action and, therefore, is bound. The latter is pure consciousness, free and eternal. The same tree means the human body, where they both reside. The supreme Self is achieved through truth, knowledge, meditation and brahmacharya, practiced constantly. The second section says that those who long for objects of desires are born again and again, whereas the desires of those sages who are devotedly engaged in realization of the Atman vanish away, here in this life. The Atman is gained by those who strive for it with vigor, purity and austerity. Whoever knows Brahman becomes Brahman himself.

### Peace Invocation

Om! O gods, may our ears hear auspicious words. May we, who are good in worship, see auspicious things with our eyes. May we, who sing your praise, live our allotted span of life in perfect health and strength.

May Indra of ancient fame confer success in our study of the Upanishad. May all-knowing Pusha, god of the earth, confer prosperity on us. May Garuda, the destroyer of evil, be well disposed toward us. May Brihaspati ensure our welfare in the study of this scripture. Om. Peace, Peace, Peace.

\*\*\*

## CHAPTER 1

### Section 1.1

Amongst all the gods Brahma, the creator and protector of the universe, was the first to be born. He imparted the knowledge of Brahman, the basis of all knowledge, to his eldest son Atharvan. [1.1.1]

A long time ago Atharvan taught that supreme knowledge of Brahman to Angir. Angir passed it on to Satyavaha Bharadvaja, and Satyavaha Bharadvaja revealed it to Angiras. [1.1.2]

Once Shaunaka, the famous householder, approached Angiras with due respect and asked, "Sir, what is that knowledge, knowing which everything in this world is known?" [1.1.3]

Angiras replied to him: As the knowers of the Vedas have said, their are two kinds of knowledge, namely, the higher and the lower. [1.1.4]

Of these, the lower knowledge is the knowledge of the *Rigveda, Yajurveda, Samaveda, Atharvaveda*, phonetics, rituals, grammar, etymology, prosody and astronomy. On the other hand, the higher knowledge is that by which one knows the changeless Reality, that is Brahman. [1.1.5]

That Brahman is invisible, ungraspable, without origin and without attributes. He has neither eyes nor ears, neither hands nor feet. He is eternal, of many forms, all-pervading, very subtle and imperishable. The wise perceive Him as the source of all creation. [1.1.6]

As a spider emits and withdraws a web, as plants grow from the soil, and as hair grows over the human body, so does the universe spring out from the eternal Brahman. [1.1.7]

When Brahman willed, the material cause of creation was produced, from it came the primordial energy, from the primordial energy came the mind, from the mind came the five elements, from the elements came many worlds, and from the action of the beings in these worlds came their chain of cause and effects, that is, the reward and punishments of their action. [1.1.8]

Brahman is omniscient, seer of all and ocean of knowledge. Of Him only are born Brahma, all the creatures and their source of nourishment. [1.1.9]

### Section 1.2

Whatever the sages have described about the rituals and their fruits, in the sacred hymns of the three Vedas, are true. O seekers of the truth, perform them constantly. Those meritorious actions indeed are the path to the joyful worlds. [1.2.1]

When the sacrificial fire is well lit and the flames begin to rise, offer the oblations with faith, in the center of the flames. [1.2.2]

If the Agnihotra sacrifice is not performed as prescribed, that is, if it is not done during the first moon, the full moon, the four months of Autumn, harvest time, also if it is done without guests, without offerings to the Vishvadevas (feeding of birds and animals), and if it is not done according to scriptural injunctions, the performer's chances of attaining the seven worlds are destroyed. (The seven desirable higher worlds are: Bhu, Bhuva, Sva, Maha, Jana, Tapa and Satya.) [1.2.3]

The fire god has seven waving tongues. They are called the Black, the Fierce, the Swift-mind, the Red, the Smoke-colored, the Scintillating, and the All-shining. [1.2.4]

He who offers oblations to these shining flames at the appropriate time is led by these oblations, as the sun's rays, to the world of Indra, the Lord of the gods. [1.2.5]

The bright offerings welcome the sacrificer, carry him along the sun's rays, and praise him with pleasant words by saying that that world of Brahma is won by him due to his meritorious deeds. [1.2.6]

(After praising the rituals of the sacrifices, now the Upanishad tells about their limitations.)

Alas! But these sacrifices, with their eighteen members (sixteen priests, the sacrificer and his wife), make a frail boat. The deluded, who regard them as the highest deeds, remain subject to cycles of birth and death. [1.2.7]

Living in deep ignorance, yet thinking themselves wise and learned, the deluded go round and round, like the blind led by the blind, suffering time and again. [1.2.8]

(This mantra also occurs in the *Katha Upanishad.* See *Katha Upanishad* 1.2.5.)

Fools, dwelling in the very midst of ignorance, yet vainly considering themselves wise and learned, go round and round stumbling hither and thither, like the blind guided by the blind. [1.2.9]

The deluded, thinking that performing sacrifices (yajnas) and acts of charity are the highest religious deeds, do not know anything better. Having enjoyed the fruits of their good deeds in the high heavens, they fall back to human birth or even lower birth. [1.2.10]

Those who live in the forest with austerity and devotion, leading peaceful lives as mendicants, become freed from all impurities and achieve the immortal world of that imperishable Brahman (even in this life). [1.2.11]

A man devoted to spiritual life should carefully examine the demerits of attaining these ephemeral worlds gained by good deeds, and should become indifferent to them. The eternal Brahman cannot be achieved by created ephemeral deeds. He, with sacrificial fuel in hand, should approach a preceptor who is well versed in the scriptures and established in Brahman. [1.2.12]

When a disciple, whose mind is pacified and senses are controlled, approaches a learned preceptor with due respect and humility, the preceptor will impart the knowledge of the true and imperishable Brahman to him. [1.2.13]

## CHAPTER 2

### Section 2.1

Brahman is the ultimate Truth. Just as from a blazing fire thousands of sparks are formed, similarly, from the imperishable Brahman manifold creatures are born and go back to It again. [2.1.1]

That self-luminous Brahman is formless, unborn, pure, without Prana and without mind. He is both within and without. He is greater than the greatest. [2.1.2]

From Him are born Prana, mind, senses, ether, air, fire, water and the earth, that supports all. [2.1.3]

He, who is the innermost Self of all, has fire as His head, the sun and moon as His eyes, the four directions as His ears, the Vedas as His voice, the wind as His breath and the universe as His heart. The earth originated from his feet. [2.1.4]

From Him came the bright heavens with the sun as the fuel (to keep them lighted), from the moon in those worlds came the rain clouds, from the clouds, the plants on the earth. From the plants, food came which formed the seed in man, which he gives to woman. In this manner all creatures are born of the all-pervading Brahman. [2.1.5]

From Him are born the Vedic hymns, devotional chants, sacrificial rites, ceremonies, sacrificial gifts, time, the sacrificer, and the worlds purified by the sun and the moon. [2.1.6]

From Him only came the gods of various orders, celestials, men, animals, birds, Prana and Apana, grains, austerity, faith, truth, brahmacharya and the law. [2.1.7]

From Him sprang the seven sense-organs, seven flames, seven kinds of fuels, seven oblations, and seven seats where move the sense-organs that lie in the cavity of heart. God has thus deposited them in groups of seven. [2.1.8]

(Here the seven senses are those that are in the head: two eyes, two ears, two nostrils and mouth. The flames are their powers of perception, the fuels are the sense-objects, the oblations are the perceptions of the sense-objects, and the seats are the nerve centers through which the senses function. The meaning of the verse is not very clear. Perhaps it is trying to say that from Brahman emerged all that we are, we perceive, we enjoy; and therefore, we should worship Him with the attitude that everything including ourselves is Him.)

From Him emerged all the oceans, mountains, various forms of rivers, all the plants and other life-sustaining elements which support the subtle body inside the gross body. [2.1.9]

O young man, the Purusha alone is all this—the sacrificial works and knowledge. He who knows Him as the supreme immortal Brahman, seated in the heart, destroys the knot of ignorance itself here. [2.1.10]

## Section 2.2

Brahman is self-effulgent and is well established in the heart. Realizing Him is the supreme goal of all. All that move, breathe, and wink are supported by Him. Know Him as the cause of all the subtle and the gross. He is beyond the knowledge of ordinary creatures. He is adorable and the highest of all. [2.2.1]

That Brahman is luminous and subtler than the subtle. Yet He supports all the worlds as well as all those who inhabit them. He is the vital force, speech and mind. He is true and He is immortal. His knowledge is the target to be penetrated by the mind. [2.2.2]

Holding the bow, that great weapon mentioned in the Upanishads, using the arrow sharpened by constant meditation, and having drawn the arrow with the mind absorbed in His thoughts, hit that target, the immutable Brahman. [2.2.3]

(What forms the bow and the arrow is mentioned in the next passage.)

Om is the bow, the Atman is the arrow, and Brahman is said to be the target. Hit the target with an undistracted mind, and like the arrow, be one with Him. [2.2.4]

Know only Him on whom are strung the earth, heaven, the inter-space, the mind and the vital force, together with all the other organs. Give up all vain talk. He alone is the bridge leading to immortality. [2.2.5]

Within the heart where all the nerves meet, like the spokes of a chariot wheel on the hub, the Atman moves by becoming multiformed (with different mental states). Meditate on the Atman as Om. May you be free from hindrances in reaching the shore beyond darkness. [2.2.6]

He who is all-knowing, omniscient, has his glory manifest in this universe, lives in the cavity of the heart—the bright city of Brahman. He is established in the mind, in food, and is carrier of the vital force and the body. The wise attain bliss and immortality by realizing Him, through their knowledge. [2.2.7]

When a person realizes Him who is both high and low (manifested or unmanifested form), the knot of the heart is untied, all doubts become solved and all actions become dissipated. [2.2.8]

Brahman is in a supreme, luminous sheath, free from taints and indivisible. He is pure and the light of lights. Him the knowers of Atman realize. [2.2.9]

There the sun does not shine, nor the moon, nor the stars. This lightning doesn't shine there either, much less the earthly fire. Everything shines reflecting His glory. This whole universe is illumined with His light. [2.2.10]

All this is the immortal Brahman. He is everywhere—above, below, in the front, at the back, to the right, to the left. All this indeed is the supreme Brahman! [2.2.11]

## CHAPTER 3

### Section 3.1

The Jivatman and the Paramatman are like two birds of golden plumage, who are inseparable companions and are perched on the same tree (the body). One of them, the Jivatman, eats the bitter and sweet fruits of karma, while the other, the Paramatman, looks on without eating. [3.1.1]

(The Jivatman and the Paramatman are the individual soul and God, respectively. The former is bound by body, mind, and action. God, on the other hand, is pure consciousness. However, the Jivatman is the image of the Paramatman, except that it is seen through the mind. Therefore, they are said to be inseparable.)

On the same tree, the individual self is deluded by ignorance of its true identity. Therefore it is sad and grieves. When he recognizes the other, the worshipful Lord as his own true Self, and beholds His glory, he grieves no more. [3.1.2]

When the seer sees the Effulgent One, who is ruler, creator and the source of Brahma, the lord of creation, then that wise one shakes off virtues and sins and unites with the Supreme. [3.1.3]

The Lord is the life of all creatures, through whom He shines (that is, He is present in all beings). Knowing this fact, one becomes wise and gives up vain talk. Reveling in the Atman, delighting in the Atman, performing pious works, he becomes distinguished amongst the knowers of Brahman. [3.1.4]

The Atman is realized through steadfastness in truth, austerity, complete knowledge and brahmacharya (celibacy). When impurities are washed away, the seers see Him within themselves. [3.1.5]

Truth alone wins, and not untruth. Truth lays out a divine path called Devayana, by which the sages, free from desires, achieve the supreme abode of truth. [3.1.6]

Brahman is vast, self-luminous, and beyond imagination. He is subtler than the subtlest, farther than the farthest. The seers realize Him in this very life, as residing in their own hearts. [3.1.7]

The eyes cannot see Him, speech cannot describe Him and the senses cannot perceive Him. He cannot be attained by austerity or karma (action) either. When one's mind becomes calm and purified, then through meditation one realizes Him. [3.1.8]

This subtle Atman within the body, where the Prana dwells with its five parts, should be known by meditation. Man's mind is interwoven with his senses. When the mind is purified (freed from the senses), the Atman is realized. [3.1.9]

A man of pure mind gets whatever worlds he wishes to achieve and whatever desires he has in his heart. Therefore, he who desires prosperity should respect a man who has realized the Atman. [3.1.10]

### Section 3.2

The sage knows the radiant Brahman to be the supreme abode of the whole universe. Those wise persons who, having become desireless, worship that knower of Brahman, transcend rebirth. [3.2.1]

He whose mind thinks of desirable things is born again to fulfill those desires. But he whose desires are pacified after realization of Brahman has no more longings for mundane objects. [3.2.2]

This Atman cannot be attained by the study of the scriptures, nor by intelligence, nor by much hearing. It is attained by him to whom It chooses to reveal Its own true form. [3.2.3]
(This mantra also occurs in the *Katha Upanishad* as mantra 1.2.23.)

The Atman is not attained by one who is weak in determination. It is not attained by the careless, nor by people of improper austerities. But the wise man who strives for It with vigor and care enters the abode of Brahman. [3.2.4]

After having attained the Atman, the sages become contented with their knowledge, established in the Self, free from attachment, and composed. Those wise and devout souls, having realized the all-pervading Atman, enter into Him, the self of all. [3.2.5]

Those who are well established in the Atman through the study of the Vedantic knowledge, practicing constantly the sannyasa yoga (monastic life), with their nature purified, after death attain immortality in Brahman and become freed from rebirth. [3.2.6]

The knowers of the Atman, after having their fifteen body-constituents (Prana, faith, ether, air, etc., as in *Prashna Upanishad* 6.4) resolved into their sources, their sense-organs gone to their respective deities, have their karma and their individual soul merged in the supreme, immutable Brahman. [3.2.7]
(Ear, eye, tongue, etc., have their respective presiding deities as ether, sun, Varuna, etc.; see *Tattva Bodha*, by Shankaracharya.)

As rivers, after merging into the ocean, lose their name and form, so also the wise man, free from name and form, achieves the highest of the high, the supreme Brahman. [3.2.8]
(See *Prashna Upanishad* 6.5.)

He who knows the supreme Brahman becomes that very Brahman. In his family no one ignorant of Brahman is born. *The knots of his heart are untied* (In Upanishadic language this sentence means that one's ignorance is destroyed), and after going beyond all sorrows and sins he attains immortality. [3.2.9]

The following principle has been declared by this Vedic mantra: This Brahmavidya should be revealed only to those who are well versed in the Vedas, perform rites, are devoted to Brahman, make oblations to the fire, called Ekarshi, and take the vow of sannyasa. [3.2.10]

The Rishi Angiras spoke of this truth in ancient times. No one who has not taken the proper vows should study it. Salutations to the great Rishis. [3.2.11]

*****

# Mandukya Upanishad

## Introduction

This Upanishad derives its name after its seer, Manduka, who compiled it, and belongs to the *Atharvaveda*. It is the shortest amongst the principal Upanishads and contains only twelve mantras. However, it is one of the most difficult Upanishads to understand. It presents the essence of all the Upanishads, in a unique way. It starts with a *mahavakya*, or a sacred dictum, that this "Atman is Brahman." It also declares that Om is really this universe or Brahman. Then it analyses the whole span of human consciousness into three states, namely, the waking state (*jagrat avastha*), the dream state (*svapna avastha*), and the state of dreamless deep sleep (*sushupti avastha*). There is a fourth state called *Turiya*, which is the state of self-realization. In this state all phenomena cease, and there is nothing but peace and bliss. The Upanishad talks about a mono-syllable, Om, as the symbol of the Atman to meditate upon, made up of three sounds, A, U and M. "A" stands for Vaishvanara (the Universal person), whose field of action is the waking state. "U" stands for Taijasa (the luminous or brilliant one), whose field of action is the dream state. "M" stands for Prajna (consciousness or knowledge), whose field of action is the state of dreamless sleep. The Upanishad finally ends by asserting that the ultimate Reality is nondual, which is the central philosophy of the *Advaita* or "nondual" Vedanta.

Shri Gaudapada, who was preceptor of Govindapada (guru of Shri Shankaracharya), wrote a *Karika* or explanatory treatise on the Upanishad, to make its study easier.

## Peace Invocation

Om! O gods, may our ears hear auspicious words. May we, who are good in worship, see auspicious things with our eyes. May we, who sing your praise, live our allotted span of life in perfect health and strength.

May Indra of ancient fame confer success in our study of the Upanishad. May all-knowing Pusha, god of the earth, confer prosperity on us. May Garuda, the destroyer of evil, be well disposed toward us. May Brihaspati ensure our welfare in the study of this scripture. Om. Peace, Peace, Peace.

***

All this world is syllable Om, the imperishable Brahman. All that is past, present and future is Om. And whatever is beyond the three periods of time is Om, too. [1]

All this is surely Brahman. This Atman is Brahman. The Atman has four quarters. [2]

(*Ayam Atma Brahma* or "This Atman is Brahman," is one of the four *Mahavakyas* of the Upanishads. The four quarters are: waking state, dreaming state, state of dreamless deep sleep, and *turiya* state.)

The first quarter of the Atman is Vaishvanara, whose sphere of action is the waking state, and who is conscious of only external objects. Vaishvanara has seven body-parts and nineteen organs of knowledge. [3]

(The seven parts are: the heavens as its head, the sun its eyes, air its breath, fire its heart, water its belly, earth its feet, and ether its body. The nineteen organs of knowledge are: five organs of sense, five organs of action, five Pranas, mind, intellect, heart and ego, or sense of identity.)

The second quarter of the Atman is Taijasa, the luminous person, whose consciousness is internal. Its sphere of action is the dream state. It has seven body-parts and nineteen organs of knowledge, and enjoys subtle objects. [4]

That state is deep sleep where the person who sleeps feels no desire and sees no dreams. The third quarter of the Atman is Prajna, whose sphere of action is deep sleep. In this state all the experiences of the waking state and dream state dissolve in the experience of deep sleep. In this state cognition is reduced to an indefinite mass and is full of bliss (though the bliss is of quiescence and negative in character). This Prajna enjoys bliss and forms the gateway to the experience of the dream and waking states. [5]

This Prajna (consciousness) is the Lord, the omniscient, the inner controller, the source, the origin and dissolution of all. [6]

(From deep sleep spring the waking and the dream states. Also the latter two states dissolve in the state of deep sleep. Therefore, the state of deep sleep is said to be the Lord of all.)

The fourth quarter, Turiya, is neither conscious of the internal world, nor conscious of the external world, nor is unconscious. It is unseen, beyond empirical dealings, beyond the grasp of the organs of action, uninferable, unimaginable, indescribable. His valid proof is in the belief of the Atman, in which all phenomena cease, which is changeless, auspicious and nondual. That Atman is to be known. [7]

This Atman, described earlier, is to be identified with Om when Om is considered as a single syllable. When Om is considered as composed of its constituent letters, A, U and M, the quarters of the Atman are to be identified with the constituents. [8]

Vaishvanara (the Universal Person), having the waking state as its sphere of action, is the first letter, "A," the first constituent part of Om, because of their similarity of pervasiveness and being the first. One who knows thus, surely attains all the things he desires, and becomes the foremost. [9]

(In Sanskrit, A is the first letter of the *varnamala* or alphabet, and no letter can be pronounced without combination with A. That is why Lord Krishna says in the *Gita* that He is A amongst all the letters [*Gita*, 10.33].)

Taijasa (brilliant one), which has the dream state as its sphere of action, is the second constituent letter, "U," of Om; because of the similarity of excellence and being in between. One who knows thus, attains great knowledge and excellence. No one is born in his family who is not a knower of Brahman. [10]

(The excellence of Taijasa is in creating the world of ideas in the dream state; however, the excellence of U is not clear. The letter U in Om is in between the letters A and M, and so also is the dream state in between waking and deep sleep. Therefore, Taijasa is in between Vaishvanara and Prajna.)

Prajna, which has the sleep state as its sphere of action, is "M," the third constituent letter of Om. This is because of their commonality of measuring and absorption. One who knows thus, measures everything with his knowledge and comprehends everything in his mind. [11]

(When Om is repeatedly chanted the first two letters A and U seem to merge in, and get absorbed by, letter M. Similarly, the waking and dream states seem to get submerged in deep sleep, identified here with Prajna, and come out of it later. Therefore, M and Prajna are compared to a measuring utensil into which grain is put to measure, and poured out of it after measuring the grain.)

The whole syllable of Om is Turiya, the fourth quarter of the Atman. It is transcendental, devoid of phenomenal existence, is supreme bliss and non-dual. This Om is the Atman itself. He who knows thus, merges himself into the Atman. [12]

## Summary

| State | Microcosmic or Individual | Macrocosmic or Universal |
|---|---|---|
| Waking | Vaishvanara = Physical condition "A" of Om | Virat = Cosmic manifestation |
| Dream | Taijasa = Mental condition "U" of Om | Hiranyagarbha = Universal mind |
| Deep sleep | Prajna = Intellectual condition "M" of Om | Ishvara = God |
| Turiya | Though this is called the fourth state this is really the whole, the Brahman-Atman that encompasses all the above three states. It is transcendental, non-dual and supreme bliss. | |

*****

# Taittiriya Upanishad

## Introduction

This Upanishad occurs in the *Taittiriya Aranyaka* of the *Yajurveda*. The *Yajurveda* has two branches, namely, the *Taittiriya Yajurveda* and the *Vajasaneyi Yajurveda*. They are also called the *Krishna Yajurveda* and the *Shukla Yajurveda*, respectively. The seventh, the eighth and the ninth chapters of the *Taittiriya Aranyaka* form the *Taittiriya Upanishad*.

There is an interesting story about how the *Yajurveda* got two branches and why one branch was called the *Taittiriya Yajurveda*. Vaishampayana, a great teacher of the *Yajurveda* and a prominent disciple of the sage Vyasa, incurred some sin and then asked his disciples to perform sacrifices for atonement of his sin. His sister's son, Yajnavalkya, who was also his disciple, criticized his fellow students and decided to perform the atonement by himself. Vaishampayana was very angry with his nephew that he had such a poor opinion about his other disciples, and asked him to regurgitate the *Yajurveda* that was taught to him, in a tangible form. The other students transformed themselves into partridges (*tittiri* birds) to pick up what was thrown up by Yajnavalkya. That is how the Veda and its Upanishad got the name *Taittiriya*. Yajnavalkya was very upset and did an intense austerity to please the Sun-god. The Sun taught the same Veda to him in a different form. The new form was named *Vajasaneyi-Veda* after the Sun, who is also known as Vajasaneya. The other name of the Veda is *Shukla Yajurveda*. Shukla means white, and since the new branch of the Veda was named *Shukla*, the original version was called the black or *Krishna Yajurveda*.

The Upanishad has three *vallis* (vines), or chapters, namely "Shikshavalli," "Ananda-valli," and "Bhrigu-valli." Each chapter is divided into *anuvakas* or lessons. The very first and last lessons of the first chapter are also the *shantipatha* or peace invocation, wherein the student of the Upanishad offers his prayers to the cosmic powers—Mitra, Varuna, Aryama, Indra, Brihaspati and Vishnu—for the welfare of himself and his teacher during the study of the sacred knowledge, the Brahmavidya. Then in the second lesson the Upanishad talks about the importance of Vedic phonetics. Lesson eight talks about Om, and says that Om represents not only Brahman but also the universe. In lesson eleven the teacher, after having taught the Upanishad to his disciple, tells him about his duties as a householder. He instructs him to speak the truth, lead a righteous life, and always worship his parents, preceptor and guests.

In lesson one of the second chapter, the sentence, "The knower of Brahman attains the highest," forms the theme of the chapter. Later the lesson also defines Brahman by stating that "Brahman is truth, knowledge and infinite." Then it talks about five sheaths of the Atman, namely, the *Annamaya* (made of food), *Pranamaya* (made of energy), *Manomaya* (made of mind), *Vijnanamaya* (made of knowledge) and *Anandamaya* (made of bliss) sheaths, which are all of the shape of the body. It then defines the Bliss of Brahma, starting with the bliss of a human. It also declares that Brahman cannot be expressed by speech or mind.

In the third chapter Bhrigu approaches his father Varuna with a request to teach him about Brahman. Varuna tells him that Brahman is That which all beings are born from, are supported by and finally merge into. He hints that Brahman is known through food, Prana, eyes, ears, mind and speech. By performing austerity Bhrigu finally realizes Brahman. The Upanishad tells us that a householder should offer food and shelter to a guest with respect.

### Chapter 1: Shikshavalli
### (On Learning Phonetics)

### Lesson 1

May Mitra, Varuna, Aryama, Indra, Brihaspati and all-pervading Vishnu be blissful to us. Salutation to Brahman. O Vayu, salutation to you. You indeed are the perceptible Brahman. I shall call you alone the direct Brahman. I shall call you righteousness. I shall call you truth. May that Vayu protect me. May that Vayu protect the teacher. May he protect me. May he protect the teacher. Om. Peace, Peace, Peace.

(Lesson 1 is also the shantipatha of this Upanishad.)

## Lesson 2

Om! We shall discuss the science of pronunciation. It deals with learning about letters of the alphabet, their accent, measure, emphasis for articulation, uniformity and combination.

(An example of combination of two letters in Sanskrit is: Dev*a* + *I*sha = Dev*e*sha. Also, in the combination, *Sat* + *va* = *Sattva*, the letter t of *Sat* is the first letter, the v of *va* is the second letter, the second t in Sattva is the link or means of joining, and the resulting speech of joining them together is the combination.)

## Lesson 3

May we both, teacher and disciple, attain fame together. May our spiritual prowess grow together.

Now that we have discussed phonetics, we shall expound the sacred principle of conjunction or combination based on the five perceptible objects, namely, the worlds of the universe, the shining objects (objects producing light), learning, progeny and the (individual) body. These are called the great combinations.

The combination concerning the worlds is explained thus: The earth is like the first letter, heaven is like the second letter, air is the link, and the sky is the combination.

Now follows the combination of the shining objects. Fire is the first letter, the sun is the second letter, lightning is the link, and water is the combination.

The next one is the combination of learning. The teacher is the first letter, the student is the second letter, the imparting of the instruction is the link, and learning is the combination.

The next subject is the combination of progeny. Mother is the first letter, father is the second letter, procreation is the link, and progeny is the combination.

What follows is the combination of the body. The lower jaw is the first letter, the upper jaw is the second letter, the tongue is the link, and speech is the combination.

These are the great combinations. Anyone who meditates on these great combinations, as explained above, attains progeny, wealth in the form of cattle, spirituality, food and the heavenly world.

(The aim of a *sadhaka*, or a seeker of Brahman, is not to gain objects of enjoyment but to achieve self-realization. Therefore, when the Upanishad talks about meditating upon the five great combinations it perhaps hints that they are the examples of the great *mayashakti*, or power of creation, of the Great Lord. Thoughts about His greatness purify one's mind and one is prepared better for the path of spirituality. Even if one falls from that path due to some distraction, one achieves some materialistic rewards.)

## Lesson 4

That Om, which is the most excellent amongst the hymns of the Vedas, the Lord who has many forms and who emerged from the immortal Vedas, may He gratify me with intelligence. O Lord, may I become the receptacle of immortality, may my body be fit, may my speech be exceedingly sweet, and may I hear well through my ears. You are the sheath of Brahman and you are covered by wisdom. Please preserve my learning.

Please confer fortune on me without any delay, so that it may bring and increase my clothes, cattle, food and drink forever. May it bring prosperity and furry animals to me. May students come to me from all directions and from far off. May they come to me in the proper way and in large numbers. May the students have physical and mental control. May the students be calm.

May I become famous among people. May I become prominent among the wealthy. O gracious Lord, may I enter into you and you into me. Merging into you, who has a thousand branches, may I cleanse myself of all sins. As water flows down the slope, as months roll into a year, similarly, O Creator, may students come to me from all directions. You are the refuge. Please illuminate me and make me soaked with you.

## Lesson 5

*Bhuh, Bhuvah, Suvah*—these are the three mystical words. In addition to these, the sage Mahachamasya knew a fourth one called *Maha*. That is Brahman, That is Atman. The other gods are its limbs. Bhuh is indeed this world. Bhuvah is the intermediate space. Suvah is the other world. Maha is the sun through which all the worlds flourish. Bhuh also represents fire. Bhuvah is air. Suvah is the sun. Maha is the moon, through which all the luminaries flourish. Bhuh is the *Rigveda*, Bhuvah is the *Samaveda*, and Suvah is the *Yajurveda*. Maha is Brahman, by which all the Vedas are nourished. Bhuh is Prana, Bhuvah is Apana, Suvah is Vyana, and Maha is food. It is food that nourishes all the vital forces (Pranas). Thus the *Vyahritis* or the mystical words are divided into four groups of four each. He who knows these *vyahritis* knows Brahman. All the gods bring presents to him.

### Lesson 6

In the space within the heart resides the intelligent, immortal and golden Atman. This nipple-like growth, that hangs down between the palates, is the path of Brahman. Reaching the crown, where the roots of the hair part, it passes out by separating the skull at the time of a person's death. (By the term "nipple-like growth" the Upanishad refers to a branch of *sushumna nadi*, a hollow canal running along the spinal cord.) Then the person becomes established in fire, in air, in the sun, and in Brahman, by uttering the mystic syllables Bhuh, Bhuvah, Suvah, and Maha respectively. After attaining sovereignty, he then becomes ruler of speech, sight, hearing and mind. After that, he becomes the immortal Brahman whose body is the sky, whose real nature is truth, who revels in the vital forces (Prana), who is a great source of bliss for the mind, and who is enriched with peace and immortality. (The teacher says to his disciple:) O Prachinayogya, worhip Him in the manner described above.

### Lesson 7

One should meditate upon the elements which the universe is composed of, namely: the earth, the space between earth and heaven, heaven, the primary directions (quarters) and the intermediate directions; fire, air, the sun, the moon and the stars; and water, plants, trees, the sky and one's body. These relate to the elements. Then one should meditate upon oneself, reflecting on: Prana, Vyana, Apana, Udana and Samana; the eye, the ear, mind, speech and the sense of touch; skin, flesh, muscle, bone and marrow.

After revealing this the seer said, "the whole universe is based on a fivefold principle, and that one set of five preserves the other set of five."

## Lesson 8

Om is Brahman. Om is all this universe. Om is well known as a syllable of concurrence. Moreover, the priests ask their assistants by saying, "Om, recite to the gods." They commence singing *Samans* by Om. By uttering the words "Om shom" they recite the *shastras* (scriptures). The priest performing the sacrifice utters the encouraging words with Om. The priest called Brahma approves to proceed with the sacrifice with the word Om. One permits the performance of the Agnihotra sacrifice with the word Om. A seeker of Brahman, when about to recite the Vedas, utters "Om" thinking that he would attain Brahman. And he surely attains Brahman.

## Lesson 9

Righteousness, along with learning and teaching, should be practiced. Truth, along with learning and teaching, should be practiced. Austerity, along with learning and teaching, should be practiced. Control of the outer and inner organs, along with learning and teaching, should be practiced. Fires should be kept up, and also learning and teaching should be practiced. The Agnihotra sacrifice should be performed, and also learning and teaching should be practiced. Guests should be welcomed with respect, and also learning and teaching should be practiced. Humanitarian work should be done, and also learning and teaching should be practiced. Children and grandchildren should be raised at the ordained time, and also learning and teaching should be practiced. The sage Rathitar, who always spoke the truth, believed that truthfulness prevails. Paurushishti, who was in penance constantly, believed that austerity prevails. Naka, son of Mudgala, believed that learning and teaching of the Vedas alone is tapas (austerity); that alone is tapas.

## Lesson 10

I am the stimulator of this tree, that is, this universe. My fame is high like a mountain top. I am high, holy and the immortal Being as He is in the sun. I am the effulgent wealth. I have a fine intellect, and am immortal and immutable. This is the sacred statement of Trishanku.

## Lesson 11

After teaching the Vedas, the preceptor advises the disciple: "Speak the truth. Lead a religious life. Do not be careless about study of the Vedic scriptures. Offer desirable wealth to the teacher and do not cut off the line of progeny. Do not be inadvertent about truth. Do not deviate from righteousness. Do not neglect your well-being. Do not neglect auspicious rites. Do not ignore learning and teaching.

"Duties toward gods and forefathers should not be neglected. Consider your mother as a god. Consider your father as a god. Consider your teacher as a god. Consider your guest as a god. Perform those actions that do not bring blame, not others. Our good conduct should be followed by you, not other. You should offer seats to those Brahmanas who are praiseworthy among us, to give them rest. An offering should be made with respect, and never with disrespect. An offering should be made in accordance with your prosperity. An offering should be made with modesty. An offering should be made with fear. An offering should be made in a friendly manner.

"If you have any doubts about your actions or conduct, you should do what the Brahmanas present there would do in those matters. You should behave just as do those Brahmanas who are able to judge impartially, are experienced, independent, not cruel, and who follow the laws. As to those who are falsely accused, you should do what the Brahmanas present there would do in those matters. You should behave just as do those Brahmanas who are able to judge impartially, are experienced, independent, not cruel, and who follow the laws. This is the command, this is the instruction, this is the commandment, this is the secret instruction of the Vedas. One must follow this rule, one must be intent on following this rule."

## Lesson 12

May Mitra, Varuna, Aryama, Indra, Brihaspati and all-pervading Vishnu be blissful to us. Salutation to Brahman. O Vayu, salutation to you. You indeed are the perceptible Brahman. I shall call you alone the direct Brahman. I shall call you righteousness. I shall call you truth. May that Vayu protect me. May that Vayu protect the teacher. May he protect me. May he protect the teacher. Om. Peace, Peace, Peace.

### Chapter 2: Anandavalli
### (On Bliss)

### Lesson 1

Om! May Brahman protect us both, the preceptor and the disciple. May He nourish us both. May both of us acquire energy, through the study of the Upanishad. May this study illumine us both. May we never hate each other. Om. Peace, Peace, Peace.

Om! The knower of Brahman attains the highest. On that, this is what has been said: "Brahman is truth, knowledge and infinite." He who knows that Brahman as residing in the supreme space of heart enjoys all desirable things, in identification with the omniscient Brahman. From the Atman, which is referred to as Brahman, came the sky. From the sky emerged air. From air came fire. From fire water was created. From water came the earth. From the earth came plants. From plants came food. From food man was born. Man indeed is the product of the essence of food. He has a head, a right side, a left side, a trunk (torso), and a hind part forming the support. Here is a stanza explaining that:

### Lesson 2

All creatures that inhabit this earth are born from food. Likewise, they live on food and become merged in food. Food was created earlier than creatures. Therefore, it is called the medicine of all. Those who worship food as Brahman, get all food (i.e., material objects). Creatures are born from food. After birth they grow by food. Food is called "annam" (made from the Sanskrit root "*ad*," meaning to eat) because it is eaten and it feeds on creatures. (Brahman who is manifest in the form of food is the consumed and the consumer.)

The body, which is the physical sheath, is made of the essence of food. Within it there is an inner sheath made of Prana (the vital energy). The physical sheath is filled up with the sheath of Prana. The sheath of Prana, too, is exactly of the shape of the human body. It gets the shape of the body from the physical sheath. Prana is its head, Vyana is its right side, Apana is the left side, the sky is the trunk, and Udana is its base. There is the following stanza about it:

### Lesson 3

Gods as well as all humans and animals depend on Prana (the vital force) for their life. Prana is the life-span of all the animate world. Therefore, it is called the universal life. Those who worship Prana as Brahman attain the full span of life. Prana indeed is the life-span of all the animate world. Therefore, it is called the universal life.

The sheath of Prana (*Pranamaya kosha*) is the inner self of the physical sheath (*Annamaya kosha*). Inside the sheath of Prana, there is an inner self consisting of mind (*Manomaya kosha*). The sheath of Prana is filled up with the inner sheath of mind. The sheath of mind, too, is of the shape of the human body. It takes the shape of the human body after the sheath of Prana. The *Yajus*-mantras are its head, the *Rik*-mantras are its right side, the *Sama*-mantras are its left side, the injunctive part of the Vedas is its trunk, and the hymn portion of the *Atharvaveda* is its support. With regard to this there is a stanza as follows:

### Lesson 4

From that Brahman who is full of bliss the mind and speech turn back, without being able to describe It. If one knows Him, one is not subject to fear at any time.

Different from the sheath of mind, there is an inner self which consists of intellect (*Vijnana*) and which fills the mental sheath (*Manomaya kosha*). This too is of the shape of the human body. Its shape is identical with the human shape of the mental sheath, which encloses it. Faith is its head, righteousness is its right side, truth is its left side, yoga is its trunk, and *maha* is its support. With regard to this, too, there is the following stanza:

### Lesson 5

A man of intellect performs yajna as well as his various duties. All the gods worship intellect as Brahman. If one knows intellect as

Brahman and does not err about it, one casts aside all sins in the body and fulfills all one's desires.

Different from the sheath of intellect, there is an inner self which consists of bliss, and which fills the sheath of intellect. This sheath of bliss (*Anandamaya kosha*) is enclosed by the sheath of intellect. This too has the shape of the human body. Its shape is identical with the human shape of the sheath of intellect, which encloses it. Love is its head, joy is its right side, delight is its left side, bliss is its trunk, and Brahman is its support. Regarding this there is a stanza:

## Lesson 6

If one thinks Brahman to be non-existing one becomes non-existent. If one thinks that Brahman is an existing entity then he is considered as existing because of that knowledge.

Bliss is the inner self of the sheath of intellect. Therefore, the following questions arise, based on what is taught so far: Does a man, ignorant of Brahman, achieve Him after departing from here? Or does a man, who has the knowledge of Brahman, achieve Him after departing from here?

Brahman wished, "May I become many. Let me be born." He deliberated. After having deliberated, He created all this that exists. After creating this He entered into it. After having entered it he became with form and without form, defined and undefined, supporting and unsupporting, sentient and insentient, true and untrue. He became the entire reality. They call that Brahman Truth. Regarding this there is a stanza:

## Lesson 7

In the beginning all this was unmanifested Brahman. From that the manifested emerged. Brahman created Himself from Himself. That is why He is called the self-created. He who is known as the self-created is indeed the nectar or essence of life. By reaching that nectar the individual self becomes happy. Who indeed would breathe, and who would live if this bliss was not there in the supreme space of the heart? He alone is the cause of bliss. An aspirant becomes fearless only when he finds support in this invisible, bodyless, indescribable and supportless Brahman. Whenever he has the slightest doubt in Him, he is subject to fear. That Brahman is a cause of fear to a learned man who lacks the will to unite with Him. There is a stanza on this:

## Lesson 8

Out of His fear the wind blows, and the sun rises. Out of His fear fire, Indra, and the fifth one, Death, run.

This is an analysis of supreme bliss: Suppose there is a young man, in the prime of his youth, very noble, well learned (in the Vedas), very alert, very energetic and well built; and the entire earth laden with all riches belongs to him. Let this be one unit of human joy. One hundred such units of human joy are equal to one unit of joy of a human-gandharva, and so also of a sage free of desires. One hundred such units of a human-gandharva's joy are equal to one unit of joy of a divine-gandharva, and so also of a sage free of desires. One hundred such units of a divine-gandharva's joy are equal to one unit of joy of a mane (*pitri*), and so also of a sage free of desires. One hundred such units of a pitri's joy are equal to one unit of joy of a god born in heaven, and so also of a sage free of desires. One hundred such units of joy of a god born in heaven are equal to one unit of joy of a *karma-deva* (one who has become a god by virtue of his good deeds), and so also of a sage free of desires. One hundred such units of a karma-deva's joy are equal to one unit of joy of a god (thirty-three in number, namely, eight Vasus, eleven Rudras, twelve Adityas, Indra, and Prajapati), and so also of a sage free of desires. One hundred such units of a deva's joy are equal to one unit of joy of an Indra, and so also of a sage free of desires. One hundred such units of Indra's joy are equal to one unit of joy of Brihaspati, and so also of a sage free of desires. One hundred such units of Brihaspati's joy are equal to one unit of joy of Prajapati, and so also of a sage free of desires. One hundred such units of Prajapati's joy are equal to one unit of joy of Brahma, and so also of a sage free of desires. (See mantra 4.3.33 of the *Brihadaranyaka Upanishad* for a similar definition of supreme bliss.)

He who is in this human body, and He who is in the sun, are one. He who knows thus, after departing from this world, attains the *Annamaya, Pranamaya, Manomaya, Vijnanamaya,* and *Anandamaya* selves. With regard to that there is a stanza:

### Lesson 9

After knowing the bliss of that Brahman, from which the mind and speech turn back without being able to describe It, a man of knowledge is not fearful of anything. Such a learned man is not afflicted by thoughts like why he did not perform good deeds or why he performed bad deeds. He who is thus enlightened redeems his Self from both these thoughts. Such is the secret instruction.

## Chapter 3: Bhriguvalli
### (On Bhrigu's Enlightenment)

### Lesson 1

Bhrigu Varuni approached his father Varuna and requested, "O reverend sir, teach me about Brahman."

Varuna said, "Food, Prana, sight, hearing, mind and speech are the aids in the knowledge of Brahman. Try to know That from which all beings are born, by which they remain alive, towards which they move, and into which they merge. Know That to be Brahman."

Then Bhrigu performed austerity, after which, . . .

### Lesson 2

He thought food is Brahman, because all beings are born from food, remain alive by food, move towards food and then merge into food. Having thus reflected he again approached his father Varuna and said, "Reverend sir, teach me about Brahman."

His father said, "Seek to know Brahman through austerity. Austerity is Brahman."

Bhrigu performed austerity, after which, . . .

### Lesson 3

He thought Prana is Brahman, because all beings are born from Prana, remain alive by Prana, move towards Prana and then merge into Prana. Having thus reflected he again approached his father Varuna and said, "Reverend sir, teach me about Brahman."

His father said, "Seek to know Brahman through austerity. Austerity is Brahman."

Bhrigu performed austerity, after which, . . .

### Lesson 4

He thought mind is Brahman, because all beings are born from mind, remain alive by mind, move towards mind and then merge into mind. Having thus reflected he again approached his father Varuna and said, "Reverend sir, teach me about Brahman."

His father said, "Seek to know Brahman through austerity. Austerity is Brahman."

Bhrigu performed austerity, after which, . . .

### Lesson 5

He thought *vijnana* (intellect) is Brahman, because all beings are born from vijnana, remain alive by vijnana, move towards vijnana and then merge into vijnana. Having thus reflected he again approached his father Varuna and said, "Reverend Sir, teach me about Brahman."

His father said, "Seek to know Brahman through austerity. Austerity is Brahman."

Bhrigu performed austerity, after which, . . .

### Lesson 6

He thought bliss is Brahman, because all beings are born from bliss, remain alive by bliss, move towards bliss and then merge into bliss. This knowledge sought by Bhrigu and imparted by Varuna is established in the cavity of the heart. He who knows thus, becomes firmly established, becomes possessor and enjoyer of food, and becomes great in progeny, cattle, sacred wisdom and fame.

### Lesson 7

One should take a vow not to condemn food. Prana is verily food. The body is the consumer of food. The body is established on Prana (vital force), and Prana is established on the body. One food is established on another food. He who knows thus, becomes firmly established, becomes possessor and enjoyer of food, and becomes great in progeny, cattle, sacred wisdom and fame.

## Lesson 8

One should take a vow not to discard food. Water is verily food. Fire is the consumer of food. Fire is established on water. Water resides on fire. One food is established on another food. He who knows thus, becomes firmly established, becomes possessor and enjoyer of food, and becomes great in progeny, cattle, sacred wisdom and fame.

## Lesson 9

One should take a vow to grow plenty of food. The earth is verily food. The sky is the consumer of food. The sky is established in the earth and the earth is established in the sky. One food is established on another food. He who knows thus, becomes firmly established, becomes possessor and enjoyer of food, and becomes great in progeny, cattle, sacred wisdom and fame.

## Lesson 10

One should take a vow not to refuse anyone shelter at one's house. Therefore, one should collect plenty of food by any means. The householder should declare that food is prepared for the guest. The food that is prepared and offered in the best manner returns to the giver in the best manner. The food that is prepared and offered in the medium manner returns to the giver in the medium manner. And the food that is prepared and offered in the lowest manner returns to the giver in the lowest manner. (The best, the medium and the lowest manners also mean in young, middle and old ages, respectively.) To one who knows thus, the result comes as described above.

One should meditate upon Brahman as preservation in speech, as preservation in Prana and Apana, as action in the hands, as movement in the feet, and as discharge in the anus. These are the meditations on Brahman on the human plane.

On the divine plane, Brahman is to be meditated upon as satisfaction in rain, as energy in lightning, as fame in cattle, as light in the stars, as procreation, immortality, and joy in the generative organ, and as everything in the sky.

If one meditates upon Brahman as the support, one is supported. If one meditates upon Brahman as great, one achieves greatness. If one meditates upon Him as mind, one becomes a great thinker. If one meditates upon Him as bowing down, all enjoyable things come bowing down to one. If one meditates upon Him as the Supreme, one attains supremacy. If one meditates upon Him as a destructive power, one's adversaries that envy one die, and so do the enemies whom one dislikes. He who is in this human body, and He who is in the sun, are one. He who knows thus, after departing from this world, attains the *Annamaya, Pranamaya, Manomaya, Vijnanamaya,* and *Anandamaya* selves. He roams over these worlds enjoying whatever food he wants and assuming whatever form he wishes, singing the following Sama: O, Wonderful! O, Wonderful! O, Wonderful! I am food! I am food! I am food! I am the eater! I am the eater! I am the eater! I am the unifier! I am the unifier! I am the unifier! I am the first born of the universe! I came to exist even prior to the gods! I am the navel of immortality! Who gives me away protects me! I, as food, eat him who eats food all by himself! I destroy the entire universe! My brightness is like that of the sun! He who knows thus, gets the results mentioned. This is the sacred doctrine.

*****

# Aitareya Upanishad

## Introduction

The *Aitareya Upanishad* belongs to the *Rigveda* and is part of the *Aitareya Aranyaka*. It is attributed to the sage Mahidasa Itareya. It is said that his father was a Brahmana, but his mother, Itara, was a non-Brahmana by caste. Itara saw that when Mahidasa was a child, his father allowed his children from his Brahmana wives to sit on his lap in a sacrificial assembly, but denied that privilege to Mahidasa. She was very hurt by this discrimination against her son. She prayed to the goddess Earth, who imparted highly enlightening knowledge to Mahidasa. Mahidasa Itareya became a renowned sage and revealed a part of the Veda, which is known by his name.

This Upanishad tells us that the Atman is Brahman, the Creator of the universe. It also tells how a Jivatman is transferred from the father and enters the mother's womb. Then it is born in this world, and takes birth again and again, until it realizes its true nature as the Atman. It talks about a *rishi* called Vamadeva who came to know all about his previous births when he was still in his mother's womb. He then flew to liberate himself, like a hawk flying high in the sky. The Upanishad says that Brahman is realized through *Prajnana*, the knowledge of Brahman. It says that *knowledge itself is Brahman*, and this is the most important message of the Upanishad.

## Peace Invocation

May my speech be in coordination with my mind, and may my mind be in coordination with my speech. O Self-effulgent One, reveal Yourself to me. May my speech and mind both be carriers of the Veda to me. May not whatever I heard be forgotten by me. I shall join day and night together through this study. I shall speak the truth. I shall speak the real. I shall speak the truth. May that Brahman protect me; may that Brahman protect the teacher. May He protect me and my teacher. Om. Peace, Peace, Peace.

***

## CHAPTER 1

### Section 1.1

In the beginning there was only Atman (i.e., Brahman). There was nothing else that existed. The Atman thought: Let me create the worlds. Thus He created the worlds, namely, *Ambhas* (the super celestial region of waters), *Marichi* (the heavens with celestial lights), *Mara* (the world of mortals), and *Apah* (the subterranean region of water). That which is above heaven and is supported by it is Ambhas. The sky is Marichi. This earth is Mara. The world below the earth is Apah.

The Atman thought: Now here are the worlds. Let me now create the protectors of these worlds. He then gathered a lump in the form of a human from the water and gave shape to it. He started planning in regard to this Purusha (the Virat Atman or the aggregate Being). As he started thinking, a mouth of the Purusha split open, just as an egg opens. From the mouth emerged speech, and from speech came Fire. Then the two nostrils were formed. From the nostrils came out the power of smell, and from smell came out Air. Then the two eyes were formed. From the eyes emerged the power of sight, and from sight came out the Sun. Then the two ears were formed. From the ears came out the power of hearing, and from hearing came out the directions. Then the skin was formed. From the skin came out the sense of touch, and from the sense of touch came out plants and trees. Then the heart was formed. From the heart came out the mind, and from the mind came out the Moon. Then the navel was formed. From the navel came out the Apana (down breathing), and from the Apana came out Death. Then the generative organs were formed. From the generative organs came out the seed (semen), and from the seed came out water. (Fire, Air, Sun, etc., are the presiding deities of the sense organs.)

## Section 1.2

These presiding deities, after they were created, fell into the ocean. (The ocean symbolizes the mundane world, where we go through the cycles of birth and death, until we realize the Atman.) The Creator subjected the Purusha to hunger and thirst. The deities spoke to the Creator thus: "Please provide us with an abode where we can stay and eat food."

He brought a cow for them. They said: "This is not sufficient for us at all."

Then He brought a horse. "This is not sufficient for us," they said. For them He brought a man. They said, "This one is well created." And man is well created indeed.

He then said to the deities, "Enter into your respective abodes."

Fire, transforming into speech, entered the mouth. Air, becoming the sense of smell, entered the nostrils. The Sun, having become sight, entered the eyes. The directions, becoming the sense of hearing, entered the ears. The plants and trees, having become the sense of touch, entered the skin. The Moon entered the heart in the form of mind. The god of death entered the navel after becoming Apana. Water entered the generative organs after becoming semen. Hunger and thirst said to Him, "Assign a place for us."

He said, "I assign you to these deities (fire and the other gods dwelling in the mouth) and make you partners with them."

Therefore, to whatever god an offering is made, hunger and thirst become partners in it.

## Section 1.3

Then the God thought: These are the senses and the deities of the senses. Let me create food for them. He pondered over the water. From the water came out an organic matter that was food. The food that was thus created turned back and wanted to run away. The Purusha, the first embodied being, wanted to catch it with speech (because he did not know any other way of eating food to satisfy his hunger). But he did not succeed in catching it with speech. If he had succeeded in catching it with speech, then one would be able to satisfy hunger merely by uttering the name of food. He then tried to grasp the food with the sense of smell. He did not succeed in grasping it with smell. If he had succeeded in grasping it by smelling, then one would have become satisfied merely by smelling food. He then tried to get the food with the eyes. He did not succeed in taking it with the eyes. If he had succeeded in taking it with the eyes, then one would have become satisfied merely by seeing food. He then tried to grasp the food with the ears. He did not succeed in grasping it with ears. If he had succeeded in grasping it by ears, then one would have become satisfied merely by hearing of food. He then tried to grasp the food with the sense of touch. He did not succeed in grasping it with touch. If he had succeeded in grasping it by touch, then one would have become satisfied merely by touching food. He then tried to grasp the food with the mind. He did not succeed in grasping it with the mind. If he had succeeded in grasping it by the mind, then one would have become satisfied merely by thinking of food. He then tried to grasp the food with the procreative organ. He did not succeed in grasping it with it. If he had succeeded in grasping it by the procreative organ, then one would have become satisfied merely by ejecting food. He then tried to grasp the food with Apana. He succeeded in it. Thus it is Apana which eats the food. It is the chief cause of supporting life by food.

He, the Creator, thought: How can this (body with senses) remain without me? By which of the two ways (i.e., head or feet) should I enter it? If utterance is made by the mouth, smelling by the sense of smell, seeing by the eyes, hearing by the ears, feeling by touch, thinking by the mind, digesting by Apana, ejecting by the procreative organs, then what am I? After making an opening in the skull, He indeed entered the body through this door. This entrance is called *vidriti* (the door with a slit opening). It is a place of joy. For Him there are three abodes and three states of dream.

(The Jivatman or individual soul which enters the body, as a king entering his city, has three places of residence. They are: the sense of sight in the waking state, the mind in the dreaming state, and the space within the heart in the state of deep sleep. The three places of residence are also: the body of the father, the womb of the mother, and one's own body. The three states of dream are: waking, dream, and deep sleep.)

He manifested all beings and identified Himself with them. He perceived this very Purusha (the Jivatman, the individual soul) as Brahman, that encompasses all. Therefore, His name is Idandra. Although He is Idandra, He is called by his indirect name, Indra. The gods like to be called by their indirect names. (In civilized societies the elders, namely, father, mother, teacher, etc., do not like to be called by their direct names by their children or disciples.)

## CHAPTER 2

### Section 2.1

The soul is first conceived in man. His semen is extracted from all his limbs as their essence. He holds this essence of his self in his own body. When he casts his semen in his wife, then he procreates it. That is his first birth. That semen becomes part of his wife, as if it were her own body part. Therefore, the fetus does not hurt her. She protects this self that has entered her womb. She, as a nourisher, has to be nourished herself. The mother bears the child in her womb until birth. The father protects the child before it is born, at birth and after birth. That child whom he has protected before birth, at birth and later is truly his own self. So is this world of progeny continued without break. That is the second birth of his self. Now the son, as the self of his father, replaces his father for performance of virtuous deeds. Then his other self, the father, after his duties are over, and due to old age, departs, and takes birth again. That is his, the son's, third birth. (Here, the father's birth as the third birth of the son is merely indicative of the father and son being identified as links of the same chain of progeny. It is not meant to be literally true.)

Referring to this there is a Vedic verse declared by the sage Vamadeva: While lying in the womb of my mother I came to know of the births of all the gods. A hundred iron citadels held me down. But I broke them and came out like a hawk, with the force of knowledge of the Atman. Vamadeva, who had known thus, became identified with the Supreme. He obtained all desirable things in this world itself, and after ascending higher up, after the end of the body, attained immortality.

## CHAPTER 3

### Section 3.1

What is it that we worship as Atman? Which of the two is it—the Parabrahman or the Aparabrahman? Is it that by which one sees, or that by which one hears, or that by which one smells, or that by which one speaks, or that by which one tastes the sweet or sour?

It is the heart and the mind, as described in the Vedas. It is perception, direction, understanding, knowledge, intelligence, retentiveness, insight, firmness, thinking, freedom of thought, mental suffering, memory, imagination, vitality, desire, ambition and such, all these are the names of consciousness. This One is Brahma, Indra, Prajapati, all the gods, the five great elements: earth, air, sky, water and fire. This is a mixture of various kinds of creatures from the smallest organism to the largest animals, those born of eggs, of womb, of heat and of shoots, namely, horses, cows, men, elephants and all the rest of the living beings that walk, fly or do not move. All these have consciousness or Prajna. The universe has Prajnana as its eye and its end. The whole universe is founded on Prajna, and therefore, *Prajnana is Brahman* (consciousness is Brahman). One who has realized this intelligent Atman, transcends this world, and having fulfilled all his desires in the yonder world of heaven, definitely becomes immortal.

*****

# Chhandogya Upanishad

## Introduction

This is a very large Upanishad. This Upanishad appears in the *Chhandogya Brahmana* of the *Samaveda*. "Chhanda" means "to please;" and the melody of the Saman is certainly pleasant to the ears and the heart. That is why Lord Krishna declares in the *Gita*, "I am the *Samaveda* among the Vedas." "Chhandoga" means one who sings the Saman, or the Sama Gana. It is said that just as the *Katha Upanishad* forms the basis for the *Bhagavadgita*, the *Chhandogya Upanishad* constitutes the chief authority for the *Brahma Sutra*, written by Veda Vyasa.

Chapter 1 tells us that the syllable "Om" is the most appropriate name of the Supreme Being. Therefore, one should meditate upon Om, which is also called the "Udgitha." Prana (vital energy) in the body, and the sun in the universe, represent Om. Chapter 2 of the Upanishad declares that everywhere in nature there is Sama Gana being recited continuously. Saman and "good" are synonymous. In the yajna there are five elements of the Saman, namely, Himkara, Prastava, Udgitha, Pratihara and Nidhana. Among the worlds, in nature, among the seasons, among the animals and among the senses there is fivefold Saman. The Chapter also talks about sevenfold Saman. One should meditate upon fivefold Saman and sevenfold Saman. In Chapter 3, the sun is considered as the honey of the gods, because the sun embodies the result of all the sacrifices. It gives pleasure to the gods as does honey. Chapter 4 has the story of Satyakama, who had perhaps a questionable parentage. But, because he tells the truth that he was not aware of what family he belonged to, the teacher Haridrumata Gautama accepts him as his disciple. Satyakama is later taught about Brahman by a steer, fire, a swan and a Madgu bird. Satyakama, when he himself becomes a knower of Brahman (a Brahmajnanin), teaches Upakosala about Brahman. He says the Atman is immortal, fearless and is Brahman itself. In Chapter 5, the Upanishad teaches us that Prana

93

(also defined as breath or the vital force) is superior to all other senses of the body. The fifth chapter also has the story of Shvetaketu, who is unable to answer the questions by King Pravahana. The king later teaches the knowledge of Brahman to Shvetaketu's father, Gautama. By that time, that knowledge of Brahman was taught only to Kshatriyas. In the same Chapter there is a story of King Ashvapati, who was studying the Vaishvanara Atman. To him went five learned householders to learn more about the Atman. The king tells them that heaven, sun, air, sky, water and earth are all parts of the Vaishvanara Atman. In Chapter 6, Uddalaka Aruni teaches his son Shvetaketu about the origin of this creation and about the Atman. He utters the famous *Mahavakya*, "You are That (Atman)." In Chapter 7, Narada approaches Sanatkumara and confesses that he had learned all the scriptures, sciences and arts, yet he had not realized the Atman. Sanatkumara explains to Narada that only something infinite can be a source of happiness. A finite thing cannot give happiness. The Atman within us is infinite and is blissful. Chapter 8 tells us that our heart is the city of Brahman or Atman, and that is where we should try to find Him.

### Peace Invocation

Om! May my limbs, speech, Prana, sight, hearing and all the sense organs be strong. Everything is Brahman, revealed in the Upanishads. May I never deny Brahman and may Brahman never deny me. Let there be no rejection of Brahman by me and may Brahman never reject me. May all the virtues spoken of in the Upanishads reside in me, who is devoted to the Atman. Om. Peace, Peace, Peace.

\*\*\*

### CHAPTER 1

### Section 1.1

One should meditate upon the syllable "Om," which is the symbol of Brahman, and is chanted loudly. It is explained here. [1.1.1]

The essence of all beings is the earth, the essence of the earth is water, the essence of water is vegetation, the essence of vegetation is man, the essence of man is speech, the essence of speech is Rik, the essence of Rik is Sama, and the essence of Sama is Om (with loud chanting). [1.1.2]

This Om is called the "Udgitha" and is the supreme essence of all the essences mentioned above. It has the highest place in the chain of the eight essences, namely, earth, water, vegetation, man, speech, Rik, Sama and Udgitha. [1.1.3]

Which one is Rik, which is Sama, and which is "Udgitha"? This will be discussed now. [1.1.4]

Speech alone is Rik. Prana is Sama. Speech and Prana form a couple, and also Rik and Sama form another couple. [1.1.5]

Just as a couple produces progeny, speech together with Prana or vital breath produces the syllable "Om." Also Rik or prayer with Sama (music) gives birth to the syllable "Om." Thus each member of the couple complements the other. [1.1.6]

One who knows "Om" as the fulfiller of all desires and meditates on it thus, surely has all his desires fulfilled. [1.1.7]

Whenever one assents to give, one signifies it by uttering "Om." Therefore, Om is the syllable of assent. Assent is the indication of prosperity, because only a prosperous person agrees to give. One who meditates upon this syllable "Om" as a symbol of prosperity, endows himself with more prosperity. [1.1.8]

With "Om" only, the three Vedas (*Rik, Yajus* and *Sama*) begin. Om only, causes one to listen, recite and sing aloud. With the worship of, with the greatness of and with the essence of this syllable the universe functions. [1.1.9]

One who knows the true meaning of Om and one who does not know, both perform actions. But its knowledge and ignorance have different effects. Actions performed with knowledge, faith and meditation are more potent. This is the importance of the greatness of the syllable "Om." [1.1.10]

## Section 1.2

Once the gods and the demons, both descendants of Prajapati, were engaged in a fight. During that fight the gods decided to perform the sacrificial rites done by the Udgatri priests. They thought they would defeat the demons with the power they would acquire through the sacrificial rites. [1.2.1]

(The gods are the people who believed in purification of the senses by performing scriptural duties. On the other hand, the demons were those who opposed it and believed in sensual pleasures. It may also be an allegory, that reminds us that sometimes there is a fight within every one of us between our righteous and unrighteous nature.)

Then the gods meditated on Om, the Udgitha, as the deity of Prana connected with the nose. The demons pierced the nose with evil. That is why one smells not only the sweet but also the foul smell. [1.2.2]

Then the gods meditated on the Udgitha as the deity of speech, and the demons pierced speech with evil. That is why one speaks truth as well as untruth. [1.2.3]

Then the gods meditated on the Udgitha as the deity of the eye, and the demons pierced it with evil. That is why one sees the good as well as the evil. [1.2.4]

Then the gods meditated on the Udgitha as the deity of the ear, and the demons pierced it. That is why one hears both pleasant and unpleasant sounds. [1.2.5]

Then the gods meditated on the Udgitha as the deity of the mind, and the demons pierced it. That is why one thinks both good and evil thoughts. [1.2.6]

Then the gods meditated on the Udgitha as the deity of Prana in the mouth. The demons struck against it and were destroyed, like a lump of clay hitting a hard rock. [1.2.7]

Just as a lump of clay striking against a rock is destroyed, so will he who wishes to hurt or do evil to the knower of the purity of Prana be destroyed, because he (the knower of Prana) is like a hard rock. [1.2.8]

In the presence of Prana in the mouth, one smells neither sweet nor foul, because Prana is sinless. That is why whatever it eats or drinks, it maintains the other Pranas with it. At the time of death, when Prana departs, one indeed opens the mouth as if inviting Prana to enter the mouth again. [1.2.9]

Angiras meditated upon Prana in the mouth as Om, or Udgitha. That is why Prana is considered as "angiras," which means essence (*ras*) of the body parts (*angas*). [1.2.10]

Similarly, Brihaspati meditated upon Prana in the mouth as Om. That is why Prana is considered as Brihaspati, because speech is "Brihati," or great, and Prana is its lord (*pati*). [1.2.11]

Similarly, Ayasya meditated upon Prana in the mouth as Om. That is why Prana is considered as Ayasya, because "aya" means going through, and "asya" means mouth—Prana that goes through the mouth. [1.2.12]

Also Baka, the son of Dalbha, meditated upon Prana in the mouth as Om, and became the Udgatri-singer of the dwellers of the Naimisha forest. He fulfilled their desires by singing Om. [1.2.13]

He who knows Prana thus and meditates on Om, looking upon it as Prana, obtains all desirable objects. This is the description of the meditation with reference to the body, namely, "adhyatma," where the Atman resides. [1.2.14]

## Section 1.3

Next the meditation upon Om with reference to the gods, that is, "adhidaivata," is described here. Just as in the body Prana represents "Udgitha," or Om, so in the solar system the sun represents it. One should meditate upon the sun, who gives heat, as Udgitha. When he rises for the benefit of all creatures, it is as if he sings aloud the Udgitha and dispels darkness and fear. [1.3.1]

Prana and the sun are similar in that the former keeps the body warm and the latter keeps the solar system warm. Prana is called the "Svara," which means the one which goes. The sun is called "Svara" as well as "Pratyasvara," meaning that which goes and comes back, because the sun sets and rises again. Therefore, one should meditate on Prana and the sun as Udgitha, or Om. [1.3.2]

One should meditate on Vyana as Udgitha. That which one breathes in is Prana and that which one breathes out is Apana. The junction of Prana and Apana, or control of the breath inside, is called Vyana. Vyana also is speech. Therefore, one produces speech when one neither breathes in nor breathes out. [1.3.3]

Speech is Rik indeed. One pronounces Rik when one neither breathes in nor breathes out. That which is Rik is also Saman. Therefore, when one neither breathes in nor breathes out one sings the Saman. That which is Saman is also the Udgitha. Therefore, when one neither breathes in nor breathes out, one sings the Udgitha. [1.3.4]

Therefore, whatever works require strength, like kindling fire by friction, running a race, or bending a strong bow, are all performed without breathing in or breathing out, that is, in the Vyana state. Therefore, one should meditate on Vyana as Udgitha. [1.3.5]

It is necessary that we give some thought to the three syllables, namely, "ut," "gi" and "tha," of "Udgitha." Prana is "ut," which means to arise, because through Prana one arises. Speech is "gi," because speech is called "gira," or word. Food is "tha," which means to be established, because all this is established on food. [1.3.6]

Also heaven is "ut," the sky is "gi" and the earth is "tha." Or the sun is "ut," the air "gi" and fire "tha." Similarly, the *Samaveda* is "ut," the *Yajurveda* is "gi" and the *Rigveda* is "tha." He who knows and meditates on the three syllables of Udgitha thus, receives the milk of the cow, that is, speech. He becomes rich with food and enjoyer of food. [1.3.7]

Now follows the explanation of the method by which wishes are fulfilled: One should meditate on the objects that will fulfill the desires, and those objects are the Saman, by means of which one proceeds to sing in praise of the Lord. [1.3.8]

One should reflect upon the Rik (Veda-mantra by which one wants to praise the Lord), upon the sage who perceived it and upon the deity to whom one wants to pray. [1.3.9]

One should reflect upon that meter (*chhanda*) by which one wants to praise the Lord; and one should reflect upon the hymn (group of chhandas or *stoma*) with which one proceeds to sing the prayer. [1.3.10]

One should concentrate in the direction toward which one wants to face to sing one's prayer. [1.3.11]

Lastly, approaching the Atman, avoiding all faults, reflecting upon one's desired object, one should sing a prayer to the Lord, and one's desire will be surely fulfilled. [1.3.12]

### Section 1.4

The syllable "Om" is "Udgitha" indeed. One should meditate on Om and sing it loudly. Of this the explanation follows. [1.4.1]

The gods being afraid of Death, took refuge in the three Vedas (that is, they performed the Vedic rituals to avoid death). They covered themselves with the "chhandas," or the hymns. That is why the hymns are called chhandas, which means to cover. [1.4.2]

Just as a fisherman sees a fish in water, so did Death see that the gods were submerged in the Vedic rites, which are perishable along with their fruits. The gods realized the motive of Death after they were purified by the Vedic rites and, therefore, became engaged in the meditation of the syllable Om. [1.4.3]

When one learns the Rik, the Yajus or the Saman one loudly pronounces "Om." The syllable Om is indeed the sound which removes death and fear. Meditating upon the sound "Om," the gods became immortal and fearless. [1.4.4]

He who knows the syllable as the destroyer of death and fear, worships it, meditates upon it and achieves immortality, just as the gods did. [1.4.5]

## Section 1.5

Now, Udgitha is Pranava (Om) and Pranava is Udgitha. That sun in the sky is Udgitha and also Pranava, because he moves along chanting "Om." (People set to work with the rise of the sun as if the sun chants Om to signify the start of the day). [1.5.1]

Kaushitaki said to his son, "I meditated upon the sun as Udgitha, and as a result I have you as my only son. If you reflect upon the rays of the sun as Udgitha, you will certainly have many sons." This is the meditation with reference to the gods (*adhidaivata*). [1.5.2]

Here is the meditation with reference to the body: One should meditate upon Prana in the mouth as Udgitha because one moves along chanting "Om." [1.5.3]

Kaushitaki said to his son, "I meditated upon Prana as Udgitha, and as a result I have you as my only son. If you meditate upon manifold Pranas as Udgitha for many sons, you will have them too." [1.5.4]

Udgitha is indeed Pranava and Pranava is Udgitha. Therefore, even if one (a Samavedin) wrongly chants it, it is rectified by the act done from the seat of the Hotri priest. (Om is Pranava for the Rigvedins and Udgitha for the Samavedins). [1.5.5]

## Section 1.6

(Note: Except seventy mantras, all the mantras of the *Samaveda* are taken from the *Rigveda*. That is why, in the following mantras of the Upanishad, it is repeatedly said that the *Samaveda* rests [is dependent] on the *Rigveda*.)

The earth is Rik and the fire is Saman. Just as the fire rests on the earth, so does the Saman rest upon the Rik. This Saman rests upon that Rik. Therefore, the Saman is sung as resting on the Rik. (In other words, the earth and the fire represent the *Rigveda* and the *Samaveda*, respectively. There is so much similarity between the *Rigveda* and the *Samaveda*. That is why the Saman is sung using the hymns of the *Rigveda*.) The earth is "sa," the fire is "ama," and jointly they make "Sama." [1.6.1]

Or, the sky and the air represent the *Rigveda* and the *Samaveda*, respectively. Just as the air rests in the sky, so does Saman rest upon the Rik. Therefore, the Saman is sung as the hymns of the Rik. The sky is "sa," the air is "ama," and jointly they make "Sama." [1.6.2]

Or, heaven and the sun represent the *Rigveda* and the *Samaveda*, respectively. Just as the sun rests in heaven, so does Saman rest upon the Rik. Therefore, the Saman is sung as the hymns of the Rik. Heaven is "sa," the sun is "ama," and jointly they make "Sama." [1.6.3]

Or, the constellations and the moon represent the *Rigveda* and the *Samaveda*, respectively. Just as the moon rests in the constellations, so is the Saman sung as the hymns of the Rik. The constellations are "sa," the moon is "ama," and jointly they make "Sama." [1.6.4]

The white light and the extremely dark blue light of the sun represent the *Rigveda* and the *Samaveda*, respectively. Just as the dark blue light rests in the white light, so does the Saman rest upon the Rik. Therefore, the Saman is sung as the hymns of the Rik. [1.6.5]

Or, the white light of the sun is "sa," and the extremely dark blue light is "ama," and jointly they make "Sama." That "Person" brilliant as gold, who is within the sun, who is with golden beard and hair, is exceedingly bright even to the very tips of his nails. [1.6.6]

His eyes are like petals of a red lotus. His name is "Ut" (above). He is so named because he is above all sins. One who knows this about Him rises above all sins. [1.6.7]

Rik and Saman are His two songs of praise. He, the bright person in the sun, is Udgitha. Since the priest is the singer of this "Ut," he is the Udgata. This Person, "Ut," controls the worlds which are above the sun, as well as the desires of the gods. This is the meditation upon the Udgitha with reference to the gods. [1.6.8]

## Section 1.7

Now, here is the meditation with reference to the body: Speech and Prana (breath) represent the *Rigveda* and the *Samaveda*, respectively. Just as speech rests on the breath, so does the Saman rest upon the Rik. (The nose, the source of breath, is above the mouth, the source of speech.) Therefore, the Saman is sung with the help of the hymns of the Rik. Speech is "sa," Prana is "ama," and they together make "Sama." [1.7.1]

Or, the eye and the image represent the *Rigveda* and the *Samaveda*, respectively. Just as the image rests in the eye, so does the Saman rest on the Rik. Therefore, the Saman is sung as the hymns of the Rik. The eye is "sa," the image is "ama," and jointly they make "Sama." [1.7.2]

Or, the ear and the mind represent the *Rigveda* and the *Samaveda*, respectively. Just as the mind rests on the ear, so does the Saman rest on the Rik. Therefore, the Saman is sung as the hymns of the Rik. The ear is "sa," the mind is "ama," and jointly they make "Sama." [1.7.3]

Or, the white light of the eye and the blue light, which is extremely dark, represent the *Rigveda* and the *Samaveda*, respectively. Just as the blue light rests on the white light, so does the Saman rest on the Rik. Therefore, the Saman is sung as the hymns of the Rik. The white light is "sa," the blue light is "ama," and jointly they make "Sama." [1.7.4]

This Person who is seen within the eye is indeed Rik, Saman, Uktha (hymn), Yajus and Brahman. The form of this Person seen in the eye is the same as the form of that Person seen in the sun. Their songs are the same and their names are the same, namely, "Ut." [1.7.5]

That Person is the lord of all the worlds below. He also has control over all the desirable objects a man wants. Those who sing on the Vina (lute) sing of Him alone, and thereby become endowed with wealth. [1.7.6]

He who sings Saman in praise of the deity thus, sings in praise of both, namely, the Person in the eye and the Person in the sun. Through the Person in the sun the singer attains the worlds beyond that sun, and also the desired objects of the gods. [1.7.7]

Similarly, through this Person in the eye, one attains worlds that are extended below this earth, as well as the desired objects of men. That is why the Udgatri priest should ask the sacrificer thus: [1.7.8]

"What desired objects shall I request for you by singing the Saman?" This is so because he alone is capable of obtaining desired objects, who knowing thus, sings the Saman. [1.7.9]

### Summary of Sections 6 and 7 in tabular form:

| Meditation with reference to the gods: | | Meditation with reference to the body: | |
|---|---|---|---|
| **Rik** | **Sama** | **Rik** | **Sama** |
| Earth | Fire | Speech | Breath |
| Sky | Air | Eye | Image |
| Heaven | Sun | Ear | Mind |
| Constellations | Moon | | |
| White light | Blue light | White light | Dark light |
| Purusha in the sun | | Purusha in the eye | |

### Section 1.8

Once upon a time three men, namely, Shilaka the son of Shalavata, Chaikitayana of the Dalbhya family, and Pravahana the son of Jivala, who were well versed in the Udgitha, said, "We are indeed well versed in the Udgitha. So let us have a discussion on it." [1.8.1]

"Sure," they said, and sat down. Then Pravahana Jaivali said, "You two dear sirs, speak first. I would like to listen to what two Brahmanas have to say." [1.8.2]

Then Shilaka Shalavatya said to Chaikitayana Dalbhya, "Let me ask you this."
"Go ahead," the latter said. [1.8.3]

Shilaka: "What is the basis of the Saman?"
Chaikitayana: "Tone."
"What is the basis of tone?"
"Breath," he replied.
"What is the basis of breath?"
"Food," he said.
"What is the basis of food?"
"Water," he said. [1.8.4]

"What is the basis of water?" Shilaka asked.
"The heavenly world," Chaikitayana replied.
"What is the basis of the heavenly world?"
"One should not think beyond the heavenly world, because the Saman itself is praised as heaven." [1.8.5]

Then Shilaka Shalavatya said to Chaikitayana Dalbhya, "O Dalbhya, your Saman is not well based. If now someone were to tell you, 'Your head should fall down,' surely your head would fall down." [1.8.6]

Dalbhya said, "Well sir, then I would like to know about it from you."
"Sure," said Shalavatya.
"Tell me, what is the basis of the heavenly world?"
"This world."
"What is the basis of this world?"
"One should not go beyond this world as the support of the Saman. We should establish the Saman in this world as its support, because the Saman is praised as the support." [1.8.7]

Then Pravahana Jaivali said to him, "O Shalavatya, your Saman has an end. If someone were to say, 'Your head should

fall down,' surely your head would fall down."
"Then, sir, let me learn about it from you."
"Sure," Jaivali said. [1.8.8]

## Section 1.9

Shalavatya asked, "What is the basis of this world?"
"Space," said Pravahana. "All these creatures arise from space and return to space. Space is indeed greater than these beings. Space is the ultimate abode." [1.9.1]

This (space) indeed is the "Udgitha," the highest and the best. It is endless. Knowing this, one who meditates on the Udgitha becomes the highest and the best, and obtains the highest and the best of the worlds. [1.9.2]

Atidhanva Shaunaka taught this knowledge about Udgitha to his disciple Udarashandilya and said, "As long as the knowledge of Udgitha continues among your descendants, so long will they have the highest and the best lives in this world." [1.9.3]

In the other world, too, they will enjoy similar status. One who knows thus and meditates on the Udgitha—his life in this world surely becomes the highest and the best, and so also in the other world. [1.9.4]

## Section 1.10

In the land of the Kurus, once when the crops were destroyed by a hailstorm, Ushasti Chakrayana lived with his young wife as a beggar in the village of mahouts (elephant drivers). [1.10.1]

He begged food from a mahout, who was eating black beans of an inferior quality. The mahout told him that he had no more left than what he was eating. [1.10.2]

Ushasti requested him to share some of them with him. The mahout gave him some of the beans and offered him his water too.

He refused the water and said that he could not drink the impure water which was left over by someone else. [1.10.3]

(In India, the leftover food from someone else's plate or water from someone else's pitcher/glass is considered impure.)

The mahout said, "Then were not those beans also impure because they were my leftover food?"

Ushasti said, "If I had not eaten them I would have died of hunger. Now I can afford to get pure water from anywhere else." [1.10.4]

Ushasti, after he had eaten, brought the leftover beans for his wife. By that time she had already obtained her food by alms, and hence saved them for later use. [1.10.5]

The next morning when he got up he said, "If I could get some food from somewhere, I could get the strength to earn some more wealth. A king is going to perform a yajna for which he may appoint me the priest." [1.10.6]

His wife said, "Dear, here are the beans you brought yesterday."

He ate them and left to join the yajna. [1.10.7]

There he saw the singing priests and sat down near them. Then he addressed the *Prastotri* priest thus: [1.10.8]

(In the Vedic sacrifice or yajna, Udgatri, Prastotri, and Pratihartri are different kinds of priests assigned to sing different stotras or prayers, namely, Udgitha, Prastava and Pratihara, respectively.)

"O Prastotri, if you sing the Prastava without knowing the deity that belongs to the Prastava, your head will fall off." [1.10.9]

Similarly he addressed the Udgatri priest, "O Udgatri, if you sing the Udgitha without knowing the deity that belongs to the Udgitha, your head will fall off." [1.10.10]

Similarly he addressed the Pratihartri priest, "O Pratihartri, if you sing the Pratihara without knowing the deity that belongs to the Pratihara, your head will fall off." [1.10.11]

## Section 1.11

Thereupon the principal of the yajna, the king, said to him, "Revered sir, I would like to know who you are."
"I am Ushasti Chakrayana," he said. [1.11.1]

The king said, "Sir, I searched for you for all these priestly offices. Not finding you I have chosen others. [1.11.2]

"Sir, please take all these priestly offices for me."
"So be it," he said, "and with my permission let them sing the hymns. But you should give me the same amount of wealth as you give them."
"Very well," said the sacrificer. [1.11.3]

Then the Prastotri priest approached him and said, "Sir, you said to me, 'O Prastotri, if you sing the Prastava without knowing the deity that belongs to the Prastava, your head will fall off.' Which is that deity?" [1.11.4]

"Prana," said Ushasti, "because all beings merge in Prana (during dissolution) and rise out of Prana (during creation). This is the deity that belongs to the Prastava. If you had sung the Prastava without knowing that deity, your head would have fallen off, after you had been warned by me." [1.11.5]

Then the Udgatri priest approached him and said, "Sir, you said to me, 'O Udgatri, if you sing the Udgitha without knowing the deity that belongs to the Udgitha, your head will fall off.' Which is that deity?" [1.11.6]

"The sun," said Ushasti, "because all beings sing the praise of the sun when he rises. This is the deity that belongs to the Udgitha. If you had sung the Udgitha without knowing that deity, your head would have fallen off, after you had been warned by me." [1.11.7]

Then the Pratihartri priest approached him and said, "Sir, you said to me, 'O Pratihartri, if you sing the Pratihara without knowing the deity that belongs to the Pratihara, your head will fall off.' Which is that deity?" [1.11.8]

"Food," said Ushasti, "because all beings live by partaking of food only. This is the deity that belongs to the Pratihara. If you had sung the Pratihara without knowing that deity, your head would have fallen off, after you had been warned by me." [1.11.9]

### Section 1.12

Next starts the Udgitha as seen by the dogs:
Once Dalbhya Baka, also known as Maitreya Glava, went out for the study of the Vedas. [1.12.1]

After he had finished his studies a white dog appeared before him. Then some other dogs came and surrounded the white dog. They asked the white dog, "Sir, we are hungry. Please obtain food for us by singing." [1.12.2]

The white dog said to them, "Come here to me tomorrow morning."
Dalbhya Baka or Maitreya Glava also kept a watch for them. [1.12.3]

Just as the priests in the yajna recite, and singing the Bahispavamana hymns move along clasping one another's hand, even so did the dogs move along. Then they sat down and began to utter "*himkara*" in the following manner: [1.12.4]

"Om, let us eat. Om, let us drink. May the god Varuna, Prajapati and Savitri bring us food here. O lord of food, please bring food here. Yes, please bring it. Om." [1.12.5]

### Section 1.13

Indeed this world is the syllable "hau," the air is the syllable "hai," the moon is the syllable "atha," the Atman is the syllable "iha," and the fire is the syllable "i." [1.13.1]
(The syllables "hau," "hai," etc., are the sounds in nature that a devotee of Brahman associates with different forms of His.)

The sun is the syllable "u," invocation is the syllable "e," the Vishvadevas are the syllable "auhoyi," Prajapati is the syllable "him," Prana is the Stobha "svara," food is the Stobha "ya," and Virat is the Stobha "vak." [1.13.2]

("Stobha" is a technical term for the chanted interjection in a hymn.)

The undefinable and variable thirteenth Stobha is the syllable "hum." [1.13.3]

For him who meditates on the syllables of the Stobha, speech yields the milk. He who knows this sacred doctrine of the Samans, becomes rich in food and an enjoyer of food. [1.13.4]

## CHAPTER 2

### Section 2.1

Om, meditation on the whole Saman is good. Anything that is good is called Saman; anything that is not good is Asaman. [2.1.1]

When people say, "He approached him with Saman," they actually mean, "He approached him with a good motive." And when they say, "He approached him with Asaman," they mean to say, "He approached with an evil motive." [2.1.2]

Again, when something is good for them, people say, "This is Saman for us." And when it is not good, then they say, "Oh, this is Asaman for us." [2.1.3]

When one knows Saman as good and meditates on it thus, all good qualities come to one and serve one. [2.1.4]

### Section 2.2

One should consider the five worlds as five parts of the Saman and meditate on them. The earth is the syllable "him," the fire is "Prastava," the sky is "Udgitha," the sun is "Pratihara," and heaven is "Nidhana." (These syllables are the five parts of the Saman.) [2.1.1]

Among the lower worlds heaven is the syllable "him," the sun is "Prastava," the sky is "Udgitha," the fire is "Pratihara," and the earth is "Nidhana." [2.2.2]

The worlds in ascending and descending order belong to him who, knowing it thus, meditates on the fivefold Saman in the worlds. [2.2.3]

### Section 2.3

One should meditate on the fivefold Saman as rain. The wind that precedes it and blows to the east is the syllable "him," the forming of the cloud is "Prastava," the shower is "Udgitha," lightning and thunder are "Pratihara." [2.3.1]

The ceasing of rain is "Nidhana." There is a rain of happiness for him who, knowing it thus, meditates on the fivefold Saman as rain, and he causes a rain of happiness for others. [2.3.2]

### Section 2.4

One should meditate on the fivefold Saman as all the waters. The gathering of the clouds is the syllable "him," when it rains is "Prastava," the flow of waters to the east is "Udgitha," and the flow to the west is "Pratihara." The ocean is "Nidhana." [2.4.1]

One does not drown in water who, knowing it thus, meditates on the fivefold Saman as the waters, and he becomes rich in water. [2.4.2]

### Section 2.5

One should meditate on the fivefold Saman as the seasons. The spring is the syllable "him," the summer is "Prastava," the rainy season is "Udgitha," the autumn is "Pratihara," and the winter is "Nidhana." [2.5.1]

The seasons serve him who, knowing it thus, meditates on the fivefold Saman as the seasons, and bestow all objects of enjoyment. [2.5.2]

## Section 2.6

One should meditate on the fivefold Saman as the animals. The goats are the syllable "him," the sheep are "Prastava," the cows are "Udgitha," the horses are "Pratihara," and man is "Nidhana." [2.6.1]

The animals belong to him who, knowing it thus, meditates on the fivefold Saman as the animals, and he becomes rich in animals. [2.6.2]

## Section 2.7

One should meditate on the best and the highest fivefold Saman as the senses. The nose (the organ of smell) is the syllable "him," the mouth (the organ of speech) is "Prastava," the eye is "Udgitha," the ear is "Pratihara," and the mind is "Nidhana." These are surely the best and the highest. [2.7.1]

His life becomes the best and the highest who, knowing it thus, meditates on the fivefold Saman as the senses, and he attains the best and the highest worlds. So much for the meditation on the fivefold Saman. [2.7.2]

## Section 2.8

Now begins the meditation on the sevenfold Saman. One should meditate on the sevenfold Saman as speech. Whatever in speech is "hum," that is the syllable "him;" whatever is "pra," that is Prastava; whatever is "a," that is Adi. [2.8.1]

Whatever in speech is "ut," that is Udgitha; whatever is "prati," that is Pratihara; whatever is "upa," that is Upadrava; and whatever is "ni," that is Nidhana. [2.8.2]

Speech yields milk (brings immense benefit) for him who, knowing it thus, meditates on the sevenfold Saman as speech, and he becomes rich in food and enjoyer of food. [2.8.3]

## Section 2.9

Next, one should meditate upon the sevenfold Saman as the sun. The sun is Saman because he remains always the same. He is the same to all because each one thinks, "He faces me." [2.9.1]

It should be known that all these beings are dependent on the sun. What he is before rising, is "Himkara." On that the animals are dependent. As they participate in the Himkara part of this Saman, they make a sound "him" before sunrise. (Here the sun is seen as "Himkara," a part of the Saman.) [2.9.2]

The form of the sun immediately after its rise, is "Prastava." The humans are dependent on that. As they participate in the Prastava part of this Saman, they are desirous of praise. [2.9.3]

The form of the sun as it looks at the time of assembling its rays, is "Adi." The birds depend on this. As they participate in the Adi part of this Saman, they can fly in the sky unsupported. [2.9.4]

The form of the sun that appears at midday, is "Udgitha." The gods are dependent on this. As they participate in the Udgitha part of this Saman, they are the best amongst the offspring of Prajapati. [2.9.5]

The form of the sun that appears between midday and late afternoon, is "Pratihara." The fetuses are dependent on this. As they participate in the Pratihara part of this Saman, they are held in the womb and do not fall down. [2.9.6]

The form of the sun that appears between late afternoon and sunset, is "Upadrava." The wild animals depend on this. As they participate in the Upadrava part of this Saman, they run away to the forest for safety when they see a human being. [2.9.7]

The form of the sun that appears just after sunset, is "Nidhana." The fathers depend on this. As they participate in the Nidhana part of this Saman, people lay them aside. (People lay down *Pindas* or oblations of round balls of boiled rice for them during the Shraddha ceremony, a special ceremony of offerings to the fathers.) [2.9.8]

In this section the day is divided into five equal parts, which are enjoyed by different species of creatures as tabulated below in the chart:

| Time of Day | Part of Saman | Creature Associated |
|---|---|---|
| Sunrise | Himkara | Animals |
| Forenoon | Prastava | Humans |
| Midday | Udgitha | Gods |
| Afternoon | Pratihara | Fetuses |
| Sunset | Upadrava | Wild animals |

## Section 2.10

Indeed one should meditate upon the sevenfold Saman, which has all its parts equal and which leads beyond death. "Himkara" and "Prastava" each have three syllables. Therefore, they are equal to each other. [2.10.1]

"Adi" has two syllables, "Pratihara" has four syllables, and if we take one syllable from Pratihara to Adi, they become equal to each other. [2.10.2]

"Udgitha" has three syllables, "Upadrava" has four syllables, and to make them equal, each made of three syllables, one syllable has to be dropped (from Upadrava). [2.10.3]

"Nidhana" has three syllables, and this too is equal to the others. These are the twenty-two syllables of the sevenfold Saman. [2.10.4]

One reaches the sun by the number twenty-one. (According to the Vedas, twelve months, five seasons, considering Hemanta and Shishira as one, and three worlds make twenty, and the sun itself is the twenty-first.) With the twenty-second syllable, one conquers the world beyond the sun. That world is free from misery and is full of bliss. [2.10.5]

One who, knowing the Saman thus (so blissful), meditates on the sevenfold Saman, which has all its parts equal and which leads beyond death, reaches the sun. [2.10.6]

### Section 2.11

The mind is Himkara, speech is Prastava, the eye is Udgitha, the ear is Pratihara and Prana is Nidhana. This is the Gayatra Saman woven in the senses. [2.11.1]

One who thus knows the Gayatra Saman, as woven in the senses, obtains perfect senses, reaches the full length of life, lives a glorious life, is endowed with good offspring and a large number of cattle, and attains name and fame. His holy vow is that he would be very high-minded. [2.11.2]

### Section 2.12

What one rubs (to produce the sacrificial fire) is Himkara. The smoke produced by that is Prastava. Its flame is Udgitha. The embers formed are Pratihara. Extinguishing it is Nidhana. This is the Rathantara Saman woven in fire. (The Rathantara Saman is sung to produce fire for the sacrifice.) [2.12.1]

One who knows the Rathantara Saman thus, woven in fire, becomes radiant as a Brahman, is endowed with a good appetite, reaches the full length of life, lives gloriously, becomes great with offspring and cattle, and great also with fame. His holy vow is that he should neither sip nor spit facing the fire. [2.12.2]

### Section 2.13

Sending the invitation is Himkara, declaring one's vows (of marriage in front of the fire) is Prastava, abiding by the vows of marriage is Udgitha, loving the wife is Pratihara, and leading the married life is Nidhana. The Vamadevya Saman is woven in a couple. (The Vamadevya was born out of the union of air and water.) [2.13.1]

One who thus knows this Vamadevya Saman, as woven in a couple, becomes one couple and procreates. He reaches the full length of life, lives gloriously, becomes great with offspring and cattle, and great also with fame. His holy vow is that he should not despise any woman. [2.13.2]

## Section 2.14

The rising sun is Himkara, the risen sun is Prastava, the midday sun is Udgitha, the afternoon sun is Pratihara, and the setting sun is Nidhana. This is the Brihat Saman woven in the sun. [2.14.1]

One who knows this Brihat Saman thus, woven in the sun, becomes radiant, is endowed with a good appetite, reaches the full length of life, lives gloriously, becomes great with offspring and cattle, and great also with fame. His holy vow is that he should not find fault with the burning sun. [2.14.2]

## Section 2.15

The gathering of white clouds is Himkara, the forming of rain clouds is Prastava, the rains are Udgitha, lightning and thunder are Pratihara, and the ceasing of the rains is Nidhana. This is the Vairupa Saman (a Saman of different shapes) woven in the rain cloud. [2.15.1]

One who thus knows the Vairupa Saman, as woven in the rain cloud, acquires cattle of many kinds, reaches the full length of life, lives gloriously, becomes great with offspring and cattle, and great also with fame. His holy vow is that he should not find fault with the rain cloud when it rains. [2.15.2]

## Section 2.16

The spring is Himkara, the summer is Prastava, the rainy season is Udgitha, the autumn is Pratihara, and the winter is Nidhana. This is the Vairaja (variously shining) Saman woven in the seasons. [2.16.1]

One who thus knows the Vairaja Saman, as woven in the seasons, shines with offspring, reaches the full length of life, lives gloriously, becomes great with offspring and cattle, and great also with fame. His holy vow is that he should not find fault with the seasons. [2.16.2]

## Section 2.17

The earth is Himkara, the sky is Prastava, heaven is Udgitha, the quarters are Pratihara, and the ocean is Nidhana. This is the Shakvari Saman (the Saman sung in Mahanamni Riks). [2.17.1]

One who thus knows the Shakvari Saman, woven in the worlds, becomes the owner of the worlds, reaches the full length of life, lives gloriously, becomes great with offspring and cattle, and great also with fame. His holy vow is that he should not find fault with the worlds. [2.17.2]

## Section 2.18

The goats are Himkara, the sheep are Prastava, the cows are Udgitha, the horses are Pratihara, and man is Nidhana. This is the Revati Saman woven in the animals. [2.18.1]

(According to the Shruti, animals are the Revati Saman.)

One who thus knows the Revati Saman, woven in the animals, becomes the owner of animals, reaches the full length of life, lives gloriously, becomes great with offspring and cattle, and great also with fame. His holy vow is that he should not find fault with animals. [2.18.2]

## Section 2.19

The hair is Himkara, the skin is Prastava, the flesh is Udgitha, the bone is Pratihara, and the marrow is Nidhana. This is the Yajnayajniva (essence) Saman woven in the parts of the body. [2.19.1].

One who thus knows the Yajnayajniva Saman, woven in the parts of the body, is endowed with all the body parts and is not crippled with any part, reaches the full length of life, lives gloriously, becomes great with offspring and cattle, and great also with fame. His holy vow is that he should not eat fish and meat for a year, or even better, not at all. [2.19.2]

## Section 2.20

The fire is Himkara, air is Prastava, the sun is Udgitha, the stars are Pratihara, and the moon is Nidhana. This is the Rajana (effulgent) Saman woven in the deities. [2.20.1]

One who thus knows this Rajana Saman, woven in the deities, lives in the same world with the same power as these very deities or attains union with them, reaches the full length of life, lives gloriously, becomes great with offspring and cattle, and great also with fame. His holy vow is that he should not find fault with the Brahmanas. [2.20.2]

## Section 2.21

The three Vedas are Himkara, the three worlds are Prastava, the fire, air and sun are Udgitha, the stars, birds and rays are Pratihara, and the serpents, Gandharvas (the celestial singers) and fathers are Nidhana. This is the collection of Samans woven in all things. [2.21.1]

One who thus knows this collection of Samans, as woven in all things, becomes lord of all things. [2.21.2]

There is a verse about it which goes like this: That which is fivefold is in groups of three; there is nothing else greater or other than these (fifteen). [2.21.3]

One who knows that, knows all. All the directions (quarters) bring offerings to him. His holy vow is that he should meditate, "I am all." [2.21.4]

## Section 2.22

Of the Samans I choose the one that sounds pleasant to cattle. This loud singing is sacred to Agni, the undefined one to Prajapati, the defined one to Soma, the soft and smooth to Vayu, the smooth and strong to Indra, the cooing-like sound of a Kraunch bird to Brihaspati, and the coarse sounding to Varuna. One may practice all these except the one liked by Varuna. [2.22.1]

One should sing the Stotra attentively, thinking all these in mind: "By singing the Saman thus, may I obtain immortality for the gods, oblation for the fathers, hope for men, grass and water for animals, the heavenly world for the sacrificer, and food for myself." [2.22.2]

All the vowels are the embodiments of Indra, all the Ushmana (sibilant) consonants are the embodiments of Prajapati, and all the Sparsha (mute) consonants are the embodiments of Death. Therefore, if someone reproves the Udgatri priest for his pronunciation of the vowels, he should say, "I have taken my refuge in Indra; he will answer you." [2.22.3]

If someone reproves him for his pronunciation of the sibilants, he should tell him, "I have taken my refuge in Prajapati; he will crush you." And if someone should reprove him for his Sparsha consonants, he should tell him, "I have taken my refuge in Death; he will burn you up." [2.22.4]

All vowels should be pronounced clearly and strongly, with the thought, "May I impart strength to Indra." All sibilants should be pronounced neither inarticulately nor leaving out the elements of sound, but distinctly, with the thought, "May I give myself to Prajapati." All Sparsha consonants should be pronounced slowly without mixing them with other letters, with the thought, "May I withdraw myself from Death." [2.22.5]

### Section 2.23

There are three branches of religious duties: Performing yajnas, studying the Vedas and giving away gifts is the first. Austerity alone is the second. Leading a celibate student life until death, in the teacher's house, is the third. People doing these duties achieve meritorious worlds. However, one who is firmly established in Brahman becomes immortal. [2.23.1]

When Prajapati pondered on the worlds, from them came forth the three Vedas. When he pondered on the Vedas, from them came forth the three syllables, "Bhuh" (earth), "Bhuvah" (sky) and "Svah" (heaven). [2.23.2]

When he pondered on the three syllables, from them came forth the syllable "Om." Just as the whole leaf is permeated by the ribs of the leaf, so are all the worlds permeated by the syllable "Om." [2.23.3]

### Section 2.24

The expounders of Brahman say that the morning libation is of the Vasus, the midday libation is of the Rudras, and the third (evening) libation is of the Adityas and the Vishvadevas. [2.24.1]

Then where is the world of the sacrificer? How can he who does not know this fact perform yajna? Only after knowing this should he perform yajna. [2.24.2]

Before the commencement of the morning chant the sacrificer sits behind the *Garhapatya* fire, and facing north sings the Saman sacred to the *Vasus.* [2.24.3]

"O fire, open the door of this world, so that we may see you for obtaining the kingdom." [2.24.4]

Then he offers the oblation with the mantra, "Salutation to Fire, who dwells in the region of the earth and the region of the world. Obtain the world for me, the sacrificer. I am willing to go to this world." [2.24.5]

"At the end of this life, I, the sacrificer, will come here—Svaha. Unlock the door of the world." Saying this he gets up. The Vasus grant him the world related to the morning libation. [2.24.6]

Before starting the midday libation the sacrificer sits behind the *Agnidhriya* fire, facing north, and sings the Saman sacred to the Rudras. [2.24.7]

(The Agnidhriya or Dakshinagni fire is the southern fire, or fire maintained in the south end of the house.)

He says, "O fire, open the door of the sky region, so that we may see you and obtain the sovereignty of the sky." [2.24.8]

Then he offers the oblation with the mantra, "Salutation to Vayu, who dwells in the region of the sky. Obtain this region for me. I, the sacrificer, am willing to go there at the end of my life. Svaha." Saying this he gets up. The Rudras grant him the region of the sky related to the midday libation. [2.24.9-10]

Before starting the third libation the sacrificer sits behind the *Ahavaniya* fire (the fire maintained for sacrifice), facing north, and sings the Saman sacred to the Adityas and the Vishvadevas: [2.24.11]

(The Vishvadevas are a class of gods.)

"O fire, open the door of the world of heaven, so that we may see you for obtaining the sovereignty of heaven." [2.24.12]

This is the Saman sacred to the Adityas. The next one is sacred to the Vishvadevas: "O fire, open the door of the world of heaven, so that we may see you for obtaining supreme sovereignty." [2.24.13]

Then the sacrificer offers the oblation, chanting: "Salutation to you Adityas and Vishvadevas, the inhabitants of the world of heaven. Obtain that world of heaven for me, the sacrificer." [2.24.14]

"This world is to be obtained by the sacrificer. At the end of this life, I, the sacrificer, am willing to go there. Svaha. Unlock the door of the world." Saying this he gets up. [2.24.15]

The Adityas and the Vishvadevas grant him the world appropriate to the third libation. He alone knows the real strength of the sacrifice, who knows thus. [2.24.16]

## CHAPTER 3

### Section 3.1

Om. That sun indeed is the honey of the gods. Of this honey heaven is the slant bamboo (in the roof that supports the honeycomb), the sky is the honeycomb, and the rays are the eggs. [3.1.1]

The eastern rays of the sun are its eastern honey-cells, the Riks (verses of the *Rigveda*) are the bees, the rituals of the *Rigveda* are the flower, and those waters (used in the ritual) are the nectar. [3.1.2]

Those Riks pressed this *Rigveda*. From that came out fame, splendor, alertness of the senses, masculine vigor and food, as juice. [3.1.3]

That juice, after flowing, settled by the side of the sun. Surely, that is what appears as red hue of the sun. [3.1.4]

### Section 3.2

The sun's southern rays are its southern honey-cells. The Yajus verses are the bees. The *Yajurveda* is the flower, and those waters are the nectar. [3.2.1]

Those Yajus verses pressed this *Yajurveda*. From that came out fame, splendor, alertness of the senses, masculine vigor and food, as juice. [3.2.2]

It flowed and settled by the side of the sun. Surely, that is what appears as the white hue of the sun. [3.2.3]

### Section 3.3

The sun's western rays are its western honey-cells. The Samans are the bees. The *Samaveda* is the flower, and those waters are the nectar. [3.3.1]

Those Samans pressed this *Samaveda*. From that came out fame, splendor, alertness of the senses, masculine vigor and food, as juice. [3.3.2]

It flowed and settled by the side of the sun. Surely, that is what appears as the black hue of the sun. [3.3.3]

### Section 3.4

The sun's upper rays are its northern honey-cells. The mantras of the *Atharvaveda* are the bees. The Itihasa (history) and Puranas are the flower, and those waters (the results of the meditation on the Pranava) are the nectar (Brahman). [3.4.1]

Those mantras of the *Atharvaveda* pressed this Itihasa-Purana. From that came out fame, splendor, alertness of the senses, masculine vigor and food, as juice. [3.4.2]

It flowed and settled by the side of the sun. Surely, that is what appears as the black hue of the sun. [3.4.3]

### Section 3.5

The sun's upper rays are its upper honey-cells. The secret teachings are the bees. Brahman (Pranava) is the flower, and those waters are the nectar. [3.5.1]

Those secret teachings pressed this *Samaveda*. From that came out fame, splendor, alertness of the senses, masculine vigor and food, as juice. [3.5.2]

It flowed and settled by the side of the sun. Surely, that is what appears as the movement of the sun. [3.5.3]

These hues are the juice of the juices because the Vedas are the essence of the worlds, and these hues are their essence. These hues are indeed the nectar of the nectars. [3.5.4]

## Summary of Sections 3.1 through 3.5:

The sun is compared to the honey of the gods; heaven is the bamboo supporting the honeycomb; the sky is the honeycomb; the Riks, the Yajus verses, the Samans, the mantras of the *Atharvaveda*, and the secret teachings of Pranava are the bees; and the sun-rays are the eggs of the bees. The four Vedas and Pranava are flowers from which sweet juice is extracted. The juice in the form of fame, splendor, alertness of the senses, masculine vigor and food comes out of the flowers (the scriptures), which the gods achieve. These juices from different flowers (scriptures) give different colors to the honey.

## Section 3.6

That which is the first nectar (the red form) the Vasus enjoy, with Agni as their mouth. The gods neither eat nor drink; they are satisfied by only seeing this nectar (Brahman). [3.6.1]

They enter into this form and emerge out of it. (They keep on meditating on Brahman and eventually go upwards to Him.) [3.6.2]

One who knows this nectar thus, becomes one of the Vasus, and with Agni as its mouth is satisfied by only seeing this nectar. [3.6.3]

As long as the sun rises in the east and sets in the west, so long does he retain the sovereignty and kingdom of the Vasus. [3.6.4]

## Section 3.7

That which is the second nectar (of the white hue) is enjoyed by the Rudras, with Indra as their leader (or mouth). The gods neither eat nor drink. They are satisfied by only seeing the nectar. [3.7.1]

They enter into this form and emerge out of it. [3.7.2]

He who knows this nectar thus, becomes one of the Rudras, and with Indra as the leader, is satisfied by only seeing it. He enters into this form and emerges out of it. [3.7.3]

As long as the sun rises in the east and sets in the west, twice that long does the knower rise in the south and set in the north; and so long does he retain the sovereignty and heavenly kingdom of the Rudras. [3.7.4]

## Section 3.8

That which is the third nectar (of the black form) the Adityas enjoy, with Varuna as their leader. The gods neither eat nor drink. By only seeing that nectar they are satisfied. [3.8.1]

They enter into this very form and emerge out of this form. [3.8.2]

He who knows this nectar thus, becomes one of the Adityas, and with Varuna as the leader, is satisfied by only seeing this nectar. He enters into this very form and out of that he emerges. [3.8.3]

As long as the sun rises in the south and sets in the north, even twice that does he rise in the west and set in the east; and even so long does he retain the sovereignty and heavenly kingdom of the Adityas. (See the last para of the summary after Section 3.10.) [3.8.4]

## Section 3.9

That which is the fourth nectar (that is the deep black color) the Maruts (a class of gods) enjoy, with the Moon as their leader.

The gods neither eat nor drink, they are satisfied by only seeing this nectar. [3.9.1]

They enter this form of nectar and emerge from it. [3.9.2]

He who knows this nectar thus, becomes one of the Maruts, and with Soma as the leader, is satisfied by only seeing this nectar. [3.9.3]

As long as the sun rises in the west and sets in the east, twice that long does he rise in the north and set in the south; and even so long does he retain the sovereignty and heavenly kingdom of the Maruts. [3.9.4]

### Section 3.10

That which is the fifth nectar (the moving form) the Sadhyas (the scholars of the Vedas who are engaged in realizing Brahman) enjoy, with Pranava as their leader. The gods neither eat nor drink; they are satisfied by only seeing this nectar. [3.10.1]

They enter this form of nectar and emerge from it. [3.10.2]

He who thus knows this nectar becomes one of the Sadhyas, and with Pranava as the leader, is satisfied by only seeing this nectar. [3.10.3]

As long as the sun rises in the north and sets in the south, for twice that length of time does he rise above and set below; and for that length of time he retains the sovereignty and heavenly kingdom of the Sadhyas. [3.10.4]

### Summary of Sections 3.6 through 3.10:

The gods do not need food and drink. They drink five kinds of "nectars" that come out of the scriptures. A knower progresses towards perfection in five successively higher stages of spirituality, namely, Vasu, Rudra, Aditya, Marut and Sadhya. Those who drink the first nectar, namely, "fame," are called Vasus. Their leader is Agni. Those who drink the second nectar, namely, "splendor," are called Rudras. Their leader is Indra. Those who drink the third nectar, namely, "alertness of the senses," are called Adityas. Their leader is Varuna. Those who drink the fourth nectar, namely, "masculine vigor," are called Maruts. Their leader is the Moon (Soma). Those who drink the fifth nectar, namely, "food," are the Sadhyas. Their leader is Brahman.

Agni represents the mundane world. The Vasus, whose leader is Agni, are worldly people, trying to go up the ladder of spirituality. Pranava represents the higher end of spirituality. The Sadhyas, whose leader is Pranava, have almost reached perfection, and are at the higher end of the ladder of spirituality. The Rudras, Adityas and Maruts are the three in-between stages of spirituality. So man advances from being a Vasu to a Sadhya in stages, to achieve spiritual perfection.

A "Vasu" will enjoy sovereignty as long as the sun rises from the east to the west. A "Rudra" will enjoy sovereignty for twice the length of time a Vasu will enjoy it. An "Aditya" will enjoy sovereignty for twice the length of time a Rudra will enjoy it. A "Marut" will enjoy sovereignty for twice the length of time an Aditya will enjoy it. And finally, a "Sadhya" will enjoy sovereignty for twice the length of time an Aditya will enjoy it. The same idea of enjoying for "twice the length of time" is put in a different way in Sections 3.6 through 3.10. In these sections the directions of rising and setting of the sun and the knower are rotated to indicate that a Rudra enjoys the sovereignty and heavenly kingdom twice that of a Vasu, an Aditya enjoys twice that of a Rudra, a Marut enjoys twice that of an Aditya, and a Sadhya enjoys twice that of a Marut.

## Section 3.11

Then rising upward from there, the sun will neither rise nor set, but will remain in the middle. There is this verse about it (uttered by a Yogi who possessed the knowledge of the "Doctrine of Honey" described in the above sections): [3.11.1]

Never does this happen there. Never did the sun set nor rise there. O gods, by this assertion of truth, may I not fall from Brahman. [3.11.2]

For him who knows the Brahman of the Upanishads the sun neither rises nor sets. For him there is perpetual day. [3.11.3]

Brahma (Hiranyagarbha) imparted this Doctrine of Honey to Prajapati, Prajapati to Manu, and Manu to his progeny. And the father told his son Uddalaka Aruni this very knowledge of Brahman. [3.11.4]

A father may declare to his eldest son or to any other worthy disciple this very knowledge of Brahman. [3.11.5]

And not to anyone else, even if one should offer him this sea-encircled earth full of wealth. This doctrine is certainly greater than that. [3.11.6]

## Section 3.12

Gayatri is indeed all this, whatever being exists. Speech indeed is Gayatri, for speech sings (*gayati*) and protects (*trayate*) from all this that exists. [3.12.1]

Gayatri is like this earth. All beings are established on this earth and do not transcend it (are protected and supported by this earth). [3.12.2]

Just as the earth is like Gayatri, so is this body in respect of this person, because its senses are established in this body and they do not transcend it. (The earth and the body both are made of the same five elements.) [3.12.3]

Just as this body is with respect to this person, so is the heart within this body, because these senses are indeed established in the heart and do not transcend it. [3.12.4]

This Gayatri is four-footed (beings, earth, body and heart) and sixfold (speech, beings, earth, body, heart and Prana). (Also Gayatri has four quartets with six syllables each, making 24 letters in all.) This Gayatri is expressed in the following Rik: [3.12.5]

Such is the greatness of this Gayatri. Yet the Person (Brahman, whose praise the Gayatri sings) is even greater than this. All this world is a quarter of Him. Immortality in heaven constitutes the other three of His quarters. [3.12.6]

That which is Brahman is this sky (Akasha) outside the body. That which is Akasha outside the body is also Akasha inside the body. That which is Akasha inside the body is also within the heart. This Brahman is all-filling and unchanging. One who knows Him thus, obtains all-filling and unchanging prosperity. [3.12.7-9]

## Section 3.13

The heart has five doors, guarded by the gods. At the eastern door of the heart is Prana. Prana is the eye (in the body); Prana is the sun (in the cosmos). This Prana should be meditated upon as brightness and as the source of food. One who meditates thus, becomes bright and an eater of food. [3.13.1]

At the southern door of the heart is Vyana. Vyana is the ear (in the body); Vyana is the moon (in the cosmos). This Vyana should be meditated upon as prosperity and fame. One who meditates thus, becomes prosperous and famous. [3.13.2]

At the western door of the heart is Apana. Apana is speech; Apana is fire. This Apana should be meditated upon as the holy effulgence born of sacred wisdom, and as the source of food. One who meditates thus, becomes radiant with the holy effulgence born of sacred wisdom, and also an eater of food. [3.13.3]

At the northern door of the heart is Samana. Samana is mind; Samana is the rain-god (Parjanya). This Samana should be meditated upon as fame and grace. One who meditates thus, becomes famous and graceful. [3.13.4]

At the upper door of the heart is Udana. Udana is air; Udana is the sky. This Udana should be meditated upon as strength and nobility. One who meditates thus, becomes strong and noble. [3.13.5]

These are the five persons under Brahman, the sentinels of the heavenly world. One who knows these five persons under Brahman as the sentinels of the heavenly world has born in his family a hero, and he himself reaches the heavenly world. [3.13.6]

The light of Brahman that shines above this heaven, on the surface of all the worlds, on the best and the highest worlds, is also the light that shines within the body of this man. This light can be seen like a perception of warmth, when one touches the body. It can be heard, even with closed ears, like one hears the sound of a chariot, or the bellowing of a bull, or the sound of a blazing fire. One should meditate on this light as seen and heard. One who meditates on this light thus, becomes handsome and illustrious. [3.13.7]

## Section 3.14

Indeed all this universe is Brahman. From Him all things originate, into Him they all dissolve, and by Him they are sustained. On Him one should meditate with tranquillity (of mind and body). One is what one resolved to be. One will become, after departing this world, what one resolves to become. Therefore, let one cultivate resolution. [3.14.1]

He permeates the mind, His body is Prana, His nature is consciousness, He is infallible, His own form is like Akasha (the sky), His creation is all that exists, His desires are all pure, He possesses all the pleasant odors and tastes, He pervades all that exists, He is without speech, and He is free from agitation and eagerness. [3.14.2]

This Atman of mine residing in the heart is smaller than a grain of rice, of barley, a mustard seed, a grain of millet or a kernel of a grain of millet. This Atman of mine is also larger than the earth, the sky, heaven or all these worlds. [3.14.3]

His creation is all that exists, His desires are all pure, He possesses all the pleasant odors and tastes, He pervades all this, He is without speech, He is free from agitation and eagerness. He is my Atman residing in the heart. He is Brahman. On departing this world I shall merge in Him. The sage Shandilya said that one who possesses this faith has no further doubt. [3.14.4]

## Section 3.15

Here the universe is compared with the chest containing wealth. The universe, with the sky as its hollow and the earth as its bottom, does not decay (lasts for a long time). The quarters (directions) are its corners, and heaven is its upper lid. The chest of this nature is the container of wealth. All the worlds rest in it. [3.15.1]

Of that chest, the eastern quarter is called *Juhu*, the southern is called *Sahamana*, the western is called *Rajni*, and the northern is called *Subhuta*. The air is their calf. He who knows this air, the calf of the quarters, thus as immortal, never weeps in mourning for his son. I, wishing my son's longevity, worship this air, the calf of the quarters. May I never weep to mourn for my son. [3.15.2]
(The father wishes that his son, with a long life, outlives him. Meditating upon the Purusha or the Universal Person, with the threefold world and the four quarters as his consorts and air as the child, one should repeat the following mantra.)

I take refuge in the imperishable chest for such and such and such. (For the sake of long life of my son, such and such.) [Repeat the name of the son three times in place of the word "such."] I take refuge in Prana for such and such and such. I take refuge in Bhuh (earth) for such and such and such. I take refuge in Bhuvah (sky) for such and such and such. I take refuge in Svah (heaven) for such and such and such. [3.15.3]

When I said, "I take refuge in Prana," it is because all these beings that exist are indeed Prana. Therefore, I took refuge in this only. [3.15.4]

When I said, "I take refuge in Bhuh," I meant really this: "I take refuge in the earth, sky and heaven." [3.15.5]

When I said, "I take refuge in Bhuvah," I meant this: "I take refuge in Fire, Air and Sun." [3.15.6]

When I said, "I take refuge in Svah," I meant this: "I take refuge in the *Rigveda*, *Yajurveda* and *Samaveda*." Yes, that is what I meant. [3.15.7]

## Section 3.16

In this Section a man is compared with the sacrifice called Somayaga. It has three libations: the first in the morning, the second in the midday and the third in the evening. The mantras related to these three libations are Gayatri, Trishtubha and Jagati. Gayatri has 24 syllables, Trishtubha has 44 syllables and Jagati has 48 syllables. A man's life-span is divided into three parts lasting 24, 44 and 48 years, respectively. These stages of human life are compared with the three libations of Somayaga. The respective gods related to these mantras are: Agni and the Vasus for the first, Indra and the Rudras for the second, and the Vishvadevas and Adityas for the last.

Man is really like a yajna (sacrifice). The first twenty-four years he passes are the morning libation related to the Gayatri mantra, because the Gayatri mantra too has twenty-four syllables. The related gods of the morning libation are the Vasus. The Pranas indeed are the Vasus because they keep beings alive (*vasayanti*). [3.16.1]

During this period of life (the first twenty-four years), if any illness causes pain to the man, he should repeat this mantra: "O Pranas, O Vasus, unite this morning libation of mine with the midday libation. (That is, add the first period to the second period of life.) May I, who am a yajna, not be lost in the midst of the Vasus, who are the Pranas." After that he recovers and becomes healthy. [3.16.2]

His next forty-four years of life are the midday libation related to the Trishtubha mantra, which is made up of forty-four syllables. The Rudras are the related gods of the midday libation. The Pranas indeed are the Rudras, for they cause all this universe to weep (*rodayanti*). [3.16.3]

During this period of life, if anything causes him pain, he should repeat this mantra: "O Pranas, O Rudras, unite this midday libation of mine with the third libation. May I, who am a sacrifice, not be lost in the midst of the Rudras who are the Pranas." After that he recovers and becomes healthy. [3.16.4]

His next forty-eight years are the third libation. The Jagati mantra is made up of forty-eight syllables, and is related to the third libation. The Adityas are the related gods of the third libation. The Pranas indeed are the Adityas, for they accept (*adadate*) all this (sound, taste, etc.). [3.16.5]

During this period of life, if anything causes him pain, he should repeat this mantra: "O Pranas, O Adityas, extend this third libation of mine to a full length of life. May I, who am a sacrifice, not be lost in the midst of the Adityas, who are the Pranas." He then recovers from that and becomes healthy. [3.16.6]

Knowing this well-known doctrine of sacrifice, Mahidasa Aitareya said, "Death, why do you thus afflict me, who cannot be so killed." He lived for one hundred and sixteen years. He, too, who knows thus, lives in vigor for one hundred and sixteen years. [3.16.7]

### Section 3.17

He who eats and drinks (to sustain and) not to enjoy is like one who performs initiatory rites of a (Soma) yajna. [3.17.1]

And when one eats, drinks and enjoys, one is like him who performs "Upasadas" (a rite performed before a Soma sacrifice). [3.17.2]

While chanting the mantra called "Shastra" and the Saman called "Stotra," one laughs, eats and behaves as one of a couple. [3.17.3]

Austerity, giving gifts, uprightness, nonviolence and truthfulness are the Dakshinas (largesse) given to the priest in this sacrifice. [3.17.4]

That is why people say "will be born" (*soshyati*) and "is born" (*asoshta*). His birth is the beginning of the sacrifice and his death is the *Avabhrita* bath (the bath taken at the end of the sacrifice). [3.17.5]

Ghora Angiras expounded this well-known doctrine to Devaki's son Krishna, and said, "Such a knower should, at the time of death, repeat this triad: "You are the imperishable. You are the unchangeable. You are the subtle essence of Prana." After hearing this, Krishna had no desire for any other knowledge. There are two Rik stanzas on this: [3.17.6]

The knower of Brahman sees everywhere the supreme light of the ancient One, who is the seed of the universe.

May we reach it too, having perceived the highest light which dispels darkness. Having perceived the highest light in our own heart, we have reached that highest light, shining in all the gods. [3.17.7]

## Section 3.18

One should meditate on mind as Brahman. This meditation is with regard to the body. The Akasha (the sky) is Brahman; this is the meditation with regard to the gods. Both meditations are enjoined. [3.18.1]

This Brahman (mind) has four feet (parts): the (organ of) speech is one foot; Prana is one foot; the eye is one foot; and the year is one foot. This is with reference to the body. Then with reference to gods, Agni is one foot; Vayu is one foot; Aditya is one foot; and the quarters (directions) are one foot. Thus both meditations, with respect to the body and with respect to the gods, are prescribed by the Rishis. [3.18.2]

Speech is one of the four feet of Brahman (called mind). With the light of fire it shines and warms. One who knows thus, shines and warms with name, fame, and with the effulgence born of sacred wisdom. [3.18.3]

The organ of smell is one of the four feet of Brahman. With the light of air it shines and warms. He who knows thus, shines and warms with name, fame, and with the effulgence born of sacred wisdom. [3.18.4]

The eye is one of the four feet of Brahman. With the light of the sun it shines and warms. One who knows thus, shines and warms with name, fame, and with the effulgence born of sacred wisdom. [3.18.5]

The ear is one of the four feet of Brahman (called mind). With the light of the quarters it shines and warms. One who knows thus, shines and warms with name, fame, and with the effulgence born of sacred wisdom. [3.18.6]

## Section 3.19

This is the teaching: "The sun is Brahman." Further, before the creation, this universe was nonexistent. Then it became existent. It grew, it turned into an egg, it lay for a period of one year, and then it burst open. One half of the egg was of silver and the other half was of gold. [3.19.1]

That which was of silver is this earth; and that which was of gold is heaven. The outer shell is the mountains. The inner membrane is the clouds with mist. The veins are the rivers. The water in the lower belly is the ocean. [3.19.2]

That which was born was that sun. After he was born, a loud sound like shouting was produced. Also, all beings and all desired objects were produced. That is why during the rising and setting of the sun, sounds of loud shouts, all beings and all desired objects are produced. [3.19.3]

Pleasant sounds will reach and continue to delight him who knows the sun thus, and meditates on it as Brahman. [3.19.4]

## CHAPTER 4

### Section 4.1

Om. Once there lived Janashruti Pautrayana who made gifts with respect, gave generously, and had plenty of cooked food for others. He built rest houses everywhere, thinking that everywhere people needed food. [4.1.1]

One night Janashruti saw some swans flying by. Then he heard one swan addressing another thus: "Hey, Bhallaksha, the brightness of Janashruti Pautrayana has spread like the daylight. Do not come into contact with it. Otherwise it may burn you." [4.1.2]

Bhallaksha replied to him, "Look, you are talking about him as if he is Raikva, the cartman." Then the first said, "Who is this Raikva, the cartman?" [4.1.3]

Just as in the game of dice a player who rolls Krita (four, the highest number in the cast) wins from all other players, similarly Raikva gets the fruits of all the good deeds that other people do. [4.1.4]

Janashruti Pautrayana overheard those words. As soon as he got up in the morning he said to his attendant, "Listen, do you praise me like I am Raikva, the cartman?" He asked, "Sir, who is this Raikva, the cartman?" [4.1.5]

He repeated the words of the swan: "Just as in the game of dice a player who rolls Krita wins from all other players, similarly Raikva gets the fruits of all the good deeds that other people do." [4.1.6]

The attendant went out in search of him, but not having found him, came back. Janashruti said to him, "Look for him in places where a knower of Brahman should be found." [4.1.7]

While searching, he saw a man sitting under a cart and scratching eruptions on his skin. He asked him, "Sir, are you Raikva, the cartman?"

"Yes, Mister, I am he."

The attendant thought, "Finally I found him," and returned. [4.1.8]

## Section 4.2

On hearing about Raikva, Janashruti Pautrayana took with him six hundred cows, a gold necklace, and a chariot drawn by mules, went to Raikva and addressed him thus: [4.2.1]

"O Raikva, I have brought for you these six hundred cows, this gold necklace, and this chariot drawn by mules. Now, sir, teach me about the god whom you worship." [4.2.2]

The man answered him thus, "O Shudra, keep this gold neckless with the chariot and the cows for yourself." Then Janashruti Pautrayana again went back to Raikva with one thousand cows, a gold necklace, a chariot drawn by mules and his daughter. [4.2.3]

Janashruti said to him, "O Raikva, here are one thousand cows, a gold necklace, a chariot drawn by mules and my daughter as your wife. In addition, this village where you are staying is also for you. Now, sir, please teach me." [4.2.4]

Accepting his daughter, Raikva said, "O Shudra, you have brought so many things! By this gift of your daughter alone you are going to make me teach you." The king (Janashruti) gave away to him all the villages in the Mahavrisha country, which was later known as Raikvaparna, where Raikva lived. Raikva said to him: [4.2.5]

### Section 4.3

Air indeed is the absorber. When fire is extinguished, it is air in which it merges. When the sun sets, it is air in which it merges. When the moon sets, it is air in which it merges. [4.3.1]

When water dries up, it is air in which it is absorbed. Air absorbs everything. This is the doctrine of Samvarga (absorption) with reference to the gods. [4.3.2]

Next is the doctrine of Samvarga with reference to the body. Prana indeed is the absorber. When one sleeps, speech merges in Prana, the eyes merge in Prana, the ears merge in Prana, and the mind merges in Prana. Prana absorbs all these. [4.3.3]

These two, namely, air among the gods and Prana among the sense organs, are indeed the absorbers. [4.3.4]

Once upon a time, Kapeya Shaunaka and Kakshaseni Abhipratarin were being served with food, when a Brahmacharin (a celibate student of sacred knowledge) begged them for food. They did not give him anything. [4.3.5]

The Brahmacharin said, "Prajapati is the one god who swallows the four great ones (namely, fire, sun, moon and water as air; or also speech, ears, eyes and mind as Prana). He is the protector of the worlds. O Kapeya, O Abhipratarin, mortals do not see him (Prajapati), who lives in different forms. All this food is meant for him, and you are denying him this food. (The Brahmacharin is trying to say that he has realized the identity of Prana, i.e., Prajapati, and himself.) [4.3.6]

Reflecting upon his words, Kapeya Shaunaka approached him and said, "O Brahmacharin, He who is the self of the gods, creator of all beings, has golden teeth (has shining teeth) even though he is the devourer of everything, is the wise one, is never eaten but devours even those who cannot be eaten by any other, is immeasurable, is indeed Brahman whom we worship." Then he asked the servants to give him food. [4.3.7]

They gave him food. Krita, the highest number 4 in the dice-cast, wins (eats) the other lower numbers 3, 2 and 1. The sum total of the eater and the eaten makes 10. Similarly, the first set of five, namely, air, fire, sun, moon and water, made of eater and eaten, and the second set of five—Prana, speech, eye, ear and mind—make ten. Therefore, these ten are Virat, dwelling in all the ten quarters. [4.3.8]

## Section 4.4

Once Satyakama, son of Jabala, asked his mother, "Mother, I want to lead the life of a Brahmacharin. What family (*gotra*) do I belong to?" [4.4.1]

She told him, "Son, I do not know what family you belong to. In my youth when I worked around a great deal as a servant, I had you. So I do not know which family you belong to. I am Jabala and you are Satyakama by name. So you may call yourself Satyakama Jabala." [4.4.2]

Then he went to Haridrumata Gautama and said, "Sir, I would like to live as a Brahmacharin under you. May I come to you, sir?" [4.4.3]

He said, "My dear lad, what family do you belong to?"

He replied, "Sir, I do not know which family I belong to. I asked my mother about it and she said, 'Son, I do not know what family you belong to. In my youth when I worked around a great deal as a servant, I had you. So I do not know which family you belong to. I am Jabala and you are Satyakama by name.' So, I am Satyakama Jabala, sir." [4.4.4]

Then the teacher said to him, "Only a true Brahmana would speak like this. My dear boy, go and get the sacrificial fuel. I shall initiate you as a Brahmacharin. You have not swerved from the truth."

Having initiated him, he selected four hundred lean and weak cows and said, "Dear boy, tend these cows."

Satyakama, while driving them towards the forest, thought, "I shall not return until they are increased to one thousand in number." [4.4.5]

## Section 4.5

Eventually, a bull addressing him said, "Satyakama!"

"Yes, sir," he responded.

"Dear boy, we have become one thousand now. Take us to the teacher's house. [4.5.1]

"Also, let me teach you about the first foot of Brahman."

"Please do teach me, sir."

"The eastern quarter (direction) is one part, the western quarter is one part, the southern quarter is one part, and the northern quarter is one part. Dear boy, this indeed is one foot of Brahman, consisting of four parts, and is called Prakashavan (Radiant)." [4.5.2]

"One who knows this one foot of Brahman, thus consisting of four parts, and meditates on it as the Radiant, becomes radiant in this world. He also wins radiant worlds hereafter." [4.5.3]

## Section 4.6

"Fire will tell you of another foot of Brahman," said the bull.

The next morning at dawn, he drove the cows towards the teacher's house. In the evening, at one place where the cows stopped together, he started a fire, penned the cows, collected fuel and sat down near the fire, facing the east. [4.6.1]

The fire addressed him, "Satyakama!"
"Yes, sir," he responded. [4.6.2]

"Dear boy, let me teach you about one foot of Brahman," said the fire.
"Please do teach me, sir," he said.
"The earth is one part, the sky is one part, heaven is one part, and the ocean is one part. This indeed is one foot of Brahman, consisting of four parts, named Anantavan (Endless). [4.6.3]

"One who knows this one foot of Brahman, thus consisting of four parts, and meditates on it as the Endless, becomes endless in this world. He also wins endless worlds hereafter." [4.6.4]

## Section 4.7

The fire said, "The swan will tell you about another foot of Brahman."

The next day at dawn, he drove the cows towards the teacher's house. In the evening, at one place where the cows stopped together, he started a fire, penned the cows, collected fuel and sat down near the fire, facing the east. [4.7.1]

A swan flew to him and addressed him, "Satyakama!"
"Yes, sir," he responded. [4.7.2]

"Dear boy, let me teach you about one foot of Brahman," said the swan.

"Please do teach me, sir," he said.

"Fire is one part, the sun is one part, the moon is one part, and lightning is one part. This indeed is one foot of Brahman, consisting of four parts, named Jyotishman (Effulgent). [4.7.3]

"One who knows this one foot of Brahman, thus consisting of four parts, and meditates on it as the Effulgent, becomes effulgent in this world. He also wins effulgent worlds (the sun, the moon, etc.) hereafter." [4.7.4]

### Section 4.8

"Madgu (an aquatic bird) will tell you of another foot of Brahman," said the swan.

The next morning at dawn, he drove the cows towards the teacher's house. In the evening, at one place where the cows stopped together, he started a fire, penned the cows, collected fuel and sat down near the fire, facing the east. [4.8.1]

A Madgu bird flew to him and addressed him, "Satyakama!"

"Yes, sir," he responded. [4.8.2]

"Dear boy, let me teach you about one foot of Brahman," said the Madgu.

"Please do teach me, sir," he said.

"Prana is one part, the eye is one part, the ear is one part, and the mind is one part. This indeed is one foot of Brahman, consisting of four parts, named the Repository. [4.8.3]

"One who knows this one foot of Brahman, thus consisting of four parts, and meditates on it as the Repository, becomes a repository (abode) in this world. He also wins the repository (extensive) regions hereafter." [4.8.4]

### Section 4.9

Satyakama reached his teacher's house. The teacher addressed him, "Satyakama!"

"Yes, sir," he responded. [4.9.1]

"Dear boy, you shine like a knower of Brahman. Who taught you about Him?"

Satyakama assured him by saying, "Those other than men. I would, however, like to be taught by you, sir. [4.9.2]

"Sir, I have heard from teachers like you that the knowledge taught by one's own teacher becomes more effective."

The teacher taught him the same thing and omitted nothing. [4.9.3]

### Section 4.10

Once upon a time, Upakosala Kamalayana lived as a Brahmacharin in the house of Satyakama Jabala. For twelve years he had taken care of his fires. Satyakama had performed graduation ceremonies of the other fellow students of Upakosala and had sent them home. Upakosala had not been allowed to graduate. [4.10.1]

Satyakama's wife said to him, "This Brahmacharin has undergone severe austerities and has taken care of the fires (Garhapatya, Anvaharyapachana and Ahavaniya fires) very well. You should complete his graduation, lest the fires may curse you."

But the teacher (ignored her and) went away on travel without teaching him. [4.10.2]

Because of mental anguish Upakosala stopped eating. Then the teacher's wife asked him, "O Brahmacharin, why are you fasting? Please do eat."

He replied, "In me, a disappointed and ordinary man, there are many desires, pulling me in all directions. I am suffering from mental anguish. I cannot eat." [4.10.3]

Then the fires deliberated and said, "This Brahmacharin has undergone severe austerities and has tended us carefully. Let us teach him." Then they said to him, "Prana is Brahman, Ka (joy) is Brahman, and Kha (the sky) is Brahman." [4.10.4]

He said, "I know that Prana is Brahman, but I don't understand "Ka" and "Kha" (the inanimate objects being Brahman)."

Then they said, "What is 'Ka' is also 'Kha,' and vice versa." And they taught him about Prana and "Akasha" (the sky) within the heart. [4.10.5]

## Section 4.11

Then the Garhapatya (householder's) fire instructed him thus: "Earth, fire, food and the sun are my forms. The person seen in the sun is none other than me. [4.11.1]

"One who knows it thus, and meditates on it, destroys all his sinful deeds, wins the regions of fire, lives the full length of life gloriously, and his descendants do not perish. We protect him who meditates on it, in this world and in the next." [4.11.2]

## Section 4.12

Then the Anvaharyapachana fire (the fire produced from the Garhapatya and used for cooking) instructed him thus: "Water, the quarters, the stars and the moon are my forms. The person seen in the moon is none other than me. [4.12.1]

"One who knows it thus, and meditates on it, destroys all his sinful deeds, wins the regions of fire, lives the full length of life gloriously, and his descendants do not perish. We protect him who meditates on it, in this world and in the next." [4.12.2]

## Section 4.13

Then the Avahaniya fire (the fire produced from the Garhapatya fire and used to perform sacrifice) instructed him thus: "Prana, Akasha (the sky), heaven and lightning are my forms. The person seen in lightning is none other than me. [4.13.1]

"One who knows it thus, and meditates on it, destroys all his sinful deeds, wins the regions of fire, lives the full length of life gloriously, and his descendants do not perish. We protect him who meditates on it, in this world and in the next." [4.13.2]

## Section 4.14

The fires said, "O Upakosala! Dear boy, the knowledge of the fires and the knowledge of the Atman have been revealed to you. But the teacher will tell you the way."

The teacher came back and addressed him, "Upakosala!" [4.14.1]

"Yes, sir," he responded.

"Dear boy, your face shines like that of a knower of Brahman. Who taught you about it?"

He concealed the truth, as it were, and said, "Who would teach me here, sir?" Then, pointing to the fires, he said, "They are of this form now, but earlier they looked different."

The teacher then said, "What did they teach you, dear boy?" [4.14.2]

"This," he replied.

"Dear boy, they have told you about the worlds only, but I will tell you about That. As water does not cling to a lotus leaf, so no sin clings to him who knows it."

"Please tell me, sir."

To him he then said: [4.14.3]

## Section 4.15

"The 'person' who is seen in the eye is Atman. This is the immortal, fearless Brahman. So even if one drops clarified butter or water into the eye, it goes away by the edges. [4.15.1]

"He is called Samyad-vama (center of blessings), because all blessings come towards him. One who knows this brings all blessings. [4.15.2]

"He also is the vehicle of blessings, because he carries all blessings. One who knows this brings all blessings. [4.15.3]

"He also is the vehicle of light, because he shines in all the worlds. One who knows this shines in all the worlds. [4.15.4]

"Now such a person, whether his cremation rites are performed or not, goes to light, from light to day, from day to the bright fortnight, from the bright fortnight to the six months when the sun goes to the north, from the months to the year, from the year to the sun, from the sun to the moon, and from the moon to lightning. There a non-human person leads them to Brahman. This is the way of the gods, the way that leads to Brahman. Those who proceed by it do not return to this human whirlpool. No, they do not return." [4.15.5]

## Section 4.16

Prana (or air) that blows is yajna (sacrifice). It is yajna because it purifies everything while moving along. Mind and speech are the two paths of this yajna (Prana). [4.16.1]

The Brahma priest follows one path, the path of mind. The Hotri, Adhvaryu and Udgatri priests follow the other path, namely, speech. After the morning recitation (Prataranuvaka) is commenced, and before the ending Rik (Paridhaniya) is begun, if the Brahma priest speaks out, breaking his silence, then he follows only one path, namely speech, and the other path (is neglected and) suffers. [4.16.2]

Just as when a man walks with one leg, and a chariot moves with one wheel, both sustain injury, so also the yajna with one path (mind or speech) sustains injury. When the yajna sustains injury, the sacrificer also sustains injury. For having performed an erroneous yajna he becomes a worse sinner. [4.16.3]

However, after the Prataranuvaka is commenced and before the Paridhaniya Rik is begun, if the Brahma priest does not break his silence, then both the paths are utilized, and none suffers from injury. [4.16.4]

Just as a man walking with both legs, or a chariot moving with both wheels, moves steadily, so also the yajna and the sacrificer remain intact when both mind and speech are used. The sacrificer becomes great by performing the yajna. [4.16.5]

## Section 4.17

Prajapati brooded on the worlds. From them, thus brooded upon, he extracted their essences: fire from the earth, air from the sky, and the sun from heaven. [4.17.1]

He then brooded on these three deities. From them thus brooded upon, he extracted their essences: the Riks from fire, the Yajus-mantras from air, and the Samans from the sun. [4.17.2]

He brooded on the three Vedas. From them thus brooded upon, he extracted their essences: Bhuh (the earth) from the Riks, Bhuvah (the sky) from the Yajus-mantras, and Svah (heaven) from the Samans. [4.17.3]

Therefore, if the yajna is flawed on account of the Rik verses, one should offer an oblation in the Garhapatya fire with the mantra, "Bhuh Svaha." Thus one repairs the injury done to the yajna on the side of the Rik verses by the essence and power of the Rik verses themselves. [4.17.4]

If the yajna is flawed on account of the Yajus-mantras, one should offer an oblation in the Dakshinagni (southern) fire with the mantra, "Bhuvah Svaha." Thus one repairs the injury done to the yajna on the side of the Yajus-mantras by the essence and power of the Yajus-mantras themselves. [4.17.5]

If the yajna is flawed on account of the Samans, one should offer an oblation in the Avahaniya fire (the fire for sacrifice) with the mantra, "Svah Svaha." Thus one repairs the injury done to the yajna on the side of the Samans by the essence and power of the Samans themselves. [4.17.6]

As one joins together gold with salt, silver with gold, tin with silver, lead with tin, iron with lead, wood with iron or with leather, so does one repair the damage done to the yajna by the essence of these worlds, these deities and the three Vedas. The yajna is well healed when there is a Brahma priest who knows this. [4.17.7-8]

That yajna indeed becomes inclined to the north (the cause of attaining the northern solstice) where there is a Brahma priest knowing this. In reference to the Brahma priest knowing this, there is this song: "From whatever action of the Brahma priest the yajna becomes defective, there indeed the priest seeks for remedy." [4.17.9]

Just as a mare protects the soldier, so does only the Brahma priest protect the sacrificer. The Brahma priest who knows this protects not only the yajna but also the sacrificer and the other priests. Therefore, one should appoint only him who knows this as a Brahma priest, and not him who does not know this. [4.17.10]

## CHAPTER 5

### Section 5.1

The content of this Section is similar to that of Section 6.1 of the *Brihadaranyaka Upanishad.*

Om. Prana is the most superior and the best among the organs. He who knows the most superior and the best, becomes the most superior and the best. [5.1.1]

Speech is the richest. He who knows the richest, becomes the richest among his own people. [5.1.2]

The eye indeed is the stable basis. He who knows the stable basis, becomes stabilized in this world and in the next. [5.1.3]

The ear indeed is prosperity. He who knows prosperity, attains all desires, both divine and human. [5.1.4]

Mind is the abode (of all the organs). He who knows the abode, becomes the abode of his people. [5.1.5]

Once the senses disputed among themselves. Each said, "I am superior, I am superior." [5.1.6]

They went to Prajapati, their father, and asked, "Who is the best among us?"

He replied, "He by whose departure the body looks the worst is the best of you." [5.1.7]

Speech then departed, and having stayed away for a year, returned. He then asked, "How have you been able to live without me?"

They replied, "Like the dumb without speaking, but breathing with the breath, seeing with the eye, hearing with the ear, and thinking with the mind. Thus we lived." Then speech entered the body. [5.1.8]

The eye then departed, and having stayed away for a year, returned. He then asked, "How have you been able to live without me?"

They replied, "Like the blind without seeing, but breathing with the breath, speaking with the tongue, hearing with the ear, and thinking with the mind. Thus we lived." Then the eye entered the body. [5.1.9]

The ear then departed, and having stayed away for a year, returned. He then asked, "How have you been able to live without me?"

They replied, "Like the deaf without hearing, but breathing with the breath, seeing with the eye, speaking with the tongue, and thinking with the mind. Thus we lived." Then the ear entered the body. [5.1.10]

The mind then departed, and having stayed away for a year, returned. He then asked, "How have you been able to live without me?"

They replied, "Like children without thinking, but breathing with the breath, seeing with the eye, speaking with the tongue, and hearing with the ear. Thus we lived." Then the mind entered the body. [5.1.11]

Now when Prana was about to leave, tearing up the other senses, as a strong horse might uproot the peg to which he is tied, they gathered round him and said, "Sir, please do not depart. You are the best among us." [5.1.12]

Then speech said to him, "If I am the richest, so are you the richest." The eye said to him, "If I am the stable basis, so are you the stable basis." [5.1.13]

Then the ear said to him, "If I am prosperity, so are you prosperity." The mind said to him, "If I am the abode, so are you the abode." [5.1.14]

That is why these are not called organ of speech, eyes, ears or mind. They are called only Pranas, because Prana itself becomes all these. [5.1.15]

## Section 5.2

Prana asked the other senses (organs), "What will be my food?"

They replied, "Whatever food there is, from the bird's food to the dog's food, is all yours too." Whatever is eaten, is the food of "Ana," that is, Prana. For him who knows this, there is nothing that is not food. (This is because Prana is sustained by food only, in all creatures. "Anna," which means food, is similar to the word "ana," which is also the base of the word "Prana." "Ana" means "Prana.") [5.2.1]

Then Prana asked, "What will be my clothes?"
The senses replied, "Water."
That is why people take water, before and after taking food (as if to cover the food with water). He who knows this receives plenty of clothes and never remains without clothing. [5.2.2]

Satyakama Jabala imparted this knowledge of Prana to Goshruti Vyaghrapada and said, "If anyone imparts this knowledge even to a dry stump, then branches and leaves would sprout from it." [5.2.3]

If the knower of Prana desires to achieve greatness, he should consecrate himself on the new moon day, and then on the night of full moon stir up the mash of all herbs in a vessel of curd and honey. Then he should offer an oblation of the mash into the fire, with the mantra, "Svaha to the most superior and the best," on the spot prescribed for offerings. He should then throw what remains attached to the ladle into the mash-pot. [5.2.4]

With the mantra, "Svaha to the richest," he should offer an oblation into the fire on the spot prescribed for offerings, and then should throw what remains attached to the ladle into the mash-pot. With the mantra, "Svaha to what is stable," he should offer an oblation into the fire on the spot prescribed for offerings, and then should throw what remains attached to the ladle into the mash-pot. With the mantra, "Svaha to prosperity," he should offer an oblation into the fire on the spot prescribed for offerings, and then should throw what remains attached to the ladle into the mash-pot. With the mantra, "Svaha to the abode," he should offer an oblation into the fire on the spot prescribed for offerings, and then should throw what remains attached to the ladle into the mash-pot. [5.2.5]

Then, moving a little away from the fire and taking the mash-pot in his hands, he should recite the mantra, "You are 'Ama' (Prana) by name, all this universe rests with you, you are the most superior, the best, ruler and protector of all. Please lead me to superiority, to the richest position, to rulership and to sovereignty. I want to achieve all this." [5.2.6]

Then reciting this Rik mantra step by step, "We pray for that food pertaining to the Progenitor (as Prana)," he should sip. "We are the food of the deity (Prana)," saying this he should sip. "The best and sustainer lord," saying this he should sip. "We readily meditate upon the deity Bhaga," saying this and washing the pot shaped like a Kamsa or a Chamasa, he should drink all. Then he should lie down behind the fire on a skin or on the ground, controlling his speech and mind. If he should see a woman in a dream, he should know that his rite has succeeded. [5.2.7]

There is this verse about it: During the performance of the rites for the desired results, if the performer sees a woman in a

dream, then he should know that that is the indication of the fulfillment of his desired results. [5.2.8]

### Section 5.3

The story of Shvetaketu in the following Sections, 5.3 through 5.10, is
also given in Section 6.2 of the *Brihadaranyaka Upanishad.*

Once, Shvetaketu Aruneya went to the assembly of the
Panchalas. There, the king Pravahana Jaivali asked him, "My boy,
has your father taught you?"
"Yes, sir," he said. [5.3.1]

"Do you know where all beings go from this world?"
"No, sir."
"Do you know how they return here again?"
"No, sir."
"Do you know where the two paths, the path of the gods and
the path of the fathers, part?"
"No, sir." [5.3.2]

"Do you know why the other world is not filled up?"
"No, sir."
"Do you know why in the fifth oblation, water is called man?"
"No, sir." [5.3.3]

"Then why did you say that you have been taught? How can
he who does not know these things say that he has been taught?"
Shvetaketu was distressed and went to his father, whom he
asked, "Sir, without teaching me properly, you said that you had
finished teaching me." [5.3.4]

Shvetaketu further said, "That ordinary Kshatriya asked me
five questions and I could not answer even one of them."
His father said, "As you told me about those questions, even I
do not know the answer to any one of them. If I had known, why
would I not have taught you?" [5.3.5]

Then Shvetaketu's father, Gautama, went to the king's
(Pravahana's) palace. When he arrived there, the king made rever-

ential offerings to him. The next morning again Gautama presented himself in the king's assembly, when the latter said to him, "O revered sir, please ask for a boon of any human wealth from me."

He replied, "O king, please keep the human wealth with you. Instead, please tell me those words that you spoke about to my boy." The king was perturbed. [5.3.6]

The king commanded him to stay there for a long time. At the end of the period he said to him, "O Gautama, you have asked me about this knowledge, which was never imparted to the Brahmanas, prior to you. In all the worlds this teaching belonged to the Kshatriyas only."

Then he taught him the knowledge. [5.3.7]

## Section 5.4

"O Gautama, that heaven is a sacrificial fire, the sun is its fuel, the rays are the smoke, the day is the flame, the moon is the ember, and the stars are the sparks. [5.4.1]

"In this fire the gods offer the oblation of faith. Out of that oblation arises Soma, the king. [5.4.2]

## Section 5.5

"O Gautama, Parjanya (the god of rain) is the sacrificial fire. The air itself is its fuel, the cloud is its smoke, lightning is the flame, the thunderbolt is the ember, and the rumblings are the sparks. [5.5.1]

"In this fire the gods offer the oblation of Soma, the king. From that offering the rain arises. [5.5.2]

## Section 5.6

"O Gautama, the earth is the sacrificial fire, the year is its fuel, space is the smoke, night is the flame, the directions are the embers, and the intermediate directions are the sparks. [5.6.1]

"Into this fire the gods offer the libation of rain. From this offering arises food. [5.6.2]

## Section 5.7

"Man, O Gautama, is the sacrificial fire, speech is its fuel, Prana is the smoke, the tongue is the flame, the eye is the ember, and the ear is the spark. [5.7.1]

"Into this fire the gods offer the oblation of food. From that oblation the seed arises. [5.7.2]

## Section 5.8

"O Gautama, woman is the sacrificial fire. . . . In this fire the gods offer the libation of seed. From this offering arises the fetus. [5.8.1-2]
(Here the whole process of childbirth, from the union of a couple to the birth of a child, is nothing but holy yajna.)

## Section 5.9

"It is for this reason that in the fifth oblation water comes to be called a person. The fetus enclosed in the womb lies inside for more or less nine or ten months, and then it is born. [5.9.1]

"After birth he lives whatever length of life he has. After his death he is carried to the fire (for cremation), from where he came (that is, from fire). [5.9.2]

## Section 5.10

"Those who know this (about the five fires), and those who meditate in the forest with faith and austerity, go to light, from light to day, from day to the bright fortnight of the month, from the bright fortnight to those six months during which the sun travels northward, from those months to the year, from the year to the sun, from the sun to the moon, and from the moon to lightning. From there a person who is not human leads them on to Brahman. This is the path of the gods. [5.10.1-2]

"But those who live as householders in a village, offer sacrifices, perform works of public service and give alms, go to smoke, from smoke to night, from night to the dark fortnight of the month, from the dark fortnight to those months during which the sun travels southward. From there they do not reach the year. (The path of the gods and the path of the fathers are separated even from the cremation fire.) [5.10.3]

"From these months they go to the region of the fathers, from the region of the fathers to space, from space to the moon. That is Soma, the king. This is the food of the gods. The gods eat it. [5.10.4]

"Residing there till the fruit of their good deeds is exhausted, they return again the same way they traveled—to space, and from space into air. Having become air they become smoke, from smoke they become the white cloud. [5.10.5]

"Having become the white cloud they become the rain-bearing cloud and then they drop down as rain. Then they are born in this world as rice and barley, herbs and trees, sesame plants and beans. From there release becomes very difficult. For whoever eats that food and begets children, the latter become like them too. [5.10.6]

"Among them, those whose conduct in this world has been good quickly attain a good birth—birth as a Brahmana, or a Kshatriya, or a Vaishya. But those whose conduct has been evil will quickly attain an evil birth—birth as a dog, a pig, or a Chandala (one born from a Shudra father and a Brahmana mother). [5.10.7]

"Then, by neither of these two paths have the small creatures gone. That is why they keep repeatedly being born as small creatures. About them one may say, 'Be born and die.' This is the third state. That is why the region of the moon is never filled up. Therefore, let a man take care of himself. There is this verse about it: [5.10.8]

"The four, namely, one who steals gold, one who drinks alcohol, one who dishonors the teacher's bed, and one who injures a Brahmana, and also a fifth, namely, one who associates with them, all fall. [5.10.9]

"Moreover, one who knows these five fires thus, even if he associates with those sinners, is not tainted by their sins. He who knows this becomes clean and pure and obtains a meritorious world." [5.10.10]

## Section 5.11

Prachinashala Aupamanyava, Satyayajna Paulushi, Indradyumna Bhallaveya, Jana Sharkarakshya and Budila Ashvatarashvi —these great householders and great Vedic scholars got together and held a discussion on what is Atman and what is Brahman. [5.11.1]

They reflected among themselves, "Gentlemen, there is one Uddalaka Aruni who is studying this Universal Atman at present. Come, let us go to him." So they went to him. [5.11.2]

Uddalaka thought, "These great householders and great Vedic scholars are going to ask me questions. I may not be able to answer all their questions. Therefore, I shall direct them to another teacher." [5.11.3]

To them Uddalaka said, "Sirs, at present Ashvapati, the king of Kaikeya, is studying the Universal Atman. Come, let us go to him." So they all went to him. [5.11.4]

When they got there, the king gave each of them proper individual attention. The next morning when he got up, he said to them, "In my kingdom there is no thief, no miser, no drunkard, no man who has not installed the sacred fire, no illiterate person, and no adulterer, much less an adulteress. Sirs, I am going to perform a yajna. In it, I shall give to each of you as much wealth as I will give to each officiating priest. Sirs, please stay here." [5.11.5]

They replied, "A man should state the purpose of his coming. At present you are studying the Universal Atman. Please tell us about it." [5.11.6]

The king said to them, "Tomorrow morning I shall give you an answer." Therefore, the next morning they approached him with sacrificial fuel in their hands. The king, even without receiving them as initiated pupils, addressed them thus: [5.11.7]

### Section 5.12

"O Aupamanyava, what do you meditate on as the Atman?"
He replied, "Heaven only, revered king."
The king said, "That Atman you meditate upon is the Universal Atman called 'Sutejas' (brightly shining). That is why in your family yajnas are performed with libations of Soma juice called 'Suta,' 'Prasuta' and 'Asuta.' [5.12.1]

"One who meditates on the Universal Atman, always has plenty of food to eat and pleasant things to see. His family attains the holy effulgence of Brahman. That is why you are well to do. But heaven (which you meditate upon) is only the head of the Universal Atman. If you had not come to me your head would have fallen off." [5.12.2]

### Section 5.13

Then he addressed Satyayajna Paulushi, "O Prachinayogya (adept in the ancient), what do you meditate on as the Atman?"
He replied, "The sun only, O revered king."
"The Atman you meditate upon is the Universal Atman called 'Vishvarupa' (Cosmic-form). That is why your family has all kinds of enjoyable things. [5.13.1]

"That is why you are blessed with a chariot, maid servants, golden ornaments, plenty of food to eat and pleasant things to see. In your family there is the holy effulgence of Brahman. But it is only the eye of the Atman (the source of light for the universe). If you had not come to me, you would have become blind." (You would not have recognized the real form of Brahman.) [5.13.2]

### Section 5.14

Then the king asked Indradyumna Bhallaveya, "O descendant of Vyaghrapada, what is the Atman you meditate upon?"

"Air only, O revered king," he replied.

The king said, "The Atman you meditate upon is the Universal Atman known as 'Prithagvartman' (having a varied course, like wind). That is why offerings from different quarters come to you and many rows of chariots follow you. [5.14.1]

"One who meditates on the Universal Atman, always has plenty of food to eat and pleasant things to see. His family attains the holy effulgence of Brahman. That is why you are well to do. But air (which you meditate upon) is only the Prana (vital energy) of the Universal Atman. If you had not come to me your Prana would have departed." [5.14.2]

### Section 5.15

Then the king asked Jana Sharkarakshya, "O Sharkarakshya, what is the Atman you meditate upon?"

"The sky only, O revered king," he replied.

The king said, "The Atman you meditate upon is the Universal Atman known as 'Bahula' (the vast). That is why your offspring and wealth are vast. [5.15.1]

"One who meditates on the Universal Atman, always has plenty of food to eat and pleasant things to see. His family attains the holy effulgence of Brahman. That is why you are well to do. But the sky (which you meditate upon) is only the trunk of the Universal Atman. If you had not come to me your trunk would have broken." [5.15.2]

### Section 5.16

Then the king asked Budila Ashvatarashvi, "O descendent of Vyaghrapada, what is the Atman you meditate upon?"

"Water only, O revered king," he replied.

The king said, "The Atman you meditate upon is the Universal Atman known as 'Rayi' (wealth). That is why you are endowed with wealth and bodily strength. [5.16.1]

"One who meditates on the Universal Atman, always has plenty of food to eat and pleasant things to see. His family attains the holy effulgence of Brahman. That is why you are well to do. But water is only the bladder of the Universal Atman. If you had not come to me your bladder would have burst." [5.16.2]

### Section 5.17

Then the king asked Uddalaka Aruni, "O Gautama, what is the Atman you meditate upon?"

"The earth only, O revered king," he replied.

The king said, "The Atman you meditate upon is the Universal Atman known as 'Pratishtha' (the firm support). That is why you are well supported with offspring and cattle. [5.17.1]

"One who meditates on the Universal Atman, always has plenty of food to eat and pleasant things to see. His family attains the holy effulgence of Brahman. That is why you are well to do. But the earth is only the feet of the Universal Atman. If you had not come to me your feet would have withered away." [5.17.2]

### Section 5.18

Then he addressed them all, "Indeed you eat your food, with partial knowledge of this Universal Atman, each knowing only a part of Him differently. But one who meditates upon this Universal Atman as a whole, extending from heaven to earth and identical with himself, eats food in all the worlds, in all beings and in all selves." [5.18.1]

"Of the Universal Atman heaven is the head, the sun is the eye, wind is the breath, the sky is the trunk, water is the bladder, and the earth is the feet. The altar is his chest, the *Kusha* grass (sacrificial grass) is his hair, the Garhapatya (household) fire is the heart, the Anvaharya fire (the fire for cooking, generated from the

household fire) is the mind, and the Ahavaniya fire (the fire generated from the household fire, for sacrifice) is the mouth." [5.18.2]

### Section 5.19

"Therefore, the food that comes first should be considered as
an oblation. While eating the first bite the eater should offer it to his
Prana with the mantra, 'Svaha to Prana.' Then Prana is satisfied.
[5.19.1]

"When Prana is satisfied, the eye is satisfied; when the eye is
satisfied, the sun is satisfied; when the sun is satisfied, heaven is
satisfied; when heaven is satisfied, whatever is under the sun and
heaven is satisfied. Then the eater himself is satisfied and has offspring, cattle, food, luster and the effulgence of Brahman. [5.19.2]

### Section 5.20

"When the eater offers the second oblation, he should offer it
with the mantra, 'Svaha to Vyana.' Then Vyana is satisfied. [5.20.1]

"When Vyana is satisfied, the ear is satisfied; when the ear is
satisfied, the moon is satisfied; when the moon is satisfied, the quarters are satisfied; when the quarters are satisfied, whatever is under
the moon and the quarters is satisfied. Then the eater himself is
satisfied and has offspring, cattle, food, luster and the effulgence of
Brahman. [5.20.2]

### Section 5.21

"When the eater offers the third oblation, he should offer it
with the mantra, 'Svaha to Apana.' Then Apana is satisfied. [5.21.1]

"When Apana is satisfied, speech is satisfied; when speech is
satisfied, fire is satisfied; when fire is satisfied, the earth is satisfied;
when the earth is satisfied, whatever is under the earth and fire is
satisfied. Then the eater himself is satisfied and has offspring, cattle,
food, luster and the effulgence of Brahman. [5.21.2]

## Section 5.22

"When the eater offers the fourth oblation, he should offer it with the mantra, 'Svaha to Samana.' Then Samana is satisfied. [5.22.1]

"When Samana is satisfied, the mind is satisfied; when the mind is satisfied, Parjanya (the rain-god) is satisfied; when Parjanya is satisfied, lightning is satisfied; when lightning is satisfied, whatever is under lightning and Parjanya is satisfied. Then the eater himself is satisfied and has offspring, cattle, food, luster and the effulgence of Brahman. [5.22.2]

## Section 5.23

"When the eater offers the fifth oblation, he should offer it with the mantra, 'Svaha to Udana.' Then Udana is satisfied. [5.23.1]

"When Udana is satisfied, the skin is satisfied; when the skin is satisfied, the air is satisfied; when the air is satisfied, space is satisfied; when space is satisfied, whatever is under the air and space is satisfied. Then the eater himself is satisfied and has offspring, cattle, food, luster and the effulgence of Brahman. [5.23.2]

## Section 5.24

"If anyone, without knowing this, offers the Agnihotra (oblation to the fire), it would be like removing the embers and pouring the oblation on the ashes. [5.24.1]

"However, if one, knowing this, offers the Agnihotra to Prana, his oblation is poured to all the worlds, all beings and all selves. [5.24.2]

"One who offers the Agnihotra, knowing this, has all his sins burnt like cotton on the soft jute reed. [5.24.3]

"Knowing this, if one offers even his leftover food to a Chandala, then that food becomes his offering to the Universal Atman alone. There is this verse about it: [5.24.4]

"As hungry children look for their mother, all beings wait on the Agnihotra." [5.24.5]

(All beings expectantly wait for the mealtime of a knower of the Universal Atman, because with his eating, the whole universe becomes satisfied.)

# CHAPTER 6

## Section 6.1

Om. Once upon a time lived Shvetaketu Aruneya. His father said to him, "Shvetaketu, go and live the life of a Brahmacharin. Dear boy, there has been no one in our family who has not studied the Vedas, and is a Brahmana by birth only." [6.1.1]

He then became a student at the age of twelve, and returned home at the age of twenty-four, after studying all the Vedas. He had become greatly conceited and arrogant about his being very learned. His father said to him, "Dear son Shvetaketu, I see that you are conceited and arrogant about your being very learned. Did you ask your teacher for that teaching (about the Supreme Brahman) through which the unheard becomes heard, the unperceived becomes perceived, and the unknown becomes known?"

"Sir, what kind of teaching is that?" [6.1.2-3]

"Dear boy, just as by one lump of clay all that is made of clay is known, the apparent difference being only the name, the truth is that it is only clay. [6.1.4]

"Dear boy, just as by one nugget of gold all that is made of gold is known, the apparent difference being only the name, the truth is that it is only gold. [6.1.5]

"Dear boy, just as by a nail cutter all that is made of iron is known, the apparent difference being only the name, the truth is that it is only iron—such is that teaching, my dear boy." [6.1.6]

"I am sure my teachers did not know it. If they knew it, why would they not teach it to me? Sir, will you please teach it to me?"

"Sure, my dear son," said the father. [6.1.7]

## Section 6.2

Shvetaketu's father said, "Dear boy, in the beginning there was this Being alone, the one and only. Some say that in the beginning there was only this Non-being, the one and only. From that Non-being, Being arose. [6.2.1]

"But how could this be so, my dear boy?" said the father. "How can Being be born from Non-being? Therefore, in the beginning of creation, there was Being alone, without a second. [6.2.2]

"The Being thought, 'May I become many, may I grow forth.' Then He created fire. The fire wished, 'May I become many, may I grow forth.' It created water. That is why, whenever a man feels hot, he perspires. [6.2.3]

"That water thought, 'May I become many, may I grow forth.' It created food. Therefore, whenever it rains, an abundance of food grows. [6.2.4]

## Section 6.3

"There are only three kinds of origins of beings, as mentioned earlier. They are either born from eggs, from living beings, or from sprouts. [6.3.1]

"That Supreme Being thought, 'Let me enter into the three kinds of beings born of these three deities (namely, fire, water and food) through the Jivatman, and give them different names and forms.' [6.3.2]

"'Let me make each one of them threefold.' Thinking thus, He entered into these three deities, and through the Jivatman, made beings into different names and forms. [6.3.3]

"He made each one of them threefold. But, dear boy, understand from me how each of these three deities becomes threefold. [6.3.4]

## Section 6.4

"The red color in fire is that of fire, the white color is of water, and the black color is of food. In this way, the quality of fire vanishes from fire. The name fire is only for recognizing it by a word, but its three forms, namely, fire, water and earth (food) are real. [6.4.1]

"The red color in the sun is that of fire, the white color is of water, and the black color is of earth. In this way, the quality of the sun vanishes from the sun. The name sun is only for recognizing it by a word, but its three forms, namely, fire, water and earth are real. [6.4.2]

"The red color in the moon is that of fire, the white color is of water, and the black color is of earth. In this way, the quality of the moon vanishes from the moon. The name moon is only for recognizing it by a word, but its three forms, namely, fire, water and earth are real. [6.4.3]

"The red color in lightning is that of fire, the white color is of water, and the black color is of earth. In this way, the quality of lightning vanishes from lightning. The name lightning is only for recognizing it by a word, but its three forms, namely, fire, water and earth are real. [6.4.4]

"The ancient great householders and great Vedic scholars have said that there is nothing that anyone could point out to them as unheard, unthought or unknown, because everything is made of these three things. [6.4.5]

"Whatever appeared red was considered as a form of fire, whatever appeared white was considered as a form of water, and whatever appeared black was considered as a form of food. [6.4.6]

"Whatever appeared to be unknown was known by them to be a combination of the three deities. My dear son, now let me tell you how, in the human body, each of these three deities become threefold. [6.4.7]

### Section 6.5

"When eaten, food is divided into three parts. Its grossest element becomes the excretum, its medium grade element becomes flesh, and its most subtle element becomes mind. [6.5.1]

"When ingested, water is divided into three parts. Its grossest element becomes urine, its medium grade element becomes blood, and its most subtle element becomes Prana. [6.5.2]

"When eaten, fire in the form of oil and clarified butter is divided into three parts. Its grossest element becomes bone, its medium grade element becomes marrow, and its most subtle element becomes speech. [6.5.3]

"Dear boy, mind is made up of food, Prana is made up of water, and speech is made up of fire."
"Revered sir, please explain it to me further," said Shvetaketu.
"Sure, my dear boy," said the father. [6.5.4]

### Section 6.6

"Dear boy, when curd is churned its subtlest part rises, and that is butter. [6.6.1]

"In the same way, dear boy, of the food that is eaten, the subtlest part that rises upwards becomes mind. [6.6.2]

"Of water that is ingested, the subtlest part that rises upwards becomes Prana. [6.6.3]

"Of the fire that is eaten, the subtlest part that rises upwards becomes speech. [6.6.4]

"Therefore, dear boy, mind is made up of food, Prana is made up of water, and speech is made up of fire."
"Explain it to me further, revered sir," said the boy.
"Sure, my boy," said the father. [6.6.5]

## Section 6.7

"Dear boy, man consists of sixteen parts. If you do not eat for fifteen days but drink as much water as you like, your Prana will not depart from you, because Prana is made up of water." [6.7.1]

Shvetaketu did not eat for fifteen days, and then approached his father saying, "What should I say?"
"Dear boy, recite Riks, Yajus verses and Saman mantras."
"I do not remember them at all, sir." [6.7.2]

The father said, "Dear boy, just as a single ember the size of a firefly, left over from a large burning fire, cannot burn any more than itself, similarly of your sixteen parts, only one part is left over, and by that you cannot perceive the Vedas. First eat and then you will understand me." [6.7.3]

He ate and then approached his father. Whatever things his father asked him, he replied to all of them. [6.7.4]

The father said, "When a single ember the size of a firefly, left over from a large burning fire, is made to blaze up by adding straw, it burns much more than its size. [6.7.5]

"Similarly, of your sixteen parts, only one part remained, and being nourished by food, that has made you to perceive the Vedas. Hence the mind is made up of food, Prana is made up of water, and speech is made up of fire."
From these words of his father, Shvetaketu understood it. [6.7.6]

## Section 6.8

Once Uddalaka Aruni said to his son, Shvetaketu, "Dear boy, you must learn from me the true nature of sleep. When a man is sleeping, he becomes united with pure Being and attains his own nature. Therefore, people speak of him as sleeping (*svapiti*), because then he has attained (*apitah*) his own (*sva*) nature. [6.8.1]

"As a bird tied to a string flies in every direction and, finding no resting place elsewhere, settles down at the very place where it is tied, similarly, dear boy, the mind, after flying in different directions and finding no resting place, takes refuge in Prana only, because it is tied to Prana. [6.8.2]

"My boy, now learn from me what hunger and thirst are. When a person is hungry, it is water which leads away (flows with) the food he has eaten to different parts of his body. As they speak of the cowherd leading the cows, the horseman leading the horses, and the king leading the people, so also they speak of water as the leader of food. My dear boy, now understand that this body has sprouted from its root. How can it be without a root? [6.8.3]

"What else could be its root other than food? Dear boy, in the same manner, with food being an offshoot, look for water as its root; with water as an offshoot, look for fire as its root; and with fire as an offshoot, look for Being as the root. My boy, all these creatures have Being as their root, Being as their abode, and Being as their support. [6.8.4]

"When a person is thirsty, as they say, fire leads away what he drank. As they speak of a leader of cows, a leader of horses or a leader of men, so they speak of fire as the leader of water. Therefore, my boy, know this offshoot (water) sprung up from its root. It could not be without a root. [6.8.5]

"And what else could its root be, other than water? With water as an offshoot, look for fire as its root. With fire as an offshoot, look for Being as the root. My boy, all these creatures have Being as their root, Being as their abode, and Being as their support. When a man departs from here his speech merges in his mind, his mind in Prana, Prana in fire, and fire in the Supreme Deity. [6.8.6]

"That which is the subtle essence, which is the Self of the whole world, that is the Reality. That is the Atman. O Shvetaketu, you are That."

"Please, sir, teach me some more."

"Sure, my boy," the father said. [6.8.7]

## Section 6.9

"My dear boy, the bees make honey by collecting juices of different trees and reducing them into one essence. [6.9.1]

"And those juices possess no discrimination such as, 'I am the juice of this tree,' 'I am the juice of that tree.' Similarly these creatures, when they merge into Being, do not know that they have merged into Being. [6.9.2]

"Whatever they are in this world, a tiger, a lion, a wolf, a pig, a worm, a flying insect, a gnat, a mosquito, that they become again. [6.9.3]

"That which is the subtle essence, which is the Self of the whole world, that is the Reality. That is the Atman. O Shvetaketu, you are That."
"Please, sir, teach me some more."
"Sure, my boy," the father said. [6.9.4]

## Section 6.10

"My dear boy, these eastern rivers flow to the east, and the western ones flow to the west. Their water rises from the ocean and becomes part of the ocean again. After merging in the ocean, the waters do not know themselves as, 'I am this river or that river.' [6.10.1]

"In the same manner, my dear son, all these creatures having come from Being, do not know that they have come from Being. Whatever these creatures were here, tiger, lion, wolf, pig, worm, fly, gnat or mosquito, that they become again and again. [6.10.2]

"That which is the subtle essence, which is the Self of the whole world, that is the Reality. That is the Atman. O Shvetaketu, you are That."
"Please, sir, teach me some more."
"Sure, my boy," the father said. [6.10.3]

## Section 6.11

"If someone strikes the root of this large tree, it would bleed but still survive; if someone strikes at the middle, it would bleed but still survive; if someone strikes at its top, it would bleed but still survive. Pervaded by the living self, it stands firm, drinking its nourishment and rejoicing. [6.11.1]

"But if its living self leaves one of its branches, that dries up; if it leaves a second branch, that dries up; if it leaves a third branch, that dries up; and if it leaves the whole tree, that dries up too. [6.11.2]

"In the same manner indeed, dear son, understand this. This body dies for sure when the living self leaves it. But the living self does not die.

"That which is the subtle essence, which is the Self of the whole world, that is the Reality. That is the Atman. O Shvetaketu, you are That."

"Please, sir, teach me some more."

"Sure, my boy," the father said. [6.11.3]

## Section 6.12

"Bring me a fruit from that Banyan tree."

"Here it is, sir."

"Break it."

"It is broken, sir."

"What do you see there?"

"These extremely small seeds, sir."

"Break one of them."

"It is broken, sir."

"What do you see there?"

"Nothing at all, sir." [6.12.1]

The father said to him, "Dear son, that subtle essence that you do not perceive there—growing from that very essence this large Banyan tree stands. Believe me, my boy. [6.12.2]

"That which is the subtle essence, which is the Self of the whole world, that is the Reality. That is the Atman. O Shvetaketu, you are That."

"Please, sir, teach me some more."

"Sure, my boy," the father said. [6.12.3]

## Section 6.13

"Put this salt in water and come to me in the morning."

He did so. In the morning, the father said to him, "Please take out the salt that you put in the water last night."

Having searched for it, he did not find it. [6.13.1]

"It has completely dissolved. My dear son, please take a sip of the water from this end. How is it?"

"It is salty."

"Take a sip from the middle. How is it?"

"It is salty."

"Take a sip from the other end. How is it?"

"It is salty."

"Throw it away and then come to me."

He did so and said it was the same everywhere.

The father said to him, "Dear son, as you do not see what is present in this water, though indeed it exists in it, similarly Being indeed exists in this body. [6.13.2]

"That which is the subtle essence, which is the Self of the whole world, that is the Reality. That is the Atman. O Shvetaketu, you are That."

"Please, sir, teach me some more."

"Sure, my boy," the father said. [6.13.3]

## Section 6.14

"My dear boy, one might bring a person from Gandhara with his eyes blindfolded and abandon him in a place where there are no human beings, and that person would shout towards the east, north, south or west, saying, 'I have been brought here with my eyes blindfolded.' [6.14.1]

"If someone would remove his blindfold and tell him, 'Gandhara region is in that direction; go in that direction,' he, by asking his way from village to village and using his own judgment, would reach Gandhara region. Exactly in the same manner, in this world, a person who has found a preceptor can acquire true knowledge. For him the only delay is his liberation from his body. Thereafter he is immediately merged in Being. [6.14.2]

"That which is the subtle essence, which is the Self of the whole world, that is the Reality. That is the Atman. O Shvetaketu, you are That."

"Please, sir, teach me some more."

"Sure, my boy," the father said. [6.14.3]

## Section 6.15

"The relatives of a sick person gather around him and ask him, 'Do you know me? Do you know me?' So long as his speech has not merged in his mind, his mind in his Prana, his Prana in fire (the warmth of his body), and fire in the Supreme Being, he knows them. [6.15.1]

"But when his speech is merged in his mind, his mind in his Prana, his Prana in fire (the warmth of his body), and fire in the Supreme Being, then he does not know them. [6.15.2]

"That which is the subtle essence, which is the Self of the whole world, that is the Reality. That is the Atman. O Shvetaketu, you are That."

"Please, sir, teach me some more."

"Sure, my boy," the father said. [6.15.3]

## Section 6.16

"They (the king's officers) bring a man held by the hand, saying, 'He has stolen, he has committed a theft; heat the ax for him.' If he has really done that, then he makes himself a liar. Because he covers himself with falsehood, he faces a heated ax, is burnt and gets killed. [6.16.1]

"But if he has not done the stealing, he makes himself a truthful man. Being given to truth, and covering himself with truth, he faces the heated ax, is not burnt and is set free. [6.16.2]

"As in this case the man of truth is not burnt, similarly a man of knowledge is not born again. The whole of this world has That for its self. That is Reality. That is Atman. O Shvetaketu, you are That."

From his words, Shvetaketu understood it for good. [6.16.3]


## CHAPTER 7

### Section 7.1

Om. Narada approached Sanatkumara and said, "Sir, I have come to you for knowledge, please teach me."

He replied, "Come and tell me what you already know and I will teach you what is beyond that." [7.1.1]

"Sir, I know the four Vedas—the *Rigveda*, the *Yajurveda*, the *Samaveda* and the *Atharvaveda*, and also the Itihasa-Purana (history) as the fifth. I know grammar, from which one can understand the Vedas, the rules for worshipping the ancestors, mathematics, the science of portents, economics, logic, political science, divinity, the science of scriptural studies, physical sciences, military science, astronomy, the science related to snakes, and fine arts. I have studied all these, sir. [7.1.2]

"Sir, with all this I am only a knower of the words, not a knower of Atman. I have heard from learned persons like you that one who knows Atman crosses over sorrow. I am in a state of sorrow. Sir, please do help me overcome this sorrow."

Sanatkumara replied, "Whatever you have learned so far is only a name." [7.1.3]

"The four Vedas—the *Rigveda*, the *Yajurveda*, the *Samaveda* and the *Atharvaveda*, and also the Itihasa-Purana (history) as the fifth—all these are merely names. Grammar, the rules for worshipping the ancestors, mathematics, the science of portents, economics, logic, political science, divinity, the science of scriptural studies, physical sciences, military science, astronomy, the science related to snakes, and fine arts—all these that you mentioned are only names. Worship the name (the sciences, but that is not all). [7.1.4]

"One who worships the name as Brahman becomes free to act as he wishes, within the sphere of that name (science)."
Narada said, "Sir, is there anything superior to name?"
Sanatkumara: "Surely there is something superior to name."
Narada: "Please tell me about that, sir." [7.1.5]

## Section 7.2

"Speech surely is superior to name. Speech makes us understand the four Vedas—the *Rigveda*, the *Yajurveda*, the *Samaveda* and the *Atharvaveda*, and also the Itihasa-Purana (history) as the fifth, grammar, the rules for worshipping the ancestors, mathematics, the science of portents, economics, logic, political science, divinity, the science of scriptural studies, physical sciences, military science, astronomy, the science related to snakes, and fine arts. It also makes us understand heaven and earth, air and sky, water and fire, gods and men, cattle and birds, grass and trees, creatures down to worms, flying insects and ants, virtue and vice, true and false, good and bad, pleasant and unpleasant. If speech did not exist we would not understand virtue or vice, true or false, good or bad, pleasant or unpleasant. Speech alone makes us understand all this. Therefore, worship speech. [7.2.1]

"One who worships speech as Brahman becomes free to act as he wishes, within the sphere of speech."
Narada said, "Sir, is there anything superior to speech?"
Sanatkumara: "Surely there is something superior to speech."
Narada: "Please tell me about that, sir." [7.2.2]

## Section 7.3

"Certainly mind is superior to speech. Just as the closed hand feels two *Amalaka*, or two *Kola*, or two *Aksha* fruits, similarly the mind feels speech and name. One first determines in his mind, 'Let me learn the mantras,' then he learns them; 'Let me perform an action,' then he performs it; 'Let me have offspring and cattle,' then he gets them; 'Let me have this world and the next,' then he obtains them. Mind indeed is Atman, mind indeed is the world. Mind indeed is Brahman. Therefore, worship the mind. [7.3.1]

"One who worships the mind as Brahman becomes free to act as he wishes, within the sphere of the mind."

Narada said, "Sir, is there anything superior to mind?"

Sanatkumara: "Surely there is something superior to mind."

Narada: "Please tell me about that, sir." [7.3.2]

### Section 7.4

"Will surely is superior to mind. When one wills, one intends in one's mind. Then the mind sends forth speech, and the speech expresses it as names or words. Names form the mantra, the mantra forms action, and the three merge together. [7.4.1]

"All these, from the name to the mind, merge in the will, are made up of the will, and depend on the will. Heaven and earth willed, air and sky willed, water and fire willed. When they will, rain is produced; when rain wills, food is produced; when food wills, Prana is produced; when Prana wills, mantras are produced; when mantras will, action or yajna is produced; and when actions will, the world is produced. When the world wills, all things are produced. Therefore, worship the will. [7.4.2]

"One who worships the will as Brahman attains the worlds willed by him. He, himself being permanent, attains permanent worlds; himself being firmly established, attains firmly established worlds; himself being painless, attains painless worlds. He further becomes free to act as he wishes, within the sphere of will."

Narada said, "Sir, is there anything superior to will?"

Sanatkumara: "Surely there is something superior to will."

Narada: "Please tell me about that, sir." [7.4.3]

## Section 7.5

"Intellect is indeed superior to will. When one understands, then one wills, then intends in mind, then sends forth speech, and then expresses it as a name. Names form the mantra, and the mantra forms action. [7.5.1]

"Will, mind and speech—all these merge in intellect. They are made up of intellect and based on intellect. Even a man who knows much, but is without intellect, is considered as if he does not exist and his knowledge does not matter, because if he were really learned, he would not be without intellect. On the other hand, if a man knowing little is endowed with intellect, people want to listen to him. Intellect is the one center where all these—will, mind and speech—merge. Intellect is their soul and support. Therefore, worship intellect. [7.5.2]

"One who worships intellect as Brahman attains the worlds of intelligence. He, himself being permanent, attains permanent worlds; himself being firmly established, attains firmly established worlds; himself being painless, attains painless worlds. He further becomes free to act as he wishes, within the sphere of intellect."
Narada said, "Sir, is there anything superior to intellect?"
Sanatkumara: "Surely there is something superior to intellect."
Narada: "Please tell me about that, sir." [7.5.3]

## Section 7.6

"Concentration surely is superior to intellect. The earth, the sky, heaven, water, mountains, gods and men—all these, as it were, concentrate. Therefore, those who attain greatness among men achieve part of their greatness as a result of concentration. Lower class people quarrel, abuse and slander. But those who are great seem to obtain their greatness surely due to concentration. Therefore, O Narada, worship concentration. [7.6.1]

"One who worships concentration as Brahman becomes free to act as he wishes, within the sphere of concentration."

Narada said, "Sir, is there anything superior to concentration?"
Sanatkumara: "Surely there is something superior to concentration."
Narada: "Please tell me about that, sir." [7.6.2]

## Section 7.7

"Understanding surely is superior to concentration. Understanding alone makes us understand the four Vedas—the *Rigveda,* the *Yajurveda,* the *Samaveda* and the *Atharvaveda,* and also the Itihasa-Purana as the fifth, grammar, the rules for worshipping the ancestors, mathematics, the science of portents, economics, logic, political science, divinity, the science of scriptural studies, physical sciences, military science, astronomy, the science related to snakes, and fine arts. It also makes us understand heaven and earth, air and sky, water and fire, gods and men, cattle and birds, grass and trees, creatures down to worms, flying insects and ants, virtue and vice, true and false, good and bad, pleasant and unpleasant, food and drink, this world and the next. Understanding alone makes us understand all this. Therefore, worship understanding. [7.7.1]

"One who worships understanding as Brahman attains the world of those who understand the Vedas and have the knowledge of other subjects. He becomes free to act as he wishes, within the sphere of understanding."
Narada said, "Sir, is there anything superior to understanding?"
Sanatkumara: "Surely there is something superior to understanding."
Narada: "Please tell me about that, sir." [7.7.2]

## Section 7.8

"Strength surely is superior to understanding. A single man with strength causes a hundred men to tremble. When a man becomes strong he rises, by rising he serves wise men, by serving them he approaches nearer to them, by approaching he sees, hears, reflects, understands, acts and realizes. By strength indeed the earth exists, by strength alone the sky, heaven, mountains, gods and men, cattle and birds, grass and trees, creatures down to worms, flying insects and ants, and the world stand. Therefore, O Narada, worship strength. [7.8.1]

"One who worships strength as Brahman becomes free to act as he wishes, within the sphere of strength."
Narada said, "Sir, is there anything superior to strength?"
Sanatkumara: "Surely there is something superior to strength."
Narada: "Please tell me about that, sir." [7.8.2]

## Section 7.9

"Food surely is superior to strength. If one does not eat for ten days, he might live but does not see, hear, reflect, understand, act or realize. But when he eats food he again does see, hear, reflect, understand, act and realize. Therefore, O Narada, worship food. [7.9.1]

"One who worships food as Brahman attains the worlds full of food and drink. He becomes free to act as he wishes, within the sphere of food."
Narada said, "Sir, is there anything superior to food?"
Sanatkumara: "Surely there is something superior to food."
Narada: "Please tell me about that, sir." [7.9.2]

## Section 7.10

"Water surely is superior to food. Therefore, when there is not enough rain living beings are troubled thinking that food will be scarce. On the other hand, when it rains plenty they are joyous thinking that food will be in abundance. Water, as it were, assumes the forms of earth, sky, heaven, mountains, gods and men, cattle and birds, grass and trees, creatures down to worms, flying insects and ants. Therefore, O Narada, worship water. [7.10.1]

"One who worships water as Brahman fulfills all desires and is satisfied. He becomes free to act as he wishes, within the sphere of water."

Narada said, "Sir, is there anything superior to water?"
Sanatkumara: "Surely there is something superior to water."
Narada: "Please tell me about that, sir." [7.10.2]

### Section 7.11

"Fire surely is superior to water. It is fire indeed which heats the sky by seizing the air. Then people say, 'It is hot, it is burning hot, it might rain.' It is fire that appears first and then creates water. It is fire that causes thunder and lightning with flashes upward and across. Then people say, 'There is lightning with flashes, it is thundering, it will surely rain.' It is fire that appears first and then creates water. Therefore, worship fire. [7.11.1]

"One who worships fire as Brahman, becoming resplendent, attains resplendent worlds full of light and free from darkness. He becomes free to act as he wishes, within the sphere of fire."
Narada said, "Sir, is there anything superior to fire?"
Sanatkumara: "Surely there is something superior to fire."
Narada: "Please tell me about that, sir." [7.11.2]

### Section 7.12

"Sky is superior to fire. In the sky only, both the sun and moon, lightning, stars and fire exist. Through the sky only one calls, one hears, one responds. In the sky one rejoices, one does not rejoice. In the sky a thing is born and towards the sky it grows. O Narada, therefore, worship the sky. [7.12.1]

"One who worships the sky as Brahman indeed attains vast worlds full of light, unconfined and spacious. He becomes free to act as he wishes, within the sphere of the sky."
Narada said, "Sir, is there anything superior to the sky?"
Sanatkumara: "Surely there is something superior to the sky."
Narada: "Please tell me about that, sir." [7.12.2]

### Section 7.13

"Memory is indeed superior to the sky. If there are many people assembled at a place and if they have no memory, they would not be able to hear any sound, would not be able to think, and would not be able to recognize. If, however, they have memory, they would hear, would be able to think, and would be able to recognize. One knows one's sons and cattle through memory only. Therefore, worship memory. [7.13.1]

"One who worships memory as Brahman becomes free to act as he wishes, within the sphere of memory."
Narada said, "Sir, is there anything superior to memory?"
Sanatkumara: "Surely there is something superior to memory."
Narada: "Please tell me about that, sir." [7.13.2]

### Section 7.14

"Hope indeed is superior to memory. Kindled by hope memory recites the hymns, performs actions, desires sons and cattle, and desires this world and the next. Therefore, worship hope. [7.14.1]

"One who worships hope as Brahman has all his wishes fulfilled, and his prayers become infallible. He becomes free to act as he wishes, within the sphere of hope."
Narada said, "Sir, is there anything superior to hope?"
Sanatkumara: "Surely there is something superior to hope."
Narada: "Please tell me about that, sir." [7.14.2]

### Section 7.15

"Prana indeed is superior to hope. Just as the spokes of a wheel are connected to the hub, similarly everything in the body is dedicated to Prana. Prana moves by Prana, gives Prana, and gives to Prana. Prana is the father, the mother, the brother, the sister, the preceptor and the Brahmana. [7.15.1]

"If one answers rudely to one's father, mother, brother, sister, preceptor or a Brahmana, people say, 'Shame on you! You are indeed a slayer of your father, your mother, your brother, your sister, your preceptor, or a Brahmana.' [7.15.2]

"However, if Prana has departed from them, and one piles their bodies on the fire, pokes them with a fork to turn them around and burns them, surely nobody would call him a slayer of his father, mother, brother, sister, preceptor or a Brahmana. [7.15.3]

"Prana indeed is everything. He who sees, thinks, and knows thus, becomes a superior speaker. If someone were to tell him that he is a superior speaker, he should not be embarrassed, but rather should accept that he is a superior speaker. [7.15.4]

## Section 7.16

"But he really is a superior speaker, who is superior in speaking the truth."
Narada said, "Sir, I would like to be a superior speaker with truth."
"But one must desire to understand the truth."
"Revered sir, I desire to understand the truth." [7.16.1]

## Section 7.17

Sanatkumara: "Only he who understands speaks the truth. One who does not understand does not speak the truth. One must have a desire to understand the knowledge."
Narada: "Sir, I desire to understand the knowledge." [7.17.1]

## Section 7.18

"When one reflects, then only one understands. Without reflecting it is not possible for one to understand. Only he who reflects understands. But one must have a desire to understand reflection."
"Sir, I have a desire to understand reflection." [7.18.1]

## Section 7.19

"When one has faith, then only one reflects. Without faith it is not possible for one to reflect. Only he who has faith reflects.

But one must have a desire to understand faith."

"Sir, I have a desire to understand faith." [7.19.1]

### Section 7.20

"When one has steadfastness, then only one has faith. Without steadfastness it is not possible for one to have faith. Only he who has steadfastness has faith. But one must have a desire to understand steadfastness."

"Sir, I have a desire to understand steadfastness." [7.20.1]

### Section 7.21

"When one acts, then only one becomes steadfast. Without acting it is not possible for one to become steadfast. Only he who acts becomes steadfast. But one must have a desire to understand action."

"Sir, I have a desire to understand action." [7.21.1]

### Section 7.22

"When one obtains happiness, then only one acts. Without happiness it is not possible for one to act. Only he who is happy acts. But one must have a desire to understand happiness."

"Sir, I have a desire to understand happiness." [7.22.1]

### Section 7.23

"Only that which is infinite is happiness. There is no happiness in anything that is finite. The infinite alone is happiness. But one must have a desire to understand the infinite."

"Sir, I have a desire to understand the infinite." [7.23.1]

### Section 7.24

"Where one sees nothing else, hears nothing else, understands nothing else—that is the infinite. Where one sees something else, hears something else, understands something else—that is the finite. The infinite indeed is immortal, the finite is mortal."

"Sir, in what is the infinite established?"

"In its own greatness, or even not in its greatness. [7.24.1]

"In this world people call cows and horses, elephants and gold, servants and wives, fields and houses, 'greatness.' I do not speak of them as greatness, because in that case one thing would be established in another. [7.24.2]

## Section 7.25

"That infinite is below, that is above, that is behind, that is in front, that is to the south, that is to the north, that alone is all this. Next is the explanation of the infinite as I: I am below, I am above, I am behind, I am in front, I am to the south, I am to the north, I am indeed all this. [7.25.1]

"Next follows the explanation of the infinite as Atman. Atman alone is below, Atman is above, Atman is behind, Atman is in front, Atman is to the south, Atman is to the north, Atman alone is all this.

"Verily, he who sees this, who thinks this, understands this, rejoices in Atman, delights in Atman, unites with Atman, and merges in Atman becomes Self-ruler, and is free to act as he wishes in all the worlds. But those who think otherwise are ruled by others. They live in perishable worlds and are not free to act as they wish in all the worlds. [7.25.2]

## Section 7.26

"For him alone who sees this, who reflects this, and understands this, springs Prana from Atman, hope from Atman, memory from Atman, sky from Atman, fire from Atman, water from Atman, appearance and disappearance from Atman, food from Atman, strength from Atman, understanding from Atman, concentration from Atman, intellect from Atman, will from Atman, mind from Atman, speech from Atman, name from Atman, hymn from Atman, and action from Atman. All this springs from Atman alone. [7.26.1]

"On this there is the following verse:

"'He who sees this does not see death, illness or sorrow. He who sees this sees everything, and obtains everything everywhere.'

"He is one, he becomes three, five, seven, nine. Then again he is said to become eleven, a hundred and eleven, and a thousand and twenty.

"When the food one eats is pure, one's reflection and understanding become pure, and memory becomes strong. When memory becomes strong all the knots of the heart are loosened."

Venerable Sanatkumara showed Narada, after his impurities had been washed away, the further shore of darkness. People refer to Sanatkumara as Skanda (a learned person, Lord Shiva's son Kartikeya). [7.26.2]

## CHAPTER 8

### Section 8.1

Om. In this city of Brahman there is an abode in the shape of a small lotus. Within it there is a small space. What is within that space is what one should desire to understand. [8.1.1]

If the disciple should say to the teacher, "Now in this city of Brahman and in this abode, which is of the shape of a lotus and has a small space within it, what is there which should be sought and understood?" [8.1.2]

The teacher should reply, "As extensive as this cosmic space is, so extensive is the space within the heart. Within it both heaven and earth, both fire and air, both sun and moon, both lightning and stars are contained. Whatever there is of Him in this world and whatever is not, all that is contained within it." [8.1.3]

If they should ask him, "If in this city of Brahman is contained all this—all beings and all desires—then what is left when old age overtakes it, or when it perishes?" [8.1.4]

Then he should reply, saying that Brahman does not age with the aging of the body; it is not killed with the death of the body.

This sky within the heart is the real city of Brahman. In it all desires are contained. It is the Atman which is free from sin, old age, death, grief, hunger and thirst, and whose desire is of the truth, whose resolve is of the truth. Just so in this world people obey the orders of the ruler and live where they are attached, be it a country or a piece of land. [8.1.5]

As here on this earth anything earned by work perishes, similarly, there in the next world anything acquired by righteous deeds perishes. Therefore, for those who depart from this world without having realized the Atman and these true desires, there is no freedom in all the worlds. But for those who depart from here having realized the Atman and these true desires, there is freedom in all the worlds. [8.1.6]

### Section 8.2

If he is desirous of the world of Pitris (fathers), by his mere will Pitris come up to him; and having obtained the world of Pitris, he is happy. [8.2.1]

If he is desirous of the world of mothers, by his mere will mothers come up to him; and having obtained the world of mothers, he is happy. [8.2.2]

If he is desirous of the world of brothers, by his mere will brothers come up to him; and having obtained the world of brothers, he is happy. [8.2.3]

If he is desirous of the world of sisters, by his mere will sisters come up to him; and having obtained the world of sisters, he is happy. [8.2.4]

If he is desirous of the world of friends, by his mere will friends come up to him; and having obtained the world of friends, he is happy. [8.2.5]

If he is desirous of the world of perfumes and garlands, by his mere will perfumes and garlands come up to him; and having obtained the world of perfumes and garlands, he is happy. [8.2.6]

If he is desirous of the world of food and drink, by his mere will food and drink come up to him; and having obtained the world of food and drink, he is happy. [8.2.7]

If he is desirous of the world of song and music, by his mere will song and music come up to him; and having obtained the world of song and music, he is happy. [8.2.8]

If he is desirous of the world of women, by his mere will women come up to him; and having obtained the world of women, he is happy. [8.2.9]

Whatever object he is attached to, whatever thing he desires— by his mere will it comes to him; and having obtained it, he is happy. [8.2.10]

## Section 8.3

These true desires have a covering of what is false. Though the desires are true, there is a covering that is false. Thus if someone's near and dear departs from this world, one does not get him back or see him again. (The longings for seeing the dead relatives are untrue because they originate due to false knowledge. This latter thus acts like a covering.) [8.3.1]

Whatever one wishes for and does not get, whether it is one's living or dead relatives or anything else, one gets by going into the Atman. For here indeed one's true desires are covered with what is false. As people who are not aware of the underground hidden treasure of gold in a field walk on it again and again, but don't find it, so do all creatures here go day after day into the Brahman-world and yet do not find it, for they are carried away by untruth. [8.3.2]

This Atman resides in the heart. Its etymological explanation is this: It is called *hridayam* (heart) because the Atman lives in the heart, *hridi-ayam* ("This One is in the heart").
One who knows this goes day by day into the heavenly world. [8.3.3]

That serene Being, rising out of this body and reaching the highest, appears in his own form. The teacher said that this is the Atman, this is fearless, this is immortal, this is Brahman. The name of this Brahman is "True." [8.3.4]

The name "Satyam" is made of three syllables, "sat," "ti," "yam." *Sat* signifies the immortal, *ti* signifies the mortal, and *yam* holds the two together. Because one holds the two together with it, it is *yam*. He who knows this goes to the heavenly world day by day. [8.3.5]

## Section 8.4

This Atman is the dike, the embankment for the protection of these worlds. This dike is affected neither by day nor night, neither by old age nor death, neither by grief nor good or evil deeds. All evils turn back from it, for this world of Brahman is free from evil. [8.4.1]

Therefore, indeed, on reaching this dike, a blind person ceases to be blind, a wounded person is no longer wounded, a suffering man no longer suffers. On reaching this dike, even night appears as day, for this world of Brahman is one of eternal light. [8.4.2]

But only those who seek it through a life of Brahmacharya (a life free from lust) attain this world of Brahman. Those people have freedom to act as they wish in all the worlds. [8.4.3]

## Section 8.5

What is called yajna is really Brahmacharya, for by Brahmacharya alone one can attain the Atman. Also, what is called *Ishta* (worship) is really Brahmacharya only, for only by worshipping with Brahmacharya can one attain the Atman. [8.5.1]

What is called *Sattrayana* (a yajna session) is really Brahmacharya (a celibate life), for by Brahmacharya only one attains one's salvation from Being. Also, what is called the "vow of silence" is really Brahmacharya, for only through Brahmacharya does one understand the Atman, and then meditates. [8.5.2]

Now, what is called a "course of fasting" is really Brahmacharya, for this Atman which one attains through Brahmacharya does not perish ever. Also, what is called *Aranyayana* (the life of a hermit) is really Brahmacharya, for indeed *Ara* and *Nya* are the two oceans in the world of Brahman, in the third heaven from here. There also is the lake *Airammadiya* (making exhilarating sound), a tree showering Soma, *Aparajita* (the unconquered) city of Brahma, and the golden hall specially built by the Lord. [8.5.3]

Therefore, only to those who attain through Brahmacharya the two oceans, *Ara* and *Nya* in the world of Brahman, belongs the world of Brahman. They also achieve freedom to act as they wish in all the worlds. [8.5.4]

### Section 8.6

Now, these arteries which belong to the heart are filled with a fine substance which is reddish-brown, white, blue, yellow and red. That sun indeed is reddish-brown, white, blue, yellow and red. [8.6.1]

Just as a highway runs from one village to the other, similarly the rays of the sun extend from one world to the other. They spread out from the sun and enter the arteries. Out of these arteries they spread and enter the sun. [8.6.2]

When a person is sound asleep, peacefully and without dreams, he enters the space in his heart through these arteries. Then no evil touches him because he is filled with the brightness of the sun. [8.6.3]

When he has become very weak, and people sitting around him ask him whether he recognizes them, he surely recognizes them as long as he has not departed from his body. [8.6.4]

When he departs from this body, he proceeds upwards through these very rays, meditating on Om, if he is an enlightened soul. He travels to the sun, with the speed of mind, in a short period. That indeed is the door to the world of Brahman for an enlightened soul, and a barrier for an ignorant one. [8.6.5]

There is a verse about it:
There are a hundred and one arteries of the heart. Only one of them leads to the crown of the head. Traveling upwards through that, one achieves immortality, while the other arteries will serve for going in different directions. [8.6.6]

## Section 8.7

The Atman which is free from sin, free from old age, free from death, free from sorrow, free from hunger and thirst, whose desire is truth, whose resolve is truth—that should be sought, that should be known. He who has found that Atman and understands it attains all the worlds and all desires. Thus spoke Prajapati. [8.7.1]

The gods and the demons both heard this and said, "Let us seek that Atman by which one attains all the worlds and all desires." Then Indra from among the gods and Virochana from among the demons, without communicating with each other, went to Prajapati with sacrificial fuel in hand. [8.7.2]

They lived with him as his disciples for thirty-two years. Then Prajapati asked them, "What is the purpose of your living here?"
They replied, "Sir, to know the Atman which is free from sin, free from old age, free from death, free from sorrow, free from hunger and thirst, whose desire is truth, whose resolve is truth— that should be sought, that should be known. He who has found that Atman and understands it attains all the worlds and all desires. These are your words only. We have been living here desiring that Atman." [8.7.3]

Then Prajapati said to them, "The person which is seen in the eye is Atman. That is immortal and fearless. That is Brahman."

"But, sir, he who is perceived in water and he who is perceived in the mirror—who is he?"

"The Atman himself is perceived in all this," replied Prajapati. [8.7.4]

## Section 8.8

"Look at yourself in a pan of water, and whatever you do not understand of the Atman come and tell me."

They looked at themselves in a pan of water. Prajapati asked them, "What do you see?"

They replied, "We see ourselves as we are, the exact image even to the very hairs and nails." [8.8.1]

Then Prajapati said to them, "After you have adorned yourselves, have become well dressed and well groomed, then look again into the pan of water."

They then adorned themselves, became well dressed and well groomed, and looked into the pan of water.

Then Prajapati asked them, "What do you see?" [8.8.2]

They replied, "Sir, just as we are adorned, well dressed and well groomed, so are both of these also adorned, well dressed and well groomed."

"That is the Atman, immortal and fearless. That is Brahman," he said.

They both went away satisfied in their hearts. [8.8.3]

Prajapati looked at them and said, "They both are going away without having perceived and without having understood the Atman. Whosoever will follow such a doctrine, be they gods or demons, will perish."

Then Virochana, satisfied in his heart, went to the demons and preached that doctrine to them, that the self (body) alone is to be worshipped, and the self alone is to be served. He who worships that self and serves that self gains both worlds, this and the next. [8.8.4]

Therefore, even to this day they call a man who does not give alms, who has no faith, and who does not perform yajna, a demon, because this is the doctrine of the demons. They adorn the body of the deceased with perfume, flowers, fine clothes and ornaments, and think that thereby they will win the other world. [8.8.5]

### Section 8.9

But Indra, even before he reached the gods, saw this difficulty: "Just as this self is well adorned when this body becomes well adorned, well dressed when the body is well dressed, well groomed when the body is well groomed, it will also be blind when this body is blind, one-eyed when the body is one-eyed, crippled when the body is crippled, and perish when this body perishes. I see no good in this." [8.9.1]

With fuel in hand, he came back again. Prajapati asked him, "O Indra, you went away with Virochana, satisfied in your heart. Now, what is the purpose in your coming back?"

He replied, "Sir, this self is well adorned when this body becomes well adorned, well dressed when the body is well dressed, well groomed when the body is well groomed, and it will also be blind when this body is blind, one-eyed when the body is one-eyed, crippled when the body is crippled, and perish when this body perishes. I see no good in this." [8.9.2]

"It indeed is so, O Indra," said Prajapati. "However, I will explain this to you further. Stay with me for another thirty-two years."

He lived there for another thirty-two years. Then Prajapati said to him: [8.9.3]

### Section 8.10

"He who moves about happy in dreams is the Atman. He is the immortal, the fearless. He is Brahman."

Then Indra went away satisfied in his heart. But even before he returned to the gods he saw this difficulty: "Even though the Atman is not blind when the body is blind, not one-eyed when the body is one-eyed, does not suffer defects from the defects of the body, is not slain when the body is slain, is not lame when the body is lame, yet when they kill it or chase it, it seems as if it becomes conscious of pain and even weeps. I see no good in this." [8.10.1-2]

With fuel in hand, he came back again. Prajapati asked him, "O Indra, you went away, satisfied in your heart. Now, what is the purpose in your coming back?"

He replied, "Sir, even though the Atman is not blind when the body is blind, not one-eyed when the body is one-eyed, does not suffer defects from the defects of the body, is not slain when the body is slain, is not lame when the body is lame, yet when they kill it or chase it, it seems as if it becomes conscious of pain and even weeps. I see no good in this."

"It indeed is so, O Indra," said Prajapati. "However, I will explain this to you further. Stay with me for another thirty-two years."

He lived there for another thirty-two years. Then Prajapati said to him: [8.10.3-4]

### Section 8.11

"He who is asleep, composed, serene and without dream is the Atman—the immortal and the fearless. He is Brahman."

Then Indra went away satisfied in his heart. But even before he returned to the gods he saw this difficulty: "In truth this one does not know himself as 'I am he,' nor does he know all these beings. It seems as though he has gone to annihilation. I see no good in this." [8.11.1]

With fuel in hand, he came back again. Prajapati asked him, "O Indra, you went away, satisfied in your heart. Now, what is the purpose in your coming back?"

He replied, "Sir, in truth this one does not know himself as "I am he," nor indeed these beings. It seems he has gone to annihilation. I see no good in this." [8.11.2]

"It indeed is so, O Indra." said Prajapati. "However, I will explain this to you further, and none other than this. Stay with me for another five years."

He lived there for another five years. This made one hundred and one years. Therefore, people say that Indra lived with Prajapati for one hundred and one years, as his celibate disciple of sacred knowledge. Then Prajapati said to him: [8.11.3]

## Section 8.12

"O Indra, this body is indeed mortal and is held by death. But it is the support of this deathless, bodiless Atman. The embodied self is held by pleasure and pain. For that which associates with the body there is no freedom from pleasure and pain. But pleasure and pain do not touch one who is bodiless. [8.12.1]

"Bodiless is air; and so are clouds, lightning and thunder. All these arising from yonder space reach the highest light and appear each in its own form. [8.12.2]

"Similarly this serene one rises out of this body, reaches the highest light and appears in his own form. He is the Highest Person. He moves about laughing, playing, rejoicing with women, chariots or relatives, never remembering this body in which he was born. Like a horse yoked to a chariot is the spirit bound to this body. [8.12.3]

"Wherever the eye is turned towards space, there is that seeing person, the Atman; the eye is only the instrument for seeing. He who is cognizant of, 'I smell this,' is the Atman; the nose is for smelling. He who is cognizant of, 'I speak this,' is the Atman; the voice is for speaking. He who is cognizant of, 'I hear this,' is the Atman; the ear is for hearing. [8.12.4]

"He who is cognizant of, 'I think this,' is the Atman; the mind is his divine eye. The Atman rejoices, seeing these pleasures through his divine eye, namely, the mind. [8.12.5]

"The gods who are in the world of Brahma meditate on the Atman. Therefore, all the worlds and all desires belong to them. He who knows that Atman, and understands it, obtains all the worlds and all desires." Thus spoke Prajapati. [8.12.6]

## Section 8.13

From the dark I pass to the colored, and from the colored I pass to the dark. Shaking off evil, as a horse shakes off his hair, and shaking off the body, as the moon frees itself from the mouth of Rahu, I, an enlightened soul, obtain the uncreated world of Brahman. [8.13.1]

## Section 8.14

What is called the sky is the revealer of name and form. That within which these (name, form and the sky) are contained is Brahman. That is the immortal, that is the Atman. I come to the assembly-hall and abode of Prajapati. I am the glory of the Brahmanas, the Kshatriyas and the Vaishyas. I have obtained the glory. I am glorious among the glorious. May I never go to the reddish-white, slippery, toothless and yet devouring (womb for rebirth). [8.14.1]

## Section 8.15

Brahma told this to Prajapati, Prajapati to Manu, and Manu to mankind. He who has learned the Vedas according to the rules in a teacher's house in the time left over from doing service to the teacher, and after coming back from the teacher's house has settled down as a householder, continuing the study of the Vedas in a clean place, and who has begotten virtuous sons and concentrated all his senses on the Atman, never causing pain to any creature except at specified holy places—who behaves thus all his life, reaches the world of Brahman and does not return here again. [8.15.1]

*****

# Brihadaranyaka Upanishad

## Introduction

The *Brihadaranyaka Upanishad* appears as a whole Aranyaka of the *Shukla Yajurveda,* and forms the final portion of the *Shatapatha-Brahmana.* This is the largest of the ten Upanishads, hence the name "Brihadaranyaka," meaning "Great Aranyaka." It is also a great Upanishad as far as its spiritual contents are concerned. There are two versions of this, one in the Madhyandina Shakha and the other in the Kanva Shakha. Acharya Shankara has written a commentary only on the version in the Kanva Shakha. The whole text of this Upanishad is in prose, with a few verses in between. The Upanishad has six chapters, which are divided into forty-seven Brahmanas or sections.

In the first chapter the Rishi of the Upanishad describes how the universe was created by Prajapati. He says this whole creation is itself like the *Ashvamedha* yajna, or the horse sacrifice, which is performed only by kings. In the process of creation Prajapati first created earth, water, sun, air and fire. Then he created the year with days and nights, and the Vedas. Gods and demons are the descendants of the same Prajapati. He created the organs, namely, the speech-organ, ear, eye, nose and Prana, the last being the foremost among them. He then created the respective deities of the organs. They are: fire for the speech-organ, air for the nose, the sun for the eye, the directions for the ear and the moon for the mind. Then Prajapati created the four Varnas, namely, Brahmana, Kshatriya, Vaishya and Shudra. It is in this Upanishad that one of the four Mahavakyas, *Aham Brahmasmi* ("I am Brahman"), occurs.

In the second chapter Ajatashatru, the king of Kashi (Varanasi), teaches Gargya about Brahman. He tells him that Brahman's subtle form in the universe is air and ether, and in the human body Prana and *Hridayakasha* (the cavity in the chest). In the universe, the shining sun represents the essence of the gross form of Brahman. In the body, the rest of the body other than Prana and Hridayakasha represent the gross form of Atman. Brahman is the "Truth of truth." It can be described only thus: "It is not this, not this." In this chapter Yajnavalkya teaches his wife, Maitreyi, about Brahman. He teaches her "Madhu-vidya," or Brahmavidya.

In the third chapter Yajnavalkya, in the court of King Janaka of Videha, answers the questions of the priests Ashvala, Artabhaga Jaratkarava and Bhujyu Lahyayani on the Karmakanda of the Vedas, namely, on yajna and its fruits enjoyed by the sacrificer. Then he answers the questions of other learned vedantins, namely, Ushasta Chakrayana, Kahola Kaushitakeya, Gargi Vachaknavi and Vidagdha Shakalya on the Jnanakanda of the Vedas, namely, on the nature of Brahman. Yajnavalkya tells them that in the body Atman moves, through Prana, as the immediate and direct Brahman. He is the seer of all sights, hearer of all sounds, thinker of all thoughts and knower of all knowledge. The Atman within us is really Brahman, realizing whom, the Brahmanas give up all mundane desires and live the life of mendicants. Brahman pervades everything in this universe. Our own Atman is the controller of this universe. He is the deity within earth, within water, within fire, in the ether, in the air, in heaven, in the sun, in the directions, in the moon, in the sky, and controls them.

In the fourth chapter Yajnavalkya tries to explain to King Janaka what Brahman is. He says that the speech-organ, Prana, eye, ear, mind, and heart—all these organs are the means of realizing Brahman. Then he explains in symbolic language how a man passes through the four stages of Vaishvanara (Universal Person), Taijasa (brilliance), Prajna (consciousness) and Atman, which correspond to four states, namely, waking, dream, deep sleep and *Turiya*. He also explains how the joy in the world of Brahman is millions of times more than that of a mortal human. This is very similar to the joy of Brahman defined in the *Taittiriya Upanishad* (Chapter 2, Lesson 8).

The last two chapters are said to be later additions. The fifth chapter starts with the Shantipatha (peace invocation) given in the beginning of the Upanishad, telling that Brahman is infinite. Then through a story the Upanishad tells us that one should have self-control, and be charitable and kind to others, if one wants to achieve Brahman. The chapter also explains the importance of the *Gayatri* mantra.

In the sixth chapter there is a repetition of Sections 5.1, 5.2 and 5.3 to 5.10 of the *Chhandogya Upanishad*. Then there is a description of the process of pregnancy and childbirth, which is compared to a yajna. The Upanishad also glorifies motherhood. At the end it gives a list of teachers of the Upanishad

### Peace Invocation

The visible universe is full (infinite) and has come out of the invisible Brahman, which is also full (infinite). Even though the universe is of an infinite extension it came out of Brahman, which still remains infinite. Om. Peace. Peace. Peace!

### CHAPTER 1

### Section 1.1

The dawn is the head of the sacrificial horse, the sun is its eye, the wind is its breath, the Vaishvanara fire is its open mouth, and the year is its body. Heaven is its back, the sky its belly, the earth its hoof, the quarters its sides, the intermediate quarters its ribs, the seasons its limbs, the months and fortnights its joints, days and nights its feet, the stars its bones, the clouds its flesh. The sands are its half-digested food, the rivers are its blood-vessels, the mountains its liver and lungs, the herbs and trees its hair. The rising sun is its forepart, the setting sun its hindpart. Lightning is its yawning, thunder is its shaking, rain is its making water, and speech is its neighing. (In other words, the whole universe is the sacrificial horse.) [1.1.1]

The day is the golden cup called Mahiman decorating the front of the sacrificial horse. The source of the day is the eastern sea. The night is the silver cup called Mahiman behind the horse. Its source is the western sea. The sacrificial horse carried the gods as a steed (*haya*), the *Gandharvas* as a stallion (*vaji*), the demons as a courser (*arva*), and men as a horse (*ashva*). The sea (the Supreme Being) is its stable and its source. [1.1.2]

## Section 1.2

In the beginning there was nothing whatsoever in the universe. This universe was covered by Death (Hiranyagarbha), or hunger. Hunger is death indeed. Then He created the mind wishing to possess a mind. He then worshipped himself. While worshipping himself water was produced. He thought, "While I was worshipping, water sprang up." That is why fire is called "Arka" (from the root "*arch*," which means to worship; and *ka* means water). There is water (or happiness) for him who thus knows why fire is called "Arka." [1.2.1]

Water is "Arka" indeed. What was there as froth on the water hardened and became the earth. During that work of creation Prajapati was tired. From his fatigue and affliction came forth the essence as luster. That was fire. [1.2.2]

Prajapati divided his body in three ways. The sun made one third, air made one third, and fire made one third of his body. So his Prana was also divided in three ways. His head is the east direction, his two arms are the north-east and south-east directions, his tail is the west direction, his two hip-bones are the north-west and south-west directions, and his two flanks are the south and north directions. His back is heaven, his belly is the sky, and his breast is this earth. He is established in water. He who knows thus, stands firm wherever he goes. [1.2.3]

He wished, "May a second body be born to me." He caused the union of speech (the Vedas) with the mind. The seed that was in the union became the year. There was never any year before him. He nourished the fetus (the year) in the cosmic egg for a year and then produced him as a baby. He opened his mouth to swallow the baby (the year) as he was born. The year cried and made a sound, "Bhan!" It was this sound that became speech. [1.2.4]

He thought, "If I kill this baby I shall have very little food." Therefore, with the union of speech (the Vedas) and the mind he created all there is, namely, the *Rigveda*, the *Yajurveda*, the *Samaveda*, the meters, the yajnas, men and animals. Whatever he created he resolved to devour. He devours everything. That is why he is called Aditi. He who thus knows the import of this name Aditi becomes the eater of the universe, and the universe becomes his food. [1.2.5]

He wished, "Let me perform a great yajna again." He was tired and afflicted. While he was tired and afflicted, his glory and strength went out. The organs are really the glory and strength. His organs having gone out, his body began to swell. But his mind remained attached to the body. [1.2.6]

He wished, "May this body of mine be fit for yajna; may I be embodied through it." Because it enlarged (*ashvat*), it became known as the horse (*ashva*), and because it became fit-for-yajna (*medhya*), the horse-sacrifice was called *Ashvamedha*. He who knows Prajapati as follows, indeed knows the *Ashvamedha*: Imagining himself as a consecrated horse, who is free to roam around, he meditated. After a year he sacrificed it to himself, and assigned other animals to their respective deities. That is why even now the priests sacrifice to Prajapati the consecrated horse that is dedicated to all the deities. The sun that shines above is the *Ashvamedha*. His body is the year. This fire is the sacrificial fire (*Arka*). The three worlds are the limbs of *Arka*. The fire and the sun are *Arka* and *Ashvamedha*, respectively. These two become the same deity, Death (Hiranyagarbha). He who knows thus, conquers death. Death does not overcome him because, being Hiranyagarbha, he identifies himself with these deities. [1.2.7]

## Section 1.3

Prajapati has two kinds of descendants, the gods and the demons. The gods were few in numbers whereas the demons were numerous. There was a rivalry between them to gain the worlds. The gods decided, "Let us beat the demons through the *Udgitha* (hymns) in the *yajna*." [1.3.1]

They said to speech, "Please sing hymns for us."
"Very well," said speech, and sang hymns for them. Speech caused well-being to the gods by singing hymns, but used the good

results of correct pronunciation for itself. The demons became aware that the gods would beat them with the help of that chanting priest (speech). Therefore, they rushed to speech and pierced it with sin. Today indeed that is the sin which people incur when speech tells a lie. [1.3.2]

Then the gods said to the nose, "Please sing hymns for us."

It said, "Very well," and sang hymns for them. The nose caused well-being to the gods by singing hymns, but used the good fragrance for itself. The demons became aware that the gods would beat them with the help of that chanting priest. Therefore, they rushed to the nose and pierced it with sin. Today indeed that is the sin which people incur when the nose smells what it should not. [1.3.3]

Then the gods said to the eye, "Please sing hymns for us."

It said, "Very well," and sang hymns for them. The eye caused well-being to the gods by singing hymns, but used the good sights for itself. The demons became aware that the gods would beat them with the help of that chanting priest. Therefore, they rushed to the eye and pierced it with sin. Today indeed that is the sin which people incur when the eye sees what is wrong. [1.3.4]

Then the gods said to the ear, "Please sing hymns for us."

It said, "Very well," and sang hymns for them. The ear caused well-being to the gods by singing hymns, but used the good sound for itself. The demons became aware that the gods would beat them with the help of that chanting priest. Therefore, they rushed to the ear and pierced it with sin. Today indeed that is the sin which people incur when the ear hears what is wrong. [1.3.5]

Then the gods said to the mind, "Please sing hymns for us."

It said, "Very well," and sang hymns for them. The mind caused well-being to the gods by singing hymns, but used the good thoughts for itself. The demons became aware that the gods would beat them with the help of that chanting priest. Therefore, they rushed to the mind and pierced it with sin. Today indeed that is the sin which people incur when the mind thinks what is wrong. In this way they also tainted the other organs with sin by piercing them with sin. [1.3.6]

Then the gods said to Prana residing in the mouth, "Please sing hymns for us."

It said, "Very well," and sang hymns for them. The demons became aware that the gods would beat them with the help of that chanting priest. Therefore, they rushed to Prana and wanted to pierce it with sin. But as a clod of earth is shattered when it dashes against a rock, so did the demons get crushed and blown in all directions, and thus perished. Then the gods became their true selves and the demons were defeated. One who knows thus, becomes his true self and his adversary is defeated. [1.3.7]

The gods said, "Where was he who united us with our true selves?" Then they thought, "He is within our mouth."

Therefore, Prana is called *Ayasya Angiras* because it is the essence (*rasa*) of the limbs (*anga*), sitting (*asye*) within the mouth. [1.3.8]

That very deity is called *Dur* (distant) because death keeps at a distance from it. Death is surely away from him who knows thus. [1.3.9]

Prana removed the sin of the deities of speech, hearing, smell, etc., carried it far away to the end of the directions, and deposited it there. Sin is like the death of the deities. That is why no one should go to a person of that territory, or go to that territory, lest one should contract sin, which is a form of death. [1.3.10]

The deity Prana, after removing the sin of the other deities, which was like their death, carried them beyond death. [1.3.11]

Prana first carried speech, the foremost of the organs, beyond death. When the latter was free from death, it became the well-known fire. That fire shines after transcending death. [1.3.12]

Then it carried the nose beyond death. When the latter was free from death, it became the air. That air blows after transcending death. [1.3.13]

Then it carried the eye beyond death. When the latter was free from death, it became the sun. That sun shines after transcending death. [1.3.14]

Then it carried the ear beyond death. When the latter was free from death, it became the directions. Those directions stay there after transcending death. [1.3.15]

Then it carried the mind beyond death. When the latter was free from death, it became the moon. That moon shines after transcending death. So this deity (Prana) does indeed carry beyond death one who knows thus (meditates upon Prana as including the other organs, and that it frees them from death). [1.3.16]

Then Prana obtained food for itself by singing. For whatever food is consumed by creatures, is consumed by Prana indeed, and Prana resides in that food (converted into the body). [1.3.17]

The organs said, "Whatever food you have, you obtained for yourself by singing. Now you should share it with us."

"Well, then you should sit around facing me," said Prana.

"Very well," said the organs, and sat down encircling Prana. Therefore, any food that one eats through Prana satisfies the other organs too. He who knows thus, becomes the supporter of his kin, who sit around facing him. He is the best among them and becomes their guide and chief. He has plenty of food to enjoy. If anyone among his kinsmen tries to compete with him, he is incapable of supporting his dependents. However, if someone follows him, or wants to support his dependents under him, he is capable of doing so. [1.3.18]

This Prana is called *Ayasya Angirasa*. (*Ayasya* means that which resides in the mouth, and *Angirasa* means the essence of the limbs.) Prana is surely the essence of the limbs. If Prana leaves any limb, it dries up soon. Therefore, it is indeed the essence of the limbs. [1.3.19]

It is also called *Brihaspati* (lord of *Rich*). Speech indeed is the meter *Brihati*, and Prana is the lord of speech. Thus it is again Brihaspati. [1.3.20]

This is also the lord of Brahman. Speech is indeed Brahman, and Prana is its lord. Therefore, this is again the lord of Brahman. [1.3.21]

This Prana is Saman, too. Speech is "*Sa*," which means "she," a word of feminine gender; and Prana is "*Ama*," a word of masculine gender. It is called Saman, because it is *Sa* (speech) and *Ama* (Prana). Or, Prana is Saman (equal) because it is equal to a white ant in size, equal to a mosquito, equal to an elephant, equal to these three worlds, or equal to this universe. He who knows this Saman (Prana) attains identity with the Saman or resides in the same world with it. [1.3.22]

This Prana indeed is Udgitha (a division of the Saman). Prana is surely *Ut* (support), because this universe is supported by Prana. Speech itself is *Githa* (song). Because it is *Ut* and *Githa*, therefore it is Udgitha. [1.3.23]

On this subject there is this story:
Brahmadatta Chaikitaneya, while drinking the Soma juice, said, "If Ayasya Angiras (Prana) sings hymns through any organ other than speech, may Soma break its head." He himself sang hymns through speech and Prana only. [1.3.24]

He who knows the wealth of this Saman (Prana) surely gets wealth. Sweet tone is the wealth of the Saman. Therefore, one who wants to do the duty of a priest should desire to have a sweet voice. He should perform his priestly function through that voice enriched with sweetness. That is why in a yajna people look for a priest with a sweet voice. One who thus knows the wealth of the Saman indeed becomes wealthy. [1.3.25]

He who knows what is the gold (or correct pronunciation of the words) of the Saman obtains gold. Correct pronunciation of the Saman is indeed its gold. He who thus knows this gold of the Saman surely attains gold. [1.3.26]

He who knows the base of the Saman obtains a base for himself. Speech indeed is its base. This Prana, with its base as speech only, sings the Saman. Some others believe that it is through food that Prana gets its melody in speech. [1.3.27]

Now, therefore, the elevating chanting of the *Pavamana* hymns are presented. It is the Prastotri priest who sings the Saman.

When he sings it, the performer of the yajna should chant these three Yajus mantras: "Lead me from the unreal to the real. Lead me from darkness to light. Lead me from death to immortality." (*Asato ma sadgamaya. Tamaso ma jyotirgamaya. Mrityorma amritam gamaya.*)

When the mantra says, "Lead me from the unreal to the real," actually the "unreal" is death, and the "real" is immortality. Thus it really means, "Lead me from death to immortality," that is, "Make me immortal." In the mantra, "Lead me from darkness to light," actually darkness is death, and light is immortality. So the mantra really says again, "Lead me from death to immortality." In the mantra, "Lead me from death to immortality," the meaning is not obscure, unlike in the other cases.

Then through the other hymns the chanter should obtain edible things (materialistic things to enjoy) for himself by singing these hymns. While these hymns are being sung, the performer of the yajna should ask for any boon that he wants. Knowing thus, the chanter priest gets whatever he wants for himself and for the sacrificer, by singing. This meditation on Prana enables one to win the world. One who meditates on this Saman (Prana) thus, can hope to go beyond this world. [1.3.28]

## Section 1.4

In the beginning there was only this Prajapati (Atman) in the form of a person (Purusha). He pondered and saw none but himself. He first said, "I am he." Therefore, he got the name "I." That is why even now, when asked, first one says, "It is I," and then tells the other names that he has. Because he was the first and had burnt all his sins, he is called "Purusha." ("Pur" means before, and "ush" means to burn. Therefore, Purusha is one who had burnt his sins before creation.) He who knows thus, burns sin if it tries to overcome him. [1.4.1]

In the beginning he was alone, and therefore, he was frightened. That is why even today a lonely person is frightened. He thought, "Since there is none other than me, what should I be afraid of?" From that thought alone his fear disappeared. Fear comes only from the presence of something else. [1.4.2]

He did not like the loneliness at all. That is why even now no one likes loneliness. He wanted the company of another person. He became the size of a man and a woman embracing each other. He divided this body into two. From that, husband and wife came into being. That is why Yajnavalkya has said that this body is like one half of a two-celled seed. Therefore, this void in a man is filled by the wife. He united with her, and from that, humankind was born. [1.4.3]

She (the wife) thought, "How can he unite with me after creating me from his own self? Well, let me disappear." Then she became a cow. The other became a bull and united with her. From that cows were born. When she became a mare, he became a stallion; when she was a she-donkey, the other became a he-donkey, and he united with her. From that one-hoofed animals were born. When one became a she-goat, the other became a he-goat; when she was a ewe, he was a ram; and he united with her. From that goats and sheep were born. In this manner he created whatever exists as couples, down to ants. [1.4.4]

He knew, "I am indeed the creation, because I created all this." Thus he was known as Creation. One who knows this, becomes a creator in this creation of Prajapati. [1.4.5]

Then he churned his mouth and created fire from its source, that is, from the mouth and hands. That is why both the hand and mouth are hairless within. When people say, "Sacrifice to this god," "Sacrifice to that god," thinking that they are different gods, they are mistaken, because they are but the multiple projection of him alone. Actually he himself is all the gods. Now, whatever is liquid in this world was created from his seed. That seed is the moon. Whatever there is in the universe is either food or the eater of food. The moon represents food and fire represents the eater of food in this universe. This creation of Prajapati is a surpassing creation, because he created the gods who are even better than him. Also he created men who can become immortals, even though Prajapati himself is mortal. One who knows this, becomes a creator in this creation of Prajapati. [1.4.6]

Then, this universe was unmanifested. It manifested itself only as name and form. So, even now things are known by different names and forms. This Atman has penetrated all these bodies right up to their nail-tips, just as a razor is in its case, and fire is in its source, firewood. People cannot see the Atman because It is not present anywhere in Its complete form. When It breathes it is called Prana; when It speaks it is called speech (*Vak*); when It sees it is called the eye; when It hears it is called the ear; when It thinks it is called the mind, and so on. These are Its names according to its functions. One who meditates upon each of these organs, considering each of them as the Atman, is unwise, because without combination each individual organ is incomplete. One should meditate upon It only as the Supreme Atman. Only in It do all these organs become one. One should seek the Atman only, because one knows all other entities only through It. One who finds the Atman from its other signs, just as one finds a missing animal through its footprints, attains fame and praise. [1.4.7]

This Atman, being closer than everything, is dearer than a son, dearer than wealth, dearer than any other object. If someone says that anything else is dearer to him than the Atman, he should be told that his dear thing is perishable, because that is true. One should meditate upon the Atman alone as dear. The dear objects of one who meditates upon the Atman as dear are never destroyed. [1.4.8]

Some seekers ask, "Men think that through the knowledge of Brahman they shall achieve everything. What do they mean by this? What did Brahman know by 'Brahma-vidya' that He became all this (universe)?" [1.4.9]

In the beginning the Atman was Brahman. He knew, "I am Brahman." Knowing this he became all this (the universe). Whosoever among the gods realized Him became Brahman. This is true among the sages and among men also. The sage Vamadeva, realizing himself as That (Brahman), knew that he was Manu and the sun. Even now, whoever knows Him in a similar manner, namely, as "I am Brahman," becomes this universe. Even the gods cannot stop him from becoming the universe, because he becomes their self. On the other hand, he who worships other gods, thinking that the gods are different from him and he is different from them, is indeed ignorant. Humans are like animals to the gods. Just as animals serve humans, so do men serve the gods. When we lose even one animal, it causes inconvenience to us. There is no need to say how much trouble is caused by the loss of many animals. That is why the gods do not like it that men should realize the Atman (because then they lose so many "human-animals" that serve them). [1.4.10]

In the beginning there was only Brahman. Being alone he did not grow. He created a noble form, the Kshatriya. Among the gods who represent the Kshatriyas are Indra, Varuna, the Moon, Rudra, Parjanya, Yama, Death and Ishana. There is none superior to the Kshatriya. Hence in the *Rajasuya* yajna, the Brahmana respects the Kshatriya from a lower seat. He bestows prestige to the Kshatriya only. The Brahmana is the source of the Kshatriya. Therefore, although the king enjoys superiority in that yajna, at the end he places himself under the Brahmana alone, who is his source. He who insults the Brahamana, destroys his own source and becomes a sinner by violence against his superior. [1.4.11]

He still did not grow. Then he created the Vaishyas—those classes of gods that are described in groups, namely, the Vasus, the Rudras, the Adityas, the Vishvadevas, and the Maruts. [1.4.12]

He still did not grow. Then he created the Shudra caste, namely, Pushan (the nourisher). This earth indeed is Pushan because it nourishes all that exists on it. [1.4.13]

He still did not grow. Then he created a noble form, righteousness. It is righteousness which is the ruler of the Kshatriyas. There is nothing greater than righteousness. Even a weak person wants to defeat a strong person through righteousness, as one does with the help of a king. What is righteousness is indeed truth. That is why it is said that when one speaks the truth, he is said to be speaking what is righteous. Also, when one speaks what is righteous he is said to be speaking the truth, because both of them are but righteousness. [1.4.14]

Thus these four castes, namely, Brahmana, Kshatriya, Vaishya and Shudra, were created. Prajapati became fire among the gods and the Brahmana among men. He then became the Kshatriya, Vaishya and Shudra by establishing Kshatra-dharma, Vaishya-dharma and Shudra-dharma, respectively. (That is, by establishing or doing the respective duties of the different castes.) Therefore, the gods wish to attain their objectives through fire, and men attain their objectives through a Brahmana, because Prajapati assumed these two (superior) forms. If anyone leaves this world without realizing the Atman as one's objective, then the Atman, being unknown, does not protect one, just as the Vedas unread or good deeds unperformed do not help one. Even if a person performs plenty of meritorious works in this world, but lacks the knowledge of the Atman, the fruits of his work will become exhausted eventually. Therefore, one should meditate upon the Atman only, as one's ultimate objective. The work of one who meditates upon the Atman only, is never exhausted, because whatever he desires he creates through the Atman. [1.4.15]

A householder is himself the support (world) of all beings. By offering libations and performing yajnas he supports the gods. By reciting the Vedas he supports the sages. By offerings to the forefathers and desiring offspring he supports the forefathers. By providing shelter and food to people he supports his fellow humans. By providing fodder and water to the household animals he supports them. He is the support for other creatures, birds and even ants which get food from his house. Then all beings will wish the welfare of such a person, just as one wishes one's own welfare. All this fivefold duty is well known and thoroughly discussed. [1.4.16]

In the beginning a person was alone. Then he desired, "I should have a wife so that a child may be born to me, and I should have wealth so that I may perform rites." These are the two main desires of a person. One cannot get more than this even if one wishes. That is why even now a single man desires, "I should have a wife so that a child may be born to me, and I should have wealth so that I may perform rites." So long as he does not get each of these he thinks he is incomplete. He may feel completeness in another way too. He may think that the mind is his self, speech is his wife, Prana is his progeny, the eye is his human wealth—since he attains it with the help of the eye, the ear is his divine wealth—since he hears it through the ear, and the body is his rite—since he performs rites through the body. This is the mental yajna consisting of five factors. These five factors are present in an animal, in a human, and in whatever exists in this universe. He who knows thus, attains all this universe. [1.4.17]

## Section 1.5

The father of creation created seven kinds of food through meditation and austerity. One was common food for all beings, two were assigned to the gods, three he created for himself, and one he gave to the animals. On the last kind of food (given to the animals) depend whatever breathes and whatever does not. Why is the food not exhausted even though it is being consumed constantly? Whoever knows the cause of this eats food symbolically. He attains identity with the gods, he attains strength. On that these are the verses. [1.5.1]

The real meaning of the sentence, "The father of creation created seven kinds of food through meditation and austerity," is that the father created them through wise thoughts and hard work. "One was common food for all beings," means that the food which is eaten by all beings is the common food. One who keeps this common food for himself without sharing it with others commits sin, because the common food is created for all. The sentence, "Two were assigned to the gods," means one was meant to be "*huta*" and the other was to be "*prahuta*." *Huta* is making libations to the fire before eating anything. *Prahuta* is giving offerings to the Brahmanas and the gods. That is why people make libations to the fire and give offerings to the Brahmanas. These, *huta* and *prahuta*, are the two foods of the gods. Some hold that these two mean the new moon and the full moon yajnas. Therefore, one should not perform the *Ishti* yajna for material gains.

In the statement, "One he gave to animals," "one" means milk, because men and animals first live on milk only. That is why people make a newly born baby lick clarified butter or suckle its mother's milk; and a newly born calf is called, "non-eater of grass." The meaning of "Whatever breathes and whatever does not, all are dependent on this" is that whatever is animate and inanimate indeed depend on milk. (The non-animate objects in the universe are created by yajna in which milk is offered.) On this, it is said that by performing a milk-yajna (that is, by living on only milk) for a year, one conquers death. This saying is not perfectly correct. Actually, on whatever day one performs a milk-yajna (drinks milk and feeds milk to others), that day one conquers death again. One who knows that, offers all kinds of foods to the gods.

The answer to "Why is the food not exhausted even though it is being consumed constantly?" is that the consumer is the cause of its inexhaustibility, because he produces food again and again. The eater is reproducing food by thinking properly and by hard work. If he does not produce food, it will certainly be exhausted soon. In the statement, "(he) eats food symbolically (Pratikena)," "Pratika" means symbol. So it means, "He eats symbolically." "He attains identity with the gods, he attains strength," is a kind of praise. [1.5.2]

In the statement, "Three he created for himself," "three" means the mind, speech and Prana. God created these for himself. (These three are internal food whereas food, *huta, prahuta* and milk are external food.) People say, "My mind was elsewhere, so I did not see;" "My mind was elsewhere so I did not hear." In other words everybody sees and hears through the mind alone. Desire, resolution, doubt, faith, lack of faith, patience, impatience, modesty, intelligence and fear—all these are states of the mind. That is why if one is touched from behind one discovers it through the mind. Also, whatever sound there is is indeed speech, because it reveals objects but is not itself the object of revelation. Prana, Apana, Vyana, Udana, and Samana—all these are different forms of Prana. This body is made up of speech, mind and Prana. [1.5.3]

These are indeed the three worlds. Speech is the earth, mind is the sky, and Prana is heaven. [1.5.4]

These are the three Vedas, too. Speech is the *Rigveda*, mind is the *Yajurveda* and Prana is the *Samaveda*. [1.5.5]

These three are the gods, forefathers (*Pitri*), and men. Speech is the gods, mind is the forefathers, and Prana is men. [1.5.6]

These three are the father, mother and child. The mind is itself the father, speech is the mother, and Prana is the child. [1.5.7]

These three are also what is known, what is to be known, and what is unknown. Whatever is known is a form of speech, because speech is the knower. Speech protects him who knows this, by becoming what is known. [1.5.8]

Whatever is to be known is a form of the mind, because mind is what is to be known. The mind protects him who knows this, by becoming what is to be known. [1.5.9]

Whatever is unknown is a form of Prana, because Prana is what is unknown. Prana protects him who knows this, by becoming what is unknown. [1.5.10]

The earth is the body of speech, and this fire is its luminous form. As far as speech extends, so far does the earth extend, and so far also does this fire. [1.5.11]

Heaven is the body of this mind, and the sun is its luminous organ. As far as the mind extends, so far does heaven extend, and so far also does the sun. The two were united and from that was born Prana. It is the lord without any adversary. A second being (of equal strength) is called an adversary. No adversary exists for him who knows thus. [1.5.12]

Water is the body of this Prana, and the moon is its luminous organ. As far as Prana extends, so far does water extend, and so far does the moon. These are all equal in extent and are endless. Whoever meditates on these as limited entities conquers a limited world (is born as finite). On the other hand, whoever meditates on them as unlimited entities conquers an unlimited world. [1.5.13]

Prajapati, described as the year, has sixteen digits. The nights (lunar days) are his fifteen digits. His sixteenth digit is fixed. He waxes and wanes, as a moon, through the lunar days. Through the sixteenth digit he pervades all living beings on the new-moon night, and arises from there in the morning. Therefore, in honor of this deity one should not destroy the life of any living being, not even that of a chameleon. [1.5.14]

That Prajapati, who is described as the year and has sixteen digits, is the man who knows this. Wealth is his fifteen digits, and the body is his sixteenth digit. It is through wealth that he waxes and wanes. This body corresponds to the hub of a wheel, and wealth is its spokes. Therefore, even if a man has lost everything he possesses but is alive, people say that he is a wheel with broken spokes. [1.5.15]

There are only three worlds—the world of people, the world of the forefathers, and the world of the gods. This world of people is attainable only through a son, and not by anything else like rites (*karma*). The world of the forefathers (*Pitriloka*) is attainable through rites, and the world of the gods through meditation (*vidya*). The world of the gods is the best of the worlds. That is why meditation is praised. [1.5.16]

Now, therefore, the transfer of the duties to the son: When the father thinks that he is going to die, he says to his son, "You are Brahman, you are yajna, you are the world."

The son repeats, "I am Brahman, I am yajna, I am the world."

What the father means is, "Whatever study there is, is summed up in the word 'Brahman.' Whatever yajnas there are to be performed, are summed up in the word 'yajna;' and whatever worlds there are, are summed up in the word 'world.' All these are a householder's duty. By identifying himself with all this, he (the son) will save me from the obligations towards the world."

Therefore, they speak of an instructed son as one who leads to the worlds. That is why a father instructs his son. When a father leaves this world, he enters his son with speech, mind and Prana. If any duty has been omitted by him inadvertently, the son releases him of that burden. Therefore, he is called "putra" (son). ("*Put*" means to do, and "*tra*" means to protect.) Even after his death a father lives here through his son. The divine and immortal speech, mind and Prana pervade him. [1.5.17]

The divine speech, consisting of the earth and fire, pervades him. That is why whatever he says through the divine speech comes to be true. [1.5.18]

The divine mind, which consists of heaven and the sun, pervades him. That is why by the divine mind he becomes happy and never grieves. [1.5.19]

The divine Prana, from water and the moon, pervades him. That is the divine Prana which, while moving or not moving, neither suffers nor perishes. One who knows this, becomes the self of all beings. As is this deity Prana, so also he becomes. As all beings worship this deity Prana, so also they worship him who knows the above fact. Whatever grief these beings suffer from is confined to them only. He is not affected by it. Only good results reach him. Evil results do not affect the gods (and he has reached the godhead). [1.5.20]

Now some discussion about the vow: Prajapati created the organs. (Here the organs are called *karmas* because they are instruments of work.) They, after being created, started competing with one another. Speech vowed that it would speak, the eye resolved that it would see, the ear vowed that it would hear, and so likewise did the other organs according to their functions. Death approached them in the form of exhaustion, and overtook them. It thus restricted them. That is why speech, the eye and the ear do get tired. However, Death could not overtake Prana residing in the body. Then the other organs knew that it was the foremost amongst them, and that it does not suffer or perish, whether it moves or moves not. They also decided to assume its form, and considered it as their own self. That is why this group of organs is called "Prana." The family of the person who knows this secret is well known because of that person. Whoever competes with that person withers and ultimately dies. This discussion is with reference to the body (*adhyatma*). [1.5.21]

Now the discussion with reference to the deities: Fire vowed that it would go on burning, the sun resolved to produce heat, the moon decided to shine, and so likewise did the other deities resolve according to their divine functions. As Prana is the foremost among the organs in the body, so is *Vayu* (air) foremost among these deities. The other deities droop, but not Vayu. It is Vayu amongst the deities who never sets. [1.5.22]

There is this verse on this: That from which the sun rises and into which it sets is Prana. That is true today and will be true tomorrow. The sun rises from Vayu, the cosmic Prana, and sets on it. The gods took the vow to make Prana their leader. Therefore, we should take this single vow—just as Prana and Apana function continuously until death, in the same way we should resolve to finish the work we take in hand, lest Death should overtake us. Through that we can achieve union with the same world as this deity. [1.5.23]

## Section 1.6

This universe has three components. They are: name, form and action. Sound is the cause of names, because all names are produced by sound. Sound is a common feature to all names. It is their self because it supports (produces) all names. 1.6.1]

Now, the eye is the cause of forms, because all forms are perceived by it. The eye is a common feature to all forms. It is their self because it supports (sees) all forms. [1.6.2]

The body is the cause of actions, because all actions are performed by the body. Thus the body is a common feature to all actions. It is their self because it supports (performs) all actions. Though these components of the universe, namely, name, form and action, are three, they are actually one, and that is this body. Again, though this body is one, it is these three. The principle of immortality is hidden by Truth. Prana is the principle of immortality, and name and form are Truth. So this Prana is hidden by them. [1.6.3]

## CHAPTER 2

## Section 2.1

Om. Once there was an eloquent descendant of Garga by the name of Proud Balaki. He said to Ajatashatru, the king of Kashi (Varanasi), that he would tell him about Brahman. Ajatashatru replied to him, "For merely saying so I would give you one thousand cows. I wonder why people think that only Janaka encourages the discussion on Brahman." [2.1.1]

Balaki Gargya said, "I worship that Being who is in the sun, as Brahman."

Ajatashatru replied, "Please do not say so. I worship him as transcendent, as the head of all beings, and as radiant. He who worships him like that becomes transcendent, the head of all beings, and radiant." [2.1.2]

Gargya said, "I worship that Being in the moon as Brahman."
At this Ajatashatru replied, "Please do not say so. I worship him only as the great, white-robed, radiant Soma. He who worships him thus, has Soma pressed out profusely every day, and his food is never exhausted." [2.1.3]

Gargya said, "I worship that Being in lightning as Brahman."
To him Ajatashatru replied, "Please do not say so. I worship him only as brilliant. He who worships him thus, becomes brilliant, and his progeny become brilliant too." [2.1.4]

Gargya said, "I worship that Being in the sky as Brahman."
At this Ajatashatru said, "Please do not say so. I worship him only as full and immobile. He who worships him thus, becomes blessed with progeny and cattle, and his progeny never die out from this world." [2.1.5]

Gargya said, "I worship that Being in the air as Brahman."
At this Ajatashatru said, "Please do not say so. I worship him only as sovereign, as unconquered, and as an indomitable army. He who worships him thus, becomes victorious, unconquerable and subduer of his enemy." [2.1.6]

Gargya said, "I worship that Being in the fire as Brahman."
At this Ajatashatru said, "Please do not say so. I worship him only as tolerant. He who worships him as tolerant becomes tolerant, and his progeny become tolerant too." [2.1.7]

Gargya said, "I worship that Being in water as Brahman."
At this Ajatashatru said, "Please do not say so. I worship him only as harmonious. For he who worships him thus, everything becomes harmonious. Inharmonious things keep away from that person, and from him harmonious children are born." [2.1.8]

Gargya said, "I worship that Being in the mirror as Brahman."

At this Ajatashatru said, "Please do not say so. I worship him only as bright. He who worships him thus, becomes bright, and his progeny too become bright. He also outshines all those with whom he associates." [2.1.9]

Gargya said, "I worship that sound as Brahman, which is heard behind a person who is practicing spiritualism, when he goes."

At this Ajatashatru said, "Please do not say so. I worship it only as life. He who adores it thus, reaches the full span of life. He does not meet an untimely death." [2.1.10]

Gargya said, "I worship that Being in the directions as Brahman."

At this Ajatashatru said, "Please do not say so. I worship him only as the second and as not parting. He who worships him thus, has associates, and his retinue never parts from him." [2.1.11]

Gargya said, "I worship that Being in the darkness as Brahman."

At this Ajatashatru said, "Please do not say so. I worship him only as death. He who worships him thus, obtains a long life in this world, and untimely death does not approach him." [2.1.12]

Gargya said, "I worship that Being who is in my self, as Brahman."

At this Ajatashatru said, "Please do not say so. I worship him only as self-restrained. He who worships him thus, becomes self-restrained, and his progeny also become self-restrained."

Then Gargya became silent. [2.1.13]

Ajatashatru asked, "Is that all?"
Gargya said, "That is all."
"Brahman is not known by this much knowledge."
Gargya said, "I would like to be your disciple." [2.1.14]

Ajatashatru said, "This is a reverse process that a Brahmana should become a disciple of a Kshatriya to learn about Brahman. I will however enlighten you."

He took the other by the hands and rose. They came to a sleeping man. Ajatashatru addressed the sleeping man by various names, like, "O Great One," "O White-robed One," "O Radiant One," "O Soma." The man did not wake up. The king then shook him repeatedly and woke him up. Then the man got up. [2.1.15]

Ajatashatru asked, "Where was this person with intellect, when he was asleep? Where did he come to now?" Gargya did not know the answers to the questions. [2.1.16]

Ajatashatru said, "When this person with intellect is asleep, he withdraws the functions of his sense organs, and lies in the Supreme Self that is within the heart. When he withdraws his organs he is called '*Svapiti*,' which means 'sleeping.' Then, of course, the nose, speech, the eye, the ear and the mind are withdrawn. [2.1.17]

"When the person is in the dream state he may become a Maharaja, or a learned Brahmana, or a high class or low class person. As a Maharaja may take a retinue of his servants with him as he goes about in his kingdom at his will, so does this self take the organs and go about at will in its own way. [2.1.18]

"Again, when the self is asleep, and when it is not aware of anything, it returns to the body along the seventy-two thousand nerves called *Hita*, which branch off from the heart to all parts of the body, and stays in it. Just as a baby, or a Maharaja, or a great Brahmana lives, having reached the height of bliss, so does this self stay. [2.1.19]

"As a spider moves up and down the thread it produces, or as little sparks spread from fire, similarly from this Atman come out all organs, all worlds, all gods and all living beings. Its secret name is the Truth of truth. Prana is truth, and It is the Truth of that." [2.1.20]

## Section 2.2

Here Prana is compared with a calf, living in its abode with a pen (special place) inside, tied to a post with a rope. Ajatashatru continues his sermon.

"He who knows the calf with its abode, its pen, post and rope, destroys his seven jealous cousins. This Prana in the body is the calf, the body is its abode, the head is its pen, vigor is its post, and food is its rope. [2.2.1]

The seven cousins of Prana are the seven sense organs in the head, namely, two eyes, two ears, two nostrils and the mouth.

"These non-decaying seven deities worship Prana. Through the red lines in the eye Rudra serves it, through the water in the eye Parjanya, through the pupil the sun, through the dark portion fire, through the white portion Indra, through the lower eye-lid the earth, and through the upper eye-lid heaven. He who knows thus, never becomes short of food. [2.2.2]

"There is a verse on this: 'There is a bowl with its mouth below and rotund part above. In that bowl is placed manifold knowledge. There are seven sages sitting by its side, and speech, which utters words, is the eighth among them.'

"In the statement, 'There is a bowl with its mouth below and rotund part above,' the bowl is our head. 'In that bowl is placed manifold knowledge,' refers to the sense organs, namely, the mouth, nose, etc., which represent manifold knowledge. 'There are seven sages sitting by its side,' refers to the organs, which are like the sages. 'Speech, which utters words, is the eighth among them,' refers to the function of the mouth as uttering words in addition to enjoying taste. [2.2.3]

"These two ears are indeed Gotama and Bharadvaja, one of them being Gotama and the other Bharadvaja. These two eyes are Vishvamitra and Jamadagni, one of them being Visvamitra and the other Jamadagni. These two nostrils are Vasishtha and Kashyapa, one of them being Vasishtha and the other Kashyapa. The tongue is Atri, because food is eaten through it. 'Atri' is a familiar name derived from 'Atti' (eats). He who knows thus, becomes the enjoyer of all food, and everything becomes his food. [2.2.4]

### Section 2.3

Ajatashatru continues:
"Brahman has only two forms—gross and subtle, mortal and

immortal, limited and unlimited, or perceptible and imperceptible. [2.3.1]

"The gross form of Brahman is that which is other than air and ether. It is mortal, limited and perceptible. The essence of that form which is gross, mortal, limited and perceptible is the shining sun, because it the essence of those three elements. [2.3.2]

"Now the subtle form of Brahman is air and ether. That form is immortal, unlimited, and imperceptible. The essence of that form which is subtle, immortal, unlimited and imperceptible is that Person who governs the solar system. He is the essence of all this universe. This is with reference to the deities. [2.3.3]

"Now, with reference to the body: What is other than Prana and the cavity in the heart (*Hridayakasha*) is the gross form. It is mortal, limited and perceptible. The essence of that form which is gross, mortal, limited and perceptible is the eye, because it is the essence of those three elements. [2.3.4]

"Now, the subtle form of Brahman is Prana and *Hridayakasha* (the cavity in the heart). That form is immortal, unlimited and imperceptible. The essence of that form which is subtle, immortal, unlimited and imperceptible is that Person who is in the right eye. He is the essence of those two elements in the body. [2.3.5]

"The form of that subtle body is like this: It is as is a cloth dyed with saffron, or gray sheep's wool, or the red color of the insect Indragopa (a furry insect with dark red color seen in the ground during the rainy season), or the flame of fire, or a white lotus, or a flash of lightning. He who knows thus, attains fame like a flash of lightning. After this the description of Brahman is: 'Not this, not this,' because there is no better description than this. Now, its sacred name is, 'the Truth of truth.' Prana is truth and Brahman is the Truth of truth." [ 2.3.6]

## Section 2.4

Yajnavalkya said to his first wife Maitreyi, "My dear, I am going to renounce this life as a householder. Therefore, I would like to make a settlement of the property between you and (my other wife) Katyayani." [2.4.1]

At this Maitreyi said, "Dear, if this whole earth is filled with wealth and becomes mine, will it make me immortal?"

"No," said Yajnavalkya, "your life will be exactly like that of wealthy people, but you cannot hope to achieve immortality through wealth." [2.4.2]

Maitreyi replied, "What shall I do with that which cannot give me immortality? Sir, please tell me about that only, which you know as the means of immortality." [2.4.3]

Yajnavalkya said, "Sweetheart, you have always been dear to me, and now you ask me what is dear to my heart. Come, sit down. I shall explain it to you. But while I am explaining, pay utmost attention to it." [2.4.4]

He said, "My dear, a husband is dear to a wife not for the sake of the husband, but for the sake of her own self. Also, a wife is dear to a husband not for the sake of the wife, but for the sake of his own self. Also, sons are dear to parents not for the sake of the sons, but for the sake of the parents themselves. Wealth is dear not for the sake of wealth, but for our own sake it is dear. A Brahmana is dear not for the sake of the Brahmana, but for our own sake he is dear. A Kshatriya is dear not for the sake of the Kshatriya, but for our own sake he is dear. The worlds are dear not for the sake of the worlds, but for our own sake they are dear. The gods are dear not for the sake of the gods, but for our own sake they are dear. Beings are dear not for the sake of beings, but for our own sake they are dear. Everything else is dear not for the sake of everything else, but for our own sake it is dear. My dear Maitreyi, Atman should be seen, heard of, reflected upon, and meditated upon. When Atman is seen, heard of, reflected upon and understood, all this is known. [2.4.5]

"The Brahmana rejects one who takes him to be different from Atman. The Kshatriya rejects one who takes him to be different from Atman. The worlds reject one who takes them to be different from Atman. The gods reject one who takes them to be different from Atman. Beings reject one who takes them to be different from

Atman. Everything else rejects one who takes it to be different from Atman. This Brahmana, this Kshatriya, these worlds, these beings and everything else are only Atman. [2.4.6]

"As one is not able to grasp the particular notes by themselves of a drum that is beaten, but only by grasping the general note of the drum or the effect of particular strokes on it are those notes grasped; . . . [2.4.7]

"As one is not able to grasp the particular notes by themselves of a conch that is being blown, but only by grasping the general note of the conch or the effect of particular blowings on it are those notes grasped; . . . [2.4.8]

"As one is not able to grasp the particular notes by themselves of a *vina* (lute) that is being played on, but only by grasping the general note of the vina or the effect of particular playings on it are those notes grasped; . . . [2.4.9]

"As various forms of smoke arise from fire kindled with damp fuel, my dear, in the same way, the *Rigveda, Yajurveda, Samaveda, Atharvangiras*, history, mythology, arts, Upanishads, mantras, aphorisms, elucidations and commentaries came out of this great Being (Brahman). They indeed are the breath of It alone. [2.4.10]

"As the ocean is the merging place of all waters, as the skin is the merging place of all touches, as the nostrils are the merging place of all odors, as the tongue is the merging place of all tastes, as the eye is the merging place of all forms, as the ear is the merging place of all sounds, as the mind is the merging place of all intentions, as the intellect is the merging place of all knowledge, as the hands are the merging place of all actions, as the organ of generation is the merging place of all pleasures, as the anus is the merging place of all excretions, as the feet are the merging place of all walking, as speech is the merging place of all the Vedas, . . . [2.4.11]

"As a lump of salt thrown into water dissolves into water and cannot be taken out again, but from whichever part one takes the water, it has a salty taste, in the same way, my dear, this great, endless, infinite Being is a mass of consciousness. It emerges with these elements (the human body and its organs) and vanishes again with them. When it is gone there is no more individual consciousness. This is what I say, my dear." Thus spoke Yajnavalkya. [2.4.12]

Then Maitreyi replied, "Sir, here you have confused me when you said, 'When it is gone there is no more individual consciousness.'"

Yajnavalkya said, "I am not saying anything confusing, my dear. What I said was necessary to explain the knowledge of that great Reality. [2.4.13]

"When Atman appears with beings then there is duality. In duality one smells another, one sees another, one hears another, one speaks to another, one thinks of another, one knows another. But when everything has become Atman, then by what and whom should one smell, by what and whom should one see, by what and whom should one hear, by what and to whom should one speak, by what and of whom should one think, and by what and whom should one know? My dear, also, by what should one know the knower?" [2.4.14]

### Section 2.5

Yajnavalkya continues:

"These waters are like honey for all beings, and all beings are like honey for these waters. This shining immortal person who is in this earth, and this shining immortal person who is in one's body—he indeed is this Atman, this Immortal, this Absolute, this All. [2.5.1]

"This earth is like honey for all beings, and all beings are like honey for this earth. This shining immortal person who is in these waters, and this shining immortal person who is in one's body and exists as the seed—he indeed is this Atman, this Immortal, this Absolute, this All. [2.5.2]

"This fire is like honey for all beings, and all beings are like honey for this earth. This shining immortal person who is in this fire, and this shining immortal person who is in one's body as speech—he indeed is this Atman, this Immortal, this Absolute, this All. [2.5.3]

"This air is like honey for all beings, and all beings are like honey for this air. This shining immortal person who is in this air, and this shining immortal person who is in one's body and exists as Prana—he indeed is this Atman, this Immortal, this Absolute, this All. [2.5.4]

"This sun is like honey for all beings, and all beings are like honey for this sun. This shining immortal person who is in this sun, and this shining immortal person who is in one's body and exists as sight— he indeed is this Atman, this Immortal, this Absolute, this All. [2.5.5]

"These directions are like honey for all beings, and all beings are like honey for these directions. This shining immortal person who is in these directions, and this shining immortal person who is in one's body and exists as the ear and each occasion of hearing— he indeed is this Atman, this Immortal, this Absolute, this All. [2.5.6]

"This moon is like honey for all beings, and all beings are like honey for this moon. This shining immortal person who is in this earth, and this shining immortal person who is in one's body and exists as mind—he indeed is this Atman, this Immortal, this Absolute, this All. [2.5.7]

"This lightning is like honey for all beings, and all beings are like honey for this lightning. This shining immortal person who is in this earth, and this shining immortal person who is in one's body and exists as lightning—he indeed is this Atman, this Immortal, this Absolute, this All. [2.5.8]

"This thunder-cloud is like honey for all beings, and all beings are like honey for this thunder-cloud. This shining immortal person who is in this earth, and this shining immortal person who is in one's body and exists as sound and voice—he indeed is this Atman, this Immortal, this Absolute, this All. [2.5.9]

"This ether is like honey for all beings, and all beings are like honey for this ether. This shining immortal person who is in this earth, and this shining immortal person who is in one's body and exists as the ether in the heart (*Hridayakasha*)—he indeed is this Atman, this Immortal, this Absolute, this All. [2.5.10]

"This righteousness is like honey for all beings, and all beings are like honey for this righteousness. This shining immortal person who is in this earth, and this shining immortal person who is in one's body and exists as righteousness—he indeed is this Atman, this Immortal, this Absolute, this All. [2.5.11]

"This truth is like honey for all beings, and all beings are like honey for this truth. This shining immortal person who is in this earth, and this shining immortal person who is in one's body and exists as truth—he indeed is this Atman, this Immortal, this Absolute, this All. [2.5.12]

"This human species is like honey for all beings, and all beings are like honey for this human species. This shining immortal person who is in this earth, and this shining immortal person who is in one's body and exists as human qualities—he indeed is this Atman, this Immortal, this Absolute, this All. [2.5.13]

"This Atman is like honey for all beings, and all beings are like honey for this Atman. This shining immortal person who is in this earth, and this shining immortal person who is in one's body and exists as the Atman—he indeed is this Atman, this Immortal, this Absolute, this All. [2.5.14]

"This Atman is the Lord of all beings, the king of all beings. As all the spokes of a wheel are held at its hub, in the same way, all the gods, all the worlds, all Pranas and all the individual selves are held together in the Atman. [2.5.15]

"This indeed is known as '*Madhu-vidya*,' the knowledge described in the *Atharvaveda*, which was once imparted to the two Ashvin brothers by the sage Dadhyach. Seeing their deed, Dadhyach had said to them, 'O Ashvins in human form, seeing your daring deed for the sake of gaining knowledge, I will reveal the knowledge of the "Madhu-vidya," described in the *Atharvaveda*, to you through a horse's head on my shoulders, just as a cloud showers rain.' [2.5.16]

According to a story in the *Shatapatha Brahmana*, once the sage Dadhyach came to the Ashvins. They wanted to learn the "Madhu-vidya," described in the *Atharvaveda*, from Dadhyach, who told them that Indra had threatened to cut his head off if he taught it to anybody. The Ashvins assured him that they had a scheme to save him. They said that when he started to teach them, they would themselves cut his head off and put a horse's head on him, through which he would teach them. When Indra would come to cut his horse-head off, they would bring back his own head and replace it on him. Dadhyach agreed. Thereafter, everything went as planned.

"This indeed is known as '*Madhu-vidya,*' the knowledge described in the *Atharvaveda,* which was once imparted to the two Ashvin brothers by the sage Dadhyach. Seeing their deed, Dadhyach had said to them, 'O Ashvins, you fixed a horse's head on my shoulders in order to gain the knowledge described in the *Atharvaveda.* O Destroyers of the enemy, in fulfillment of the promise, I imparted that secret knowledge to you relating to the sun, as well as the secret meditation relating to Atman.' [2.5.17]

"This indeed is known as '*Madhu-vidya,*' the knowledge described in the *Atharvaveda,* which was once imparted to the two Ashvin brothers by the sage Dadhyach. Observing their deed, the sage said to them, 'The Lord created cities (bodies) for two-footed and four-footed beings. First, that Supreme Being entered these cities as a bird (as a subtle body). As he dwells in all the cities (*Pura*), He is called "*Purusha.*" There is nothing that is not enveloped by Him, nothing that is not pervaded by Him.' [2.5.18]

"This indeed is known as '*Madhu-vidya,*' the knowledge described in the *Atharvaveda,* which was once imparted to the two Ashvin brothers by the sage Dadhyach. The sage said, 'The Supreme Being assumed the likeness of different forms. That form of His is for His revelation. Due to "*Maya*" (false notion) the Supreme Being is perceived as manifold, because there are ten sense-organs, nay, hundreds of them, yoked to Him. That Brahman is without antecedent, without consequent, without interior and without exterior. This Atman which experiences everything, is Brahman. This is the teaching of the Vedanta.'" [2.5.19]

## Section 2.6

Now, here is the line of teachers:
Pautimashya received this knowledge of the *Shatapatha*

*Brahmana* from Gaupavana, Gaupavana from another Pautimashya, this Pautimashya from another Gaupavana, this Gaupavana from Kaushika, Kaushika from Kaundinya, Kaundinya from Shandilya, Shandilya from Kaushika and Gautama, Gautama from Agniveshya, Agniveshya from Shandilya and Anabhimlata, Anabhimlata from another Anabhimlata, this Anabhimlata from a third Anabhimlata, this Anabhimlata from Gautama, Gautama from Saitava and Prachinayogya, Saitava and Prachinayogya from Parasharya, Parasharya from Bharadvaja, Bharadvaja from another Bharadvaja and Gautama, Gautama from another Bharadvaja, this Bharadvaja from another Parasharya, this Parasharya from Baijavapayana, Baijavapayana from Kaushikayani, Kaushikayani from Ghrita-kaushika, Ghritakaushika from Parasharyayana, Parasharyayana from Parasharya, Parasharya from Jatukarnya, Jatukarnya from Asurayana and Yaska, Asurayana from Traivani, Traivani from Aupajandhani, Aupajandhani from Asuri, Asuri from Bharadvaja, Bharadvaja from Atreya, Atreya from Manti, Manti from Gautama, Gautama from another Gautama, this Gautama from Vatsya, Vatsya from Shandilya, Shandilya from Kaishorya Kapya, Kaishorya Kapya from Kumaraharita, Kumaraharita from Galava, Galava from Vidarbhikaundinya, Vidarbhikaundinya from Vatsanapat Babhrava, Vatsanapat Babhrava from Pathin Saubhara, Pathin Saubhara from Ayasya Angirasa, Ayasya Angirasa from Abhuti Tvashtra, Abhuti Tvashtra from Vishvarupa Tvashtra, Vishvarupa Tvashtra from the two Ashvins, the Ashvins from Dadhyach Atharvana, Dadhyach Atharvana from Atharvana Daiva, Atharvana Daiva from Mrityu Pradhvamsana, Mrityu Pradhvamsana from Pradhvamsana, Pradhvamsana from Ekarshi, Ekarshi from Viprachitti, Viprachitti from Vyashti, Vyashti from Sanaru, Sanaru from Sanatana, Sanatana from Sanaga, Sanaga from Parameshthin, and Parameshthin from Brahman. Brahman is eternal. Salutation to Brahman. [2.6.1-3]

## CHAPTER 3

### Section 3.1

Om. King Janaka of Videha performed a yajna in which there were many gifts. Brahmanas from Kuru and Panchala had assembled there. Janaka, king of Videha, became curious to know who was the most learned among those Brahmanas. He had kept one thousand cows for gifts, and to each cow's horn was attached gold weighing ten *padas* (ten grams). [3.1.1]

He said to them, "Venerable Brahmanas, he who is the greatest Vedic scholar among you may drive these cows home."

The Brahmanas did not dare to do so. Then Yajnavalkya said to his own student, "Samashravas, drive these cows home, my son."

The student drove them home. The other Brahmanas present were angry, and wondered how Yajnavalkya could assert that he was the greatest scholar among them. Vaideha Janaka had a Hotri (invoking) priest named Ashvala. He asked Yajnavalkya, "Yajnavalkya, are you really the greatest Vedic scholar among us?"

He replied, "I salute the greatest Vedic scholar. I only want to keep the cows."

Thereupon the priest, Ashvala, decided to question him. [3.1.2]

He asked, "Yajnavalkya, since everything is caught and overpowered by death, how should a sacrificer transcend the reach of death?"

He replied, "Through the Hotri priest and speech—looked upon as fire. The sacrificer's speech is indeed the Hotri priest. His speech is fire. Fire is the Hotri priest. That fire is the means of liberation, and liberation transcends death." [3.1.3]

He asked, "Yajnavalkya, since everything is caught and overpowered by day and night, through what does the sacrificer transcend the reach of day and night?"

"Through the priest called Adhvaryu and the eye—looked upon as the sun. The sacrificer's eye is indeed the Adhvaryu. His eye is that sun. The sun is the Adhvaryu. That sun is the means of liberation, and liberation transcends day and night." [3.1.4]

He asked, "Yajnavalkya, since everything is caught and overpowered by the bright and dark halves of the month, how should a sacrificer transcend the reach of these?"

Yajnavalkya replied, "Through the Udgatri (chanting) priest and Prana—looked upon as air. The sacrificer's Prana is indeed the Udgatri priest. His Prana is Vayu (air). Vayu is the Udgatri priest.

That Vayu is the means of liberation, and liberation is transcendence." [3.1.5]

He asked, "Yajnavalkya, since the sky is without a support, through what prop does a sacrificer attain heaven?"

Yajnavalkya replied, "Through the Brahma (superintending) priest and the mind—looked upon as the moon. The sacrificer's mind is indeed the Brahma (superintending) priest. His mind is the moon. The moon is the Brahma priest. That moon is the means of liberation, and liberation is transcendence." [3.1.6]

Ashvala asked, "Yajnavalkya, with how many classes of Riks will the Hotri priest perform this yajna today?"

"With three classes," said Yajnavalkya.

"Which are those three?"

"The preparatory, the oblational, and the laudatory hymns as the third kind."

"What does he win through them?"

"All this that has life." [3.1.7]

"How many kinds of oblations will the Adhvaryu priest offer in today's yajna?" asked Ashvala.

"Three."

"Which are those?"

"First are those that flare up when offered, then there are those that make loud noise when put in the fire, and those that go down on being offered and remain unburnt."

"What does the sacrificer win through them?"

"Through those that flare up when offered, he wins the world of the gods, because that world looks shining. Through those that make loud noise when offered, he wins the world of the fathers, because that world seems to be too noisy. Through those oblations that go down to the bottom, the sacrificer wins the world of men, because this world is indeed lower." [3.1.8]

Ashvala asked, "Yajnavalkya, through how many gods will the Brahma priest protect the yajna while sitting in the southern direction?"

"Through one."

"Which is that god?"

"It is the mind. The mind is infinite, and the Vishvadevas are infinite too. By concentration of mind he wins an infinite world." [3.1.9]

Ashvala asked, "Yajnavalkya, how many kinds of collections of Riks (hymns) will the Udgatri priest chant in the yajna today?"

"Three."

"Which are those three?"

"The preparatory, the oblational, and the laudatory collections."

"Which are those that have reference to the body?"

"Prana is the preparatory, Vyana is the laudatory, and Apana is the oblational collection."

"What does he win through them?"

"Through the preparatory collection he wins the earth, through the oblational one the sky, and through the laudatory one heaven."

Thereafter, the Hotri priest Ashvala kept quiet. [3.1.10]

## Section 3.2

Now Artabhaga Jaratkarava asked him, "Yajnavalkya, how many 'Grahas' (organs that control us) and how many 'Atigrahas' (super organs or objects) are there?"

Yajnavalkya said, "There are eight organs (Grahas) and eight objects (Atigrahas)."

"Which are those eight organs and eight objects?" [3.2.1]

"Prana (the nose) is an organ. It is dominated by its object, odor (Apana), because one smells odors through the air that is inhaled. [3.2.2]

"Speech is an organ. It is dominated by its object, name, because one pronounces names through speech. [3.2.3]

"The tongue is an organ. It is dominated by its object, taste, because one tastes through the tongue. [3.2.4]

"The eye is an organ. It is dominated by its object, color, because one sees colors through the eye. [3.2.5]

"The ear is an organ. It is dominated by its object, sound, because one hears sounds through the ear. [3.2.6]

"The mind is an organ. It is dominated by its object, desirable objects, because one thinks of desirable objects through the mind. [3.2.7]

"The hands are an organ. They are dominated by their object, work, because one performs work through the hands. [3.2.8]

"The skin is an organ. It is dominated by its object, touch, because one feels touch through the skin. These are the eight organs and eight objects." [3.2.9]

Artabhaga asked, "Yajnavalkya, since everything is the food of death (everything is destined to destruction), which is that deity whose food is death?"
"Fire is death, yet it is the food of water. One who knows thus, overcomes death." [3.2.10]
Yajnavalkya indirectly answers him by saying that fire destroys everything, but fire itself is destroyed by water.

Artabhaga asked, "Yajnavalkya, when this man dies, do his organs depart from him?"
"No," said Yajnavalkya, "they dissolve in him only. His dead body swells and lies motionless." [3.2.11]

He asked, "Yajnavalkya, when this man dies, what is that which does not leave him?"
"It is his name. The name is infinite, and infinite are the Vishvadevas. He who knows thus, wins infinite worlds through that." [3.2.12]

Artabhaga asked, "Yajnavalkya, after a man's death, when his speech is merged in fire, the nose in air, the eye in the sun, the mind in the moon, the ear in the directions, the body in the earth, the Hridayakasha (the cavity in the heart) in the ether, the hair on the body in herbs, the hair on the head in trees, and the blood and the seed are deposited in water, on what does he rest?"

"Give me your hand, O gentle Artabhaga," said Yajnavalkya, "Let both of us think about it. This topic cannot be discussed in an assembly."

They both retired and discussed it. They talked about "action" (*karma*) only, and what they praised was action only. Therefore, one becomes noble through righteous action and ignoble through unrighteous action. Artabhaga kept quiet. [3.2.13]

## Section 3.3

Then Bhujyu, the grandson of Lahya, asked, "Yajnavalkya, we were traveling through the countryside of Madra and reached the house of Patanchala Kapya. His daughter was married to a Gandharva. We asked him his name. He said he was Sudhanvan, a descendant of Angiras. We said that since he had traveled in all parts of the world, he might know where the descendants of Parikshit lived. I am asking you, too, Yajnavalkya, where do the descendants of Parikshit live?" [3.3.1]

Yajnavalkya replied, "The Gandharva must have told you that they went to where the performers of the Ashvamedha-yajna (the horse-sacrifice) go."

"But where do the performers of the Ashvamedha-yajna go?"

"This world (where they go) is at a distance equal to thirty-two times the distance traversed by the sun's chariot in a day. The earth encircles it, covering double that distance. The ocean surrounds the earth, covering double that distance. The opening between the earth and the sky, through which the descendants of Parikshit went, is as thin as the edge of a razor or a fly's wing, compared to the vastness of the universe. The Supreme Being, becoming a heavenly bird, handed the descendants of Parikshit over to Vayu (the cosmic Prana). Vayu, placing them in itself, carried them to where the performers of the Ashvamedha-yajna lived. Then the Gandharva praised Vayu. Vayu alone is Prana in the microcosm and air in the macrocosm. He who knows thus, overcomes further death."

Thereupon Bhujyu kept quiet. [3.3.2]

## Section 3.4

Then Ushasta Chakrayana asked him, "O Yajnavalkya, tell me about Brahman that is immediately present and directly perceived, which is also Atman living within all beings."

Yajnavalkya said, "This Atman of yours lives within all beings."

"Yajnavalkya, which Atman lives within all beings?"

"That which moves forward through Prana is your Atman. This which moves through Apana, Vyana and Udana is your Atman. That Atman is within all beings." [3.4.1]

Ushasta Chakrayana then said, "Yajnavalkya, you are telling me about Brahman just like somebody describing a cow or horse as, 'a cow is like this,' or, 'a horse is like that.' Tell me precisely about Brahman which is immediately present and directly perceived, the Atman that is within all beings. Yajnavalkya, who is it that is within all?"

"You cannot see the seer of all sights, you cannot hear the hearer of all sounds, you cannot think of the thinker of all thoughts, you cannot know the knower of all knowledge. It is your Atman that is within all beings. Everything besides that is perishable."

Thereupon, Ushasta kept quiet. [3.4.2]

## Section 3.5

Then Kahola Kaushitakeya said, "O Yajnavalkya, tell me about Brahman that is immediately present and directly perceived, which is also Atman living within all beings."

Yajnavalkya said, "This Atman of yours lives within all beings."

"Yajnavalkya, which Atman lives within all beings?"

"That which transcends hunger and thirst, grief and delusion, old age and death. When Brahmanas know this Atman, they give up the desires for progeny, wealth and worlds, and take up the life of wandering mendicants. Because the desire for progeny is the desire for wealth, and the desire for wealth is the desire for worlds, both these are desires after all. Therefore, after having acquired the knowledge of Brahman, a Brahmana should seek to live on its strength. After having acquired the strength and the knowledge, he becomes a man of meditation. And after having acquired meditativeness and the absence of it, he becomes a real Brahmana."

"How does the knower of Brahman conduct himself?"

"It does not matter how he conducts himself, he is a Brahmajnani indeed. Everything other than this state of Brahmanahood is perishable."

Thereupon Kahola Kaushitakeya kept quiet. [3.5.1]

## Section 3.6

Then Gargi Vachaknavi asked him, "O Yajnavalkya, all this in the earth is pervaded by water; what is water pervaded by?"

"By air, O Gargi."

"Then what pervades the air?"

"The world of the sky, O Gargi."

"What pervades the world of the sky?"

"The world of the Gandharvas, O Gargi."

"What pervades the world of the Gandharvas?"

"The world of the sun, O Gargi."

"What pervades the world of the sun?"

"The world of the moon, O Gargi."

"What pervades the world of the moon?"

"The world of the stars, O Gargi."

"What pervades the world of the stars?"

"The world of the gods, O Gargi."

"What pervades the world of the gods?"

"The world of Indra, O Gargi."

"What pervades the world of Indra?"

"The world of Prajapati, O Gargi."

"What pervades the world of Prajapati?"

"The world of Brahman, O Gargi."

"What pervades the world of Brahman?"

"O Gargi, do not question too much, lest your head should fall off. You are questioning about the deity who cannot be known through reasoning. So do not ask too much about Him."

Thereupon Gargi kept quiet. [3.6.1]

## Section 3.7

Then Uddalaka Aruni questioned him. He said, "Once we lived in the country of Madra in the house of Patanchala Kapya, while studying the scriptures on yajnas. His wife had become a devotee of a Gandharva. We asked him who he was. He said he was Kabandha Atharvana. He asked Patanchala Kapya and the students of yajna, 'Do you know, O Kapya, that thread by which this world, the other world and all beings are tied together?' Patanchala Kapya replied, 'I do not know it, sir.' The Gandharva said again to Patanchala Kapya and to the students of yajna, 'O Kapya, do you know that Inner Controller, who dwelling within, controls this world, the other world and all other beings?' Patanchala replied, 'I do not know Him, sir.' The Gandharva said again to Patanchala Kapya and to the students, 'He who knows that thread, O Kapya, and that Inner Controller—he knows Brahman, he knows the worlds, he knows the gods, he knows the Vedas, he knows beings, he knows the Atman, and he knows everything.'

"Then he explained it to them. I too know it. And, Yajnavalkya, if you take away those cows that belong to the knowers of Brahman, without knowing that thread and that Inner Controller, your head will fall off."

Yajnavalkya said, "O Gautama, I know that thread and that Inner Controller."

Uddalaka Aruni said, "Anyone may say, 'I know, I know.' Tell us what you know." [3.7.1]

Yajnavalkya said, "O Gautama, Vayu (air) is that thread. As if tied by a thread, by Vayu only, this world, the other world and all beings are held together. For this very reason they say of a dead man that his limbs are loosened, because by Vayu only, O Gautama, were they held together."

"It is indeed so, Yajnavalkya. Now tell us about the Inner Controller." [3.7.2]

"He who dwells in the earth and is within it, whom the earth does not know, whose body is the earth, who controls the earth from within, is the Inner Controller, your own Atman and immortal. [3.7.3]

"He who dwells in the water and is within it, whom the water does not know, whose body is the water, who controls the water from within, is the Inner Controller, your own Atman and immortal. [3.7.4]

"He who dwells in the fire and is within it, whom the fire does not know, whose body is the fire, who controls the fire from within, is the Inner Controller, your own Atman and immortal. [3.7.5]

"He who dwells in the sky and is within it, whom the sky does not know, whose body is the sky, who controls the sky from within, is the Inner Controller, your own Atman and immortal. [3.7.6]

"He who dwells in the air and is within it, whom the air does not know, whose body is the air, who controls the air from within, is the Inner Controller, your own Atman and immortal. [3.7.7]

"He who dwells in heaven and is within it, whom heaven does not know, whose body is heaven, who controls heaven from within, is the Inner Controller, your own Atman and immortal. [3.7.8]

"He who dwells in the sun and is within it, whom the sun does not know, whose body is the sun, who controls the sun from within, is the Inner Controller, your own Atman and immortal. [3.7.9]

"He who dwells in the directions and is within them, whom the directions do not know, whose body is the directions, who controls the directions from within, is the Inner Controller, your own Atman and immortal. [3.7.10]

"He who dwells in the moon and stars and is within them, whom the moon and stars do not know, whose body is the moon and stars, who controls the moon and the stars from within, is the Inner Controller, your own Atman and immortal. [3.7.11]

"He who dwells in the ether and is within it, whom the ether does not know, whose body is the ether, who controls the ether

from within, is the Inner Controller, your own Atman and immortal.
[3.7.12]

"He who dwells in the darkness and is within it, whom the
darkness does not know, whose body is the darkness, who controls
the darkness from within, is the Inner Controller, your own Atman
and immortal. [3.7.13]

"He who dwells in the light and is within it, whom the light
does not know, whose body is the light, who controls the light from
within, is the Inner Controller, your own Atman and immortal. This
is with reference to the deities. Now with reference to beings:
[3.7.14]

"He who dwells in all beings and is within them, whom all
beings do not know, whose body is all beings, who controls all
beings from within, is the Inner Controller, your own Atman and
immortal. This is with reference to beings. Now with reference to
the body: [3.7.15]

"He who dwells in Prana and is within it, whom Prana does
not know, whose body is Prana, who controls Prana from within, is
the Inner Controller, your own Atman and immortal. [3.7.16]

"He who dwells in (the organ of) speech and is within it,
whom speech does not know, whose body is speech, who controls
speech from within, is the Inner Controller, your own Atman and
immortal. [3.7.17]

"He who dwells in the eye and is within it, whom the eye does
not know, whose body is the eye, who controls the eye from
within, is the Inner Controller, your own Atman and immortal.
[3.7.18]

"He who dwells in the ear and is within it, whom the ear does
not know, whose body is the ear, who controls the ear from within,
is the Inner Controller, your own Atman and immortal. [3.7.19]

"He who dwells in the mind and is within it, whom the mind
does not know, whose body is the mind, who controls the mind

from within, is the Inner Controller, your own Atman and immortal. [3.7.20]

"He who dwells in the skin and is within it, whom the skin does not know, whose body is the skin, who controls the skin from within, is the Inner Controller, your own Atman and immortal. [3.7.21]

"He who dwells in the intellect and is within it, whom the intellect does not know, whose body is the intellect, who controls the intellect from within, is the Inner Controller, your own Atman and immortal. [3.7.22]

"He who dwells in the organ of generation and is within it, whom that organ does not know, whose body is that organ, who controls that organ from within, is the Inner Controller, your own Atman and immortal. He is never seen but is the seer. He is never heard but is the hearer. He is never thought but is the thinker. There is no other seer than He. There is no other hearer than He. There is no other thinker than He. There is no other knower than He. He is the Inner Controller, your own Atman and immortal. All else but Him is perishable."

Thereupon Uddalaka Aruni kept quiet. [3.7.23]

### Section 3.8

Then Gargi Vachaknavi said, "Venerable Brahmanas, I shall ask him two questions. If he answers them, none of you can defeat him in any argument about Brahman."

"Gargi, ask him." [3.8.1]

She said, "O Yajnavalkya, just as a king of Kashi (Varanasi) or Videha, son of a heroic line, might rise to fight in a battle, having strung his unstrung bow and taken in his hand two sharp enemy-piercing arrows, even so I face you with two questions."

"O Gargi, ask me." [3.8.2]

"Yajnavalkya, what pervades that which is above heaven, below the earth and between the two—heaven and earth—and that

which is said to exist in the past, in the present and in the future?"
[3.8.3]

He said, "O Gargi, the unmanifested ether pervades that
which is above heaven, below the earth and between the two—
heaven and earth—and that which is said to exist in the past, in the
present and in the future. [3.8.4]

She said, "Salutations to you, O Yajnavalkya. You have answered this for me. Now get ready for the next one."
"Ask me, O Gargi." [3.8.5]

The repetition of 3.8.3 and 3.8.4, as 3.8.6 and 3.8.7 below, is for
confirmation of the first question:
"Yajnavalkya, in the answer to my question, 'What pervades
that which is above heaven, below the earth and between the
two—heaven and earth—and that which is said to exist in the past,
in the present and in the future?' you said, 'The unmanifested ether
pervades that which is above heaven, below the earth and between
the two—heaven and earth—and that which is said to exist in the
past, in the present and in the future.'
"Now, Yajnavalkya, what pervades the unmanifested ether?"
[3.8.6-7]

He said, "O Gargi, the knowers of Brahman describe that as
the Imperishable. It is neither coarse nor fine, neither short nor
long, neither red (like fire) nor adhering (like water), neither
shadow nor darkness, neither air nor ether. It is without attachment,
taste or odor; without eyes, ears or speech; without mind, without
effulgence, without Prana and without a mouth; without a measure,
and without an inside or outside. It eats nobody nor does anybody
eat It. [3.8.8]

"Under the rule of this Imperishable, O Gargi, the sun and
moon are held in their own courses. Under the rule of this Imperishable, O Gargi, heaven and earth hold in their own positions.
Under the rule of this Imperishable, O Gargi, moments, hours, days
and nights, fortnights, months, seasons and years are maintained in
regular intervals. Under the rule of this Imperishable, O Gargi, some
rivers flow to the east from the white mountains, others to the west,

or whatever direction they flow. Under the rule of this Imperishable, O Gargi, people praise those who give, the gods depend on the sacrificer, and the Pitris on the *Darvi* offering (a special offering for the deceased forefathers). [3.8.9]

"O Gargi, without knowing this Imperishable, whosoever performs yajnas in this world, offers worship, or practices austerities for a thousand years, finds all that work only transient. O Gargi, whosoever leaves this world without knowing this Imperishable is pitiable. But he who leaves this world after knowing this Imperishable, O Gargi, is a Brahmana (knower of Brahman). [3.8.10]

"O Gargi, that Imperishable is the unseen Seer, the unheard Hearer, the unthought Thinker, the unknown Knower. There is no other seer but He, no other hearer but He, no other thinker but He, no other knower but He.

"It is this Imperishable, O Gargi, that pervades the ether." [3.8.11]

Then she said, "O venerable Brahmanas, you should consider yourselves lucky if you can get off from him with a salutation. Certainly none of you can defeat him in expounding Brahman."

After that Gargi Vachaknavi kept quiet. [3.8.12]

## Section 3.9

Then Vidagdha Shakalya questioned him, "How many gods are there, O Yajnavalkya?"

Yajnavalkya replied quoting this *Nivid*, "As many as are mentioned in the *Nivid* in praise of all the gods (Vishvadevas), that is, three hundred and three, and three thousand and three."

"Yes," said Vidagdha, "but how many gods are there really, O Yajnavalkya?"

"Thirty-three," he said.

"Yes," said Vidagdha, "but how many gods are there really, O Yajnavalkya?"

"Six," he said.

"Yes," said Vidagdha, "but how many gods are there really, O Yajnavalkya?"

"Three," he said.

"Yes," said Vidagdha, "but how many gods are there really, O Yajnavalkya?"

"Two," he said.

"Yes," said Vidagdha, "but how many gods are there really, O Yajnavalkya?"

"One and a half," he said.

"Yes," said Vidagdha, "but how many gods are there really, O Yajnavalkya?"

"One," he said.

"Yes," said Vidagdha, "which are those three hundred and three, and three thousand and three?" [3.9.1]

A *Nivid* is a set of *mantras*, in the form of laudatory hymns, showing the number of gods.

Yajnavalkya said, "Actually there are but thirty-three gods only. The others are only their manifestations."

"Who are those thirty-three?"

"The eight Vasus, eleven Rudras, and twelve Adityas. They make thirty-one, and with Indra and Prajapati make up the thirty-three." [3.9.2]

He asked, "Who are the Vasus?"

"Fire, earth, air, sky, sun, heaven, moon and stars—these are the Vasus. Because all this universe rests on them only, they are called Vasus (abodes)." [3.9.3]

"Who are the Rudras?"

"The ten organs in man, and the mind as the eleventh. When they leave this mortal body, they make one's relatives cry. Because they make them cry, they are called Rudras." (The verb root *rud* in Sanskrit means "to cry.") [3.9.4]

"Who are the Adityas?"

"The twelve months in a year are the Adityas. They take away with them everything (namely, the longevity of people and the results of their works). Since they take away everything they are called Adityas." (*Adadanah* means taking away.) [3.9.5]

"Who is Indra and which is Prajapati?"

"The thunder-cloud is Indra, and yajna is Prajapati."
"Who is the thunder-cloud?"
"The thunderbolt."
"Who is yajna?"
"The animals." [3.9.6]
(*Ashani,* "the thunderbolt," is the strength and vigor of Indra.)

"Who are the six (gods)?"
"Fire, earth, air, sky, sun and heaven—these are the six gods, because the whole world is these six." [3.9.7]

"Who are the three gods?"
"They are the three worlds, because in them all the gods exist."
"Who are the two gods?"
"Matter and Prana."
"Who is the one and a half?"
"He who blows (wind). [3.9.8]

"Regarding this some say, 'How is it that the wind which blows like one, should be one and a half?' Because when he blows, the whole world grows up; therefore, he is one and a half."
"Which is the one god?"
"Prana. He is Brahman. They call him 'That.'" [3.9.9]

"He who knows that Person whose body is the earth, whose eye is fire, whose light is the mind, and who is the main support of all bodies, O Yajnavalkya, is the knower indeed."
"I do know that Being who, as you say, is the main support of all beings. It is this Being who is in this body. Ask me more Shakalya."
"Who is its deity?"
"Nectar," said Yajnavalkya. [3.9.10]

"He who knows that Person whose abode is the desire (to create), whose eye is the intellect, whose light is the mind, and who is the main support of all beings, is indeed a knower, O Yajnavalkya."
"I know that Person who, as you say, is the main support of all beings. He is the Person with the desire (to create this universe). Shakalya, ask me more."

"Who is his deity?"

"Woman (Nature)," said Yajnavalkya. [3.9.11]

"He who knows that Person whose abode is colors, whose instrument of vision is the eye, whose light is the mind, and who is the main support of all beings, is indeed a knower, O Yajnavalkya."

"I know that Person who, as you say, is the main support of all beings. He is the Person in the sun. Shakalya, ask me more."

"Who is his deity?"

"Truth," said Yajnavalkya. [3.9.12]

"He who knows that Person whose abode is the ether, whose instrument of vision is the ear, whose light is the mind, and who is the main support of all beings, is indeed a knower, O Yajnavalkya."

"I know that Person who, as you say, is the main support of all beings. He is the Person with the ear that hears everything. Shakalya, ask me more."

"Who is his deity?"

"The directions," said Yajnavalkya. [3.9.13]

"He who knows that Person whose abode is darkness, whose instrument of vision is the intellect, whose light is the mind, and who is the main support of all beings, is indeed a knower, O Yajnavalkya."

"I know that Person who, as you say, is the main support of all beings. He is the Person with a shadow (ignorance). Shakalya, ask me more."

"Who is his deity?"

"Death," said Yajnavalkya. [3.9.14]

"He who knows that Person whose abode is colors, whose instrument of vision is the eye, whose light is the mind, and who is the main support of all beings, is indeed a knower, O Yajnavalkya."

"I know that Person who, as you say, is the main support of all beings. He is the Person in the mirror. Shakalya, ask me more."

"Who is his deity?"

"Prana," said Yajnavalkya. [3.9.15]

"He who knows that Person whose abode is water, whose instrument of vision is the intellect, whose light is the mind, and who is the main support of all beings, is indeed a knower, O Yajnavalkya."

"I know that Person who, as you say, is the main support of all beings. He is the Person in water. Shakalya, ask me more."

"Who is his deity?"

"Varuna," said Yajnavalkya. [3.9.16]

"He who knows that Person whose abode is the seed, whose instrument of vision is the intellect, whose light is the mind, and who is the main support of all beings, is indeed a knower, O Yajnavalkya."

"I know that Person who, as you say, is the main support of all beings. He is the Person identified with the son. Shakalya, ask me more."

"Who is his deity?"

"Prajapati," said Yajnavalkya. [3.9.17]

"Shakalya," said Yajnavalkya, "have these Brahmanas made you their tongs for burning coal?" [3.9.18]

(Here Yajnavalkya is teasing Shakalya by saying that the Brahmanas have made him their instrument to ask questions to him.)

"Yajnavalkya," said Shakalya, "have you insulted the Brahmanas of Kuru and Panchala, thinking that you have known Brahman? Do you even know the directions with their deities and their supports? If you know the directions with their deities and supports, . . . [3.9.19]

"Which deity is in the eastern direction?"

"The sun."

"On what does the sun rest?"

"On the eye."

"On what does the eye rest?"

"On colors, because one sees colors with the eye."

"On what do colors rest?"

"On the heart," said Yajnavalkya, "because one knows colors through the heart; hence colors rest on the heart."

"It is indeed so, Yajnavalkya." [3.9.20]

"Which deity is in the southern direction?"

"The deity Yama."

"On what does Yama rest?"

"On yajna."

"On what does yajna rest?"

"On remuneration to the priests."

"On what does remuneration rest?"

"On faith, because whenever a man has faith, he offers remuneration to the priests. Indeed remuneration rests on faith."

"On what does faith rest?"

"On the heart," said Yajnavalkya, "because one knows faith through the heart; and faith rests on the heart (mind)."

"It is indeed so, Yajnavalkya." [3.9.21]

"Which deity is in the western direction?"

"The deity Varuna."

"On what does Varuna rest?"

"On water."

"On what does water rest?"

"On the seed."

"On what does the seed rest?"

"On the heart, because when a newborn child has a strong resemblance to his father they say that he has come out from his father's heart, and has been created from his father's heart. Therefore, the seed indeed rests on the heart."

"It is indeed so, Yajnavalkya." [3.9.22]

"Which deity is in the northern direction?"

"The deity moon."

"On what does the moon rest?"

"On initiation."

"On what does initiation rest?"

"On truth. Therefore, they say to the initiated one, 'Speak the truth,' for initiation really rests on truth."

"On what does truth rest?"

"On the heart," said Yajnavalkya, "because one knows truth through the heart; and truth rests on the heart."

"It is indeed so, Yajnavalkya." [3.9.23]

"Which deity is in the fixed (overhead) direction?"

"The deity fire."

"On what does fire rest?"

"On speech."
"On what does speech rest?"
"On the heart," said Yajnavalkya.
"On what does heart rest?" [3.9.24]

"You ghost," said Yajnavalkya, "you think the heart (mind) is elsewhere than the body! If it were so, then the dogs would eat this body, or the birds would tear it apart." [3.9.25]

"On what do the body and heart (mind) rest?"
"On Prana."
"On what does Prana rest?"
"On Apana."
"On what does Apana rest?"
"On Vyana."
"On what does Vyana rest?"
"On Udana."
"On what does Udana rest?"
"On Samana. This Atman is that which has been described as, 'Not this, not this.' It is imperceptible, because It is not perceived. It is unshrinkable, because It does not shrink. It is unattachable, because It cannot be attached. It is unrestrictable, because It cannot be restricted. It does not suffer, nor perish. These are the eight bodies, eight instruments of vision, eight deities and eight Beings. I ask you of that Being who is to be known only through the Upanishads, and who projects these beings out of Himself, withdraws them into Himself, and again transcends them. If you cannot tell me clearly of Him, your head shall roll off."

Shakalya did not know Him. His head fell off, and robbers took away his bones, thinking that they were something else. [3.9.26]

Then Yajnavalkya said, "Venerable Brahmanas, any one of you who wishes, or all of you, may question me. Or I may question any one of you, or all of you."

But the Brahmanas did not dare to say anything. [3.9.27]

Then he questioned them with these verses:

"As is a huge tree in the forest, so is man indeed. His hairs are the leaves and his skin its outer bark. [3.9.28.1]

"From a man's skin flows blood, and from the bark of a tree its sap. Therefore, blood comes forth from a wounded person, as does sap from a tree that is struck. [3.9.28.2]

"Man's flesh is like the tree's inner bark, his nerves are like its tough fibers, his bones are like its wood within, and his marrow resembles its pith. [3.9.28.3]

"When a tree is felled, it sprouts again from its roots in a newer form. But from what root does a man spring up after he is cut off by death? [3.9.28.4]

"Do not say, 'From the seed,' because that is produced in a living man only. A tree indeed sprouts from the seed. After it is cut down it springs up again. [3.9.28.5]

"If a tree is pulled out with its roots, it does not grow again. From what root does a man spring forth when he is cut off by death? [3.9.28.6]

"Do you think he is born forever? No, he is born again. Who creates him again?

"It is Brahman—that which is knowledge and bliss, the ultimate resort of him who offers gifts, and of him who stands still and knows It." [3.9.28.7]

## CHAPTER 4

### Section 4.1

Om. When Janaka, the king of Videha, had taken his seat, Yajnavalkya arrived at his court. The king asked, "O Yajnavalkya, for what purpose have you come here—for some cattle or for subtle questions?"

"For both, O Emperor," he replied. [4.1.1]

"Let us hear what any one of your teachers may have told you," said Yajnavalkya.

"Jitvam Shailini told me that speech is Brahman."

"As one with a mother, a father and a teacher might say, so did Shailini tell you that speech is Brahman, because what could a person without speech attain? But has he told you its abode and support?"

"No he did not tell me."

"Brahman has only one foot, O Emperor."

"Do tell us, O Yajnavalkya."

"Speech is indeed its abode, and ether is its support; and it should be meditated upon as intelligence."

"What is intelligence, O Yajnavalkya?"

"Speech itself, O Emperor," said Yajnavalkya. "Through speech only, a friend is known. Through speech only, the *Rigveda*, the *Yajurveda*, the *Samaveda* and the *Atharvaveda*, history, Puranas, arts, Upanishads, mantras, aphorisms, explanations, commentaries, the results of yajnas, oblations, food and drink, this world, the next world and all beings are known. Speech, O Emperor, is indeed the Supreme Brahman. Speech does not desert him who, knowing this, meditates upon it. All beings seek him. Having become a god, he joins the gods."

Janaka, the king of Videha, said, "I shall give you a thousand cows with a bull as big as an elephant."

Yajnavalkya replied, "My father believed that one should not accept a gift from a student without fully instructing him." [4.1.2]

"Let us hear what any one of your teachers may have told you," said Yajnavalkya.

"Udanka Shaulbayana told me that Prana is Brahman."

"As one with a mother, a father and a teacher might say, so did Shaulbayana tell you that Prana is Brahman, because what could a lifeless person attain? But has he told you its abode and support?"

"No he did not tell me."

"Brahman has only one foot, O Emperor."

"Do tell us, O Yajnavalkya."

"Prana is indeed its abode, and ether is its support; and it should be meditated upon as something dear."

"What is something dear, O Yajnavalkya?"

"Prana itself, O Emperor," said Yajnavalkya. "One performs yajnas for an undeserving person and accepts presents from an unworthy man for the sake of Prana only. Out of love for Prana (life) only, O Emperor, one has fear of death in any direction one may go.

Prana indeed is the Supreme Brahman. Prana does not desert him who, knowing this, meditates upon it. All beings seek him. Having become a god, he joins the gods."

Janaka, the king of Videha, said, "I shall give you a thousand cows with a bull as big as an elephant."

Yajnavalkya replied, "My father believed that one should not accept a gift from a student without fully instructing him." [4.1.3]

"Let us hear what any one of your teachers may have told you," said Yajnavalkya.

"Barku Varshna told me that the eye is Brahman."

"As one with a mother, a father and a teacher might say, so did Varshna tell you that the eye is Brahman, because what could a blind person attain? But has he told you its abode and support?"

"No he did not tell me."

"Brahman has only one foot, O Emperor."

"Do tell us, O Yajnavalkya."

"The eye is indeed its abode, and ether is its support; and it should be meditated upon as something true."

"What is the essence of truth, O Yajnavalkya?"

"The eye itself, O Emperor," said Yajnavalkya. "Therefore, O Emperor, when they ask a person who has seen with his own eyes, 'Did you see?' he replies, 'Yes, I did,' and that is true. The eye indeed is the Supreme Brahman. The eye does not desert him who, knowing this, meditates upon it. All beings seek him. Having become a god, he joins the gods."

Janaka, the king of Videha, said, "I shall give you a thousand cows with a bull as big as an elephant."

Yajnavalkya replied, "My father believed that one should not accept a gift from a student without fully instructing him." [4.1.4]

"Let us hear what any one of your teachers may have told you," said Yajnavalkya.

"Gardabhivipita Bharadvaja told me that the ear is Brahman."

"As one with a mother, a father and a teacher might say, so did Bharadvaja tell you that the ear is Brahman, because what could a deaf person attain? But has he told you its abode and support?"

"No he did not tell me."

"Brahman has only one foot, O Emperor."

"Do tell us, O Yajnavalkya."

"The ear is indeed its abode, and ether is its support; and it should be meditated upon as infinite."

"What is infinity, O Yajnavalkya?"

"The directions alone, O Emperor," said Yajnavalkya. "Therefore, O Emperor, in whatever direction one may go, one never reaches its end. Hence the directions are infinite. The ear indeed is the Supreme Brahman. The ear does not desert him who, knowing this, meditates upon it. All beings seek him. Having become a god, he joins the gods."

Janaka, the king of Videha, said, "I shall give you a thousand cows with a bull as big as an elephant."

Yajnavalkya replied, "My father believed that one should not accept a gift from a student without fully instructing him." [4.1.5]

"Let us hear what any one of your teachers may have told you," said Yajnavalkya.

"Satyakama Jabala told me that the mind is Brahman."

"As one with a mother, a father and a teacher might say, so did Jabala tell you that the mind is Brahman, because what could a person with no mind attain? But has he told you its abode and support?"

"No he did not tell me."

"Brahman has only one foot, O Emperor."

"Do tell us, O Yajnavalkya."

"The mind is indeed its abode, and ether is its support; and it should be meditated upon as bliss."

"What is bliss, O Yajnavalkya?"

"The mind itself, O Emperor," said Yajnavalkya. "Because it is through the mind that a man woos a woman. A son resembling him is born of her, and he becomes the source of bliss. The mind indeed is the Supreme Brahman. The mind does not desert him who, knowing this, meditates upon it. All beings seek him. Having become a god, he joins the gods."

Janaka, the king of Videha, said, "I shall give you a thousand cows with a bull as big as an elephant."

Yajnavalkya replied, "My father believed that one should not accept a gift from a student without fully instructing him." [4.1.6]

"Let us hear what any one of your teachers may have told you," said Yajnavalkya.

"Vidagdha Shakalya told me that the heart is Brahman."

"As one with a mother, a father and a teacher might say, so did Shakalya tell you that the heart is Brahman, because what could a person with no heart attain? But has he told you its abode and support?"

"No he did not tell me."

"Brahman has only one foot, O Emperor."

"Do tell us, O Yajnavalkya."

"The heart is indeed its abode, and ether is its support; and it should be meditated upon as stability."

"What is stability, O Yajnavalkya?"

"The heart alone, O Emperor," said Yajnavalkya. "The heart is indeed the abode of all beings, and the heart is the support of all beings, because it is in the heart that all beings are established. The heart indeed is the Supreme Brahman. The heart does not desert him who, knowing this, meditates upon it. All beings seek him. Having become a god, he joins the gods."

Janaka, the king of Videha, said, "I shall give you a thousand cows with a bull as big as an elephant."

Yajnavalkya replied, "My father believed that one should not accept a gift from a student without fully instructing him." [4.1.7]


### Section 4.2

Janaka, the king of Videha, came down from his throne and said to Yajnavalkya, "Salutations to you, O Yajnavalkya. Please teach me."

Yajnavalkya said, "O Emperor, just as a man wishing to go on a long journey would secure a chariot or a boat, similarly you have prepared yourself for this journey of life with the knowledge of the Upanishads. You are honorable and wealthy. You have learned the Vedas and you have been taught the Upanishads. But where will you go when you are released from this body?"

"I do not know, sir, where I would go."

"Then I shall tell you where you will go."

"Please do tell me, sir." [4.2.1]

In the following passages Yajnavalkya tells King Janaka in symbolic language how man passes from the Vaishvanara stage to the stage of

Taijasa, then to the stage of Prajna, and finally to the stage of Atman. These stages correspond to the states of waking, dreaming, deep sleep and turiya, respectively.

"This person who is in the right eye is called Indha (the Bright One). Though he is Indha, they indirectly call him Indra. The gods are fond of indirect names and are averse to direct names. [4.2.2]

"This human form that is in the left eye is Indra's wife (Indrani), Viraj. This space within the heart is the place of their union. The mass of red flesh near the heart is their food (because food changes to flesh and makes the body). What looks like a net within the heart is their covering. The nerve that rises upward from the heart is their passage for moving. It is like a hair split into a thousand parts. Many nerves of this body, called *Hita*, are rooted in the heart. It is through these nerves that the essence of food passes when it moves. Therefore, the subtle body has finer food than the gross body. [4.2.3]

"Of the stage identified with Prajna, the eastern direction is Prana in the east, the southern direction is Prana in the south, the western direction is Prana in the west, the northern direction is Prana in the north, the overhead direction is Prana upwards, the downward direction is Prana below, and all the directions are all Pranas. Atman is described as 'Not this, not this.' It is imperceptible because It cannot be perceived, unshrinkable because It does not shrink, unattachable because It does not attach. It cannot be bound, does not suffer, and does not perish. You have attained the fearless Brahman, O Janaka."

King Janaka said, "May the fearless Brahman reach you, O venerable Yajnavalkya, who made us know the fearless Brahman. Salutations to you. Here is my empire of Videha and also myself at your feet." [4.2.4]

## Section 4.3

Yajnavalkya went to Janaka, the king of Videha. He thought that he would not say anything to him. Once earlier Janaka and Yajnavalkya had talked at the Agnihotra (oblations of milk in the fire), when Yajnavalkya had offered him a boon. Janaka had chosen to ask him any question at the right time, and Yajnavalkya had granted it to him. Now, the emperor asked him the question. [4.3.1]

"Yajnavalkya, what is the source of light for a man?"

"The sun, O Emperor. It is by the sun's light that a man sits, goes out, works and comes back."

"It is so indeed, O Yajnavalkya." [4.3.2]

"Yajnavalkya, after the sun sets what serves as light for a man?"

"The moon serves as his light. It is by the moon's light that a man sits, goes out, works and comes back."

"It is so indeed, O Yajnavalkya." [4.3.3]

"Yajnavalkya, what serves as light for a man after the sun and the moon set?"

"The fire serves as the light, O Emperor. It is by that light that a man sits, goes out, works and comes back."

"It is so indeed, O Yajnavalkya." [4.3.4]

"Yajnavalkya, what serves as light for a man after the sun and the moon both set, and the fire goes out?"

"Sound serves as his light. It is by the light of sound that a man sits, goes out, works and comes back. Therefore, O emperor, when even one's own hand is not distinctly perceived, if a sound is produced from somewhere, one can reach there."

"It is so indeed, O Yajnavalkya." [4.3.5]

"Yajnavalkya, what serves as light for a man after the sun and the moon both set, the fire goes out, and sound is hushed?"

"Atman indeed serves as his light. It is by the light of Atman that a man sits, goes out, works and comes back." [4.3.6]

"Which is Atman?"

"Atman is the infinite entity which is associated with the intellect, which lives amid the Pranas (the organs), and which is the light within one's heart. Atman is the same in all the stages of a person (namely, whether he is awake, sleeping or dreaming). It roams between the waking and the sleeping worlds of a person, It thinks and quivers, as it were. Reaching the dream world, It goes beyond the waking world, which represents death. [4.3.7]

"This Atman, at the time of birth, enters a body and is connected with evils (under the influence of the organs which are the cause of evils). At the time of death It departs from the body and gets rid of those evils. [4.3.8]

"This Atman has only two places, namely, the waking state and the deep sleep state. The dream state, which is the third place, is the junction of the two. Staying at the junction, It sees both places, the waking state and the deep sleep state. When It is in the sleep state, It sees both miseries and joy in accordance with the sequence in which It enters that state. When It enters the dream state, It takes with It some things of the waking state. Then in the dream state, It makes Its own world, with Its own light. In this state Atman becomes Its own light. [4.3.9]

"In the dream state there are neither chariots, nor animals to be hitched to them, nor roads. Yet the Atman creates them—the chariots, the horses and the roads. There are no joys, delights or pleasures there, yet It creates the joys, delights and pleasures of Its own. There are no pools, ponds or rivers there, yet It creates pools, ponds and rivers, because It is the creator. [4.3.10]

"On this there are the following verses:
'When the effulgent Atman travels through the dream state, It leaves the sleeping body. It itself is awake and witnesses the dormant ones (the organs) from there. When It returns to the waking state, It brings out Its brightness like a lonely swan. (That is when the body is awakened.) [4.3.11]

'This effulgent and immortal Atman leaves the lower nest, namely, the body, while Prana guards it, and wanders around in the dream world, like a lonely swan outside the nest. It attains Its desire as may arise. [4.3.12]

'In the dream world the Atman attains higher and lower states, and creates many forms. It enjoys the company of women, laughs, or even sees terrifying objects. [4.3.13]

'People see only Its fanciful play, but none see It.'

"It is said that a person should not be awakened suddenly, because then his Atman is roaming outside the body, and hence some of his organs may not be fully awakened. It may be difficult to cure the sleeping organs. On the other hand, others say that whatever It has seen in the waking state, It sees in the dream state too. In the dream state, however, It uses its own light (since the sun, moon, etc., are not there in the dream world)."

"Sir, I will give you a thousand cows for your teachings. Please tell me further about liberation." [4.3.14]

"After rejoicing and wandering in the dream state, and after seeing good and evil, the Atman stays in the state of deep sleep. It eventually returns to its original dream state again. However, It is never affected by whatever It sees in the dream state, because that Person (Atman) is unattached."

"It is indeed so, venerable sir. I will give you a thousand cows for your teachings. Please tell me further about liberation." [4.3.15]

"After rejoicing and wandering in the dream state, and after seeing good and evil, the Atman eventually returns to its original waking state again. However, It is never affected by whatever It sees in the dream state, because that Person (Atman) is unattached."

"It is indeed so, venerable sir. I will give you a thousand cows for your teachings. Please tell me further about liberation." [4.3.16]

"After rejoicing and wandering in the waking state, and after seeing good and evil, the Atman stays in the state of deep sleep. It eventually returns to its original state, that is, the dream or deep sleep state. [4.3.17]

"Just as a large fish swims from the eastern to the western bank, even so the Atman moves alternately to both the states— dream and waking. [4.3.18]

"As a hawk or a falcon is exhausted while flying in the sky, and finally stretching its wings heads towards its nest, even so this Purusha—the Atman—hastens to the state of deep sleep, wherein it has no desire and sees no dream. [4.3.19]

"In a man's body there are nerves called *Hita*, which are as fine as hair, and are split into a thousand parts all over the heart and the body. They are full of white, blue, brown, green and red serums. The man in his sleep, travels through these nerves and feels as if somebody is killing him, overpowering him, or an elephant is chasing him, or he is falling into a deep hole. What he sees in the dream is nothing but imaginations based on fears he has experienced in the waking state. He may also see himself as a god, or a king, or may feel that he is all this universe. Actually the last is his highest state. [4.3.20]

"That highest state is his form which transcends desire, is devoid of sin, and is fearless. Just as a man, while embracing his dear wife, is completely unaware of what is happening inside or outside, even so this man, when he embraces the Supreme Atman, knows nothing external or internal. That indeed is his form in which all objects of desire have been realized, and hence it is devoid of desires and beyond grief. [4.3.21]

"In this state (deep sleep) a father is no more a father, a mother is no more a mother, worlds are no more worlds, the gods are no more gods, the Vedas are no more Vedas. In this state a thief is no more a thief, the killer of a fetus is no more a killer, a *Chandala* is no more a *Chandala*, a *Pulkasa* is no more a *Pulkasa*, a monk is no more a monk, a recluse is no more a recluse. This form is unaffected by virtuous work or by sin, because the Atman is beyond the afflictions of the heart. [4.3.22]

(A *Chandala* was one born of a Shudra father and a Brahmana mother, and a *Pulkasa* was one born of a Shudra father and a Kshatriya mother.)

"In that state the Atman does not see. However, although it appears as if It is not seeing, It really sees, because there cannot be an absence of sight on the part of the seer, since It is imperishable. Reaching there It finds no one else to see. [4.3.23]

"In that state the Atman does not smell. However, although it appears as if It is not smelling, It really smells, because there cannot be an absence of smelling on the part of the smeller, since It is imperishable. Reaching there It finds nothing to smell. [4.3.24]

"In that state the Atman does not taste. However, although it appears as if It is not tasting, It really tastes, because there cannot be an absence of tasting on the part of the taster, since It is imperishable. Reaching there It finds nothing else to taste. [4.3.25]

"In that state the Atman does not speak. However, although it appears as if It is not speaking, It really speaks, because there cannot be an absence of speaking on the part of the speaker, since It is imperishable. Reaching there It finds no one else to speak to. [4.3.26]

"In that state the Atman does not hear. However, although it appears as if It is not hearing, It really hears, because there cannot be an absence of hearing on the part of the hearer, since It is imperishable. Reaching there It finds no one else to hear from. [4.3.27]

"In that state the Atman does not think. However, although it appears as if It is not thinking, It really thinks, because there cannot be an absence of thinking on the part of the thinker, since It is imperishable. Reaching there It finds no one else to think of. [4.3.28]

"In that state the Atman does not touch. However, although it appears as if It is not touching, It really touches, because there cannot be an absence of touching on the part of the toucher, since It is imperishable. Reaching there It finds no one else to touch. [4.3.29]

"In that state the Atman does not know. However, although it appears as if It is not knowing, It really knows, because there cannot be an absence of knowing on the part of the knower, since It is imperishable. Reaching there It finds no one else to know of. [4.3.30]

"At some place when there is another person or thing present, then only can one see another, can one smell another, can one taste a thing, can one speak to another, can one listen to another, can one think of another, can one touch another and can one know another. [4.3.31]

"Just as in the ocean there is everywhere water only, even so in the state of deep sleep there is everywhere Atman only. The Atman becomes the seer, and the one and only which is free from duality. This is the world of Brahman, O Emperor," Yajnavalkya thus taught King Janaka. "This is Its highest goal, highest glory, highest world, and highest bliss. All other beings live on a fraction of this very bliss. [4.3.32]

"If there is a person who is physically perfect, is master of others, is affluent and is endowed with all possible human pleasures, his joy represents the maximum joy of a man. One hundred times this unit of human joy equals one unit of joy of the Pitris (manes), who have won their world. One hundred units of joy of the Pitris, who have won their world, equals one unit of joy in the world of the Gandharvas. One hundred units of joy in the world of the Gandharvas equals one unit of joy of the gods, who attain godhead through their meritorious actions. One hundred units of joy of these gods equals one unit of joy of the gods by birth, as also for one who is well versed in the Vedas, sinless and devoid of desires. One hundred units of joy of the gods by birth equals one unit of joy in the world of Prajapati, as also for one who is well versed in the Vedas, sinless and devoid of desires. One hundred units of joy in the world of Prajapati equals one unit of joy in the world of Hiranyagarbha, as also for one who is well versed in the Vedas, sinless and devoid of desires. This indeed is the supreme bliss. This is in the world of Brahman, O Emperor," said Yajnavalkya.

"I will give you a thousand cows, O venerable sir. Please tell me beyond this about liberation."

At this Yajnavalkya was afraid that the brilliant king might press him to open all the secrets. [4.3.33]

The above definition of the supreme bliss is similar to the one in Lesson 8 of Chapter 2, Anandavalli, of the *Taittiriya Upanishad*.

Yajnavalkya continued, "After rejoicing, wandering, and merely seeing the results of virtues and sins in the dream state, the Atman hastens back to its previous state, that is, the waking state. [4.3.34]

"Just as a heavily loaded cart moves on creaking, even so this body carrying the Atman moves along groaning when a person is about to breathe his last. [4.3.35]

"When the body becomes weak due to old age or illness, this Atman separates Itself from Its organs, just like a ripe mango, a fig or a Pipal fruit separates from its stem. Then It hastens back, as It came, to the place from which It started—to a new life. [4.3.36]

"Just as the policemen, the caretakers of the horses, and the village heads wait with food and drink for a king during his visit to their villages, and shout, 'Here he comes, here he comes,' even so do all creatures wait for a Brahmajnani, saying, 'Here comes Brahman, here It comes.' [4.3.37]

"Just as the policemen, the caretakers of the horses, and the village chiefs gather round a king who is about to depart, even so do all the organs gather round this Atman at the time when the body is struggling for its last breath." [4.3.38]

## Section 4.4

"When the body becomes weak and unconscious, these organs come to the Atman. The Atman, withdrawing its energy from the organs completely, comes to the heart. When the Atman, which also dwells in the eye, turns back from all sides, the dying man is not able to recognize any form. [4.4.1]

"When the Atman withdraws Its energy inward, the eye is united with the subtle body, and then people say that he (the body) does not see. The tongue is united with it and they say that he does not taste. The nose is united and then they say that he does not smell. Speech is united and then they say that he does not speak. The ear is united and then they say that he does not hear. The mind is united and then they say that he does not think. The skin is united and then they say that he does not touch. The intellect is united and then they say that he does not understand. But the upper part of his heart is brightened. With that brightness the Atman departs, either through the eye, or through the head, or through other parts of the body. When It goes out, Prana accompanies It. Along with Prana all the organs accompany It. The Atman is endowed with consciousness. It passes on to and enlightens another body with that consciousness. His knowledge, fruits of action, and previous impressions follow It. [4.4.2]

"Just as a caterpillar, having reached the end of a blade of grass, and catching another blade of grass attaches itself to it, even so this Atman, discarding this body and dispelling all ignorance, takes up a new body after drawing Itself towards it. [4.4.3]

"Just as a goldsmith, taking a piece of gold, turns it into another newer and more beautiful ornament, in the same way this Atman, having discarded this body and having dispelled all ignorance, takes up a newer and more beautiful body, which could be that of a Pitri, or of a Gandharva, or of a god, or of Prajapati, or of Brahma, or of any other being. [4.4.4]

"This Atman is Brahman indeed, and is associated with knowledge, with the mind, with Prana, with the eye, with the ear, with earth, with water, with air, with ether, with fire, with and without light, with and without desire, with and without anger, with righteousness and unrighteousness. It is associated with all things. This is what is meant when it is said, 'It is associated with this and associated with that.' As a man acts and as he conducts himself, so he becomes. The doer of good becomes good and the doer of evil becomes evil. He becomes virtuous by virtuous acts and sinful by sinful acts. Some say that a man is made of desires only. He resolves what he desires, he does what he resolves, and he attains the results of what he does. [4.4.5]

"On this there is this verse:
'To whatever object a man's mind is set, to that goes his subtle body with his actions being attached to it. After exhausting the fruits of whatever actions he did in this life, he comes back from the other world to this world again for new actions.'
"So much for a man who has desires. But for a man who does not have desires, who is freed from desires, whose desires are satisfied, whose only desire is to attain Atman—his Prana does not depart elsewhere. Being Brahman he goes to Brahman. [4.4.6]

"On this there is this verse:

'When all the desires residing in the heart of a man are cast away, then the mortal becomes immortal and realizes Brahman in this very world. As the slough of a snake lies on the anthill, dead and cast away, even so lies this body. But this bodiless and immortal Atman is the Supreme Brahman only. It is the light.'"

Then Janaka, the king of Videha, said, "Sir, for this I will give you a thousand cows." [4.4.7]

"There are these verses on this:

'The subtle but outstretched and ancient path to reach Him has been found by me. I have realized it. By that path the illumined knowers of Brahman becoming emancipated, reach heaven and even beyond it. [4.4.8]

'They say that the path has many colors—white, blue, brown, green and red. This path is known through the knowledge of the Vedas. Through that path only, a person of virtuous deeds becomes a knower of Brahman and becomes one with the Supreme Light. [4.4.9]

'Those who are devoted to *avidya* ("ignorance") eventually enter into blinding darkness. But those who are engaged in mere theoretical knowledge of the Atman, without trying to realize It, enter into even greater darkness. (See *Isha Upanishad* 9.) [4.4.10]

'People who are ignorant and devoid of knowledge of the Atman go to the joyless worlds covered with blinding darkness, after their death. (See *Isha Upanishad* 3.) [4.4.11]

'If a person knows the Atman and thinks, "I am this Atman," then with what desire and for whose sake should he worry about getting a new body. [4.4.12]

'He who has realized and intimately known the Atman that has penetrated this dangerous and inaccessible place (this body), becomes the maker of the universe. He is the maker of all. Actually, Atman is all and he is the very Atman. [4.4.13]

'If in this very life we have realized the Atman, then we have achieved the desired goal. Otherwise we face a great disaster. Those who know It become immortal, but others only face misery. [4.4.14]

'When a man directly sees the effulgent Atman, the Lord of what has been and will be, he no longer criticizes It. [4.4.15]

'The gods meditate upon that Immortal Light of all lights, around whom the year revolves with its days and nights, as longevity and immortality. [4.4.16]

'I believe that Atman alone to be the immortal Brahman, on which the five species of beings (the gods, Pitris, Gandharvas, demons and Rakshasas) and the unmanifested ether rest. Knowing that Atman, I am immortal. [4.4.17]

'Those who have known It as Prana of Prana, the eye of the eye, the ear of the ear, and the mind of the mind, have surely realized the ancient Brahman which existed before creation. [4.4.18]

'Brahman is to be known by the mind alone. There is no diversity in It. He who sees diversity in It goes from death to death. [4.4.19]

'That Atman should be realized only as a homogeneous entity. It is unknowable, unchangeable and free from impurities. The Atman is superior to the Akasha (the sky), is unborn, infinite and indestructible. [4.4.20]

'After knowing about the Atman alone (through the scriptures or through a guru), the intelligent seeker of Brahman should strive for realization. He should not reflect on many words, because it is tiring for his vocal organ.' [4.4.21]

"That infinite, birthless Atman is reflected in the intellect and is amid the organs. That controller of all, the lord of all, the ruler of all, lies in the space within the heart. He does not become greater by good works nor smaller by evil works. He is the embankment that keeps different worlds apart. The Brahmanas seek to know Him by the study of the Vedas, by performing yajnas, by gifts, by penance and by fasting. On knowing Him alone does one become a man of meditation. Desiring Him alone as their world, mendicants leave their homes. The ancient sages did not desire progeny. They said, 'What shall we do with progeny—we who have attained this Atman and this world?' Having risen above the desire for sons, the desire for wealth, the desire for worlds, they wander about as mendicants. For the desire for sons is the desire for wealth, and the desire for wealth is the desire for worlds. Both these are indeed desires only.

"This Atman is described as, 'not this, not this.' He is incomprehensible, because He can never be comprehended. He is indestructible because He can never be destroyed. He is unattached because He does not attach Himself. He is unfettered, He does not suffer, He is not injured. He who knows this is not overcome by these two thoughts, namely, 'For this reason I did an evil act,' or, 'For this reason I did a good act.' He overcomes both these. Things done and things left incomplete do not bother him. [4.4.22]

"This has been stated in the following hymn:
'The eternal glory of the knower of Brahman neither increases nor diminishes by action. Therefore, one should know the nature of that glory alone. Having known it, one is not affected by evil action.'

"Therefore, one who knows it as such becomes calm, self-controlled, withdrawn, patient and collected. He sees the Atman in his own self. Sin does not overcome him, he overcomes all sins. Sin does not burn him, he burns sin. Free from sin, free from taint, free from doubt, he becomes a true knower of Brahman. O Emperor, this is the world of Brahman. You have attained it." So spoke Yajnavalkya.

"Sir, I give you the kingdom of Videha and myself for your service," replied Janaka. [4.4.23]

"That infinite, birthless Atman is the enjoyer of all foods and the bestower of wealth (the results of action). He who knows Him as such obtains fruits of everybody's action. [4.4.24]

"This Atman is infinite, birthless, undecaying, indestructible, immortal and fearless. Brahman is fearless indeed. This Atman is

Brahman Himself. He who knows the Atman as such indeed becomes the fearless Brahman." [4.4.25]

*The last verse summarizes the whole Vedanta precisely.*

The following Sections 4.5 and 4.6 are almost the same as Sections 2.4 and 2.6, respectively.

## Section 4.5

Yajnavalkya had two wives, Maitreyi and Katyayani. Of these Maitreyi was the one who used to engage in discussing Brahman, but Katyayani was a simple housewife. Once Yajnavalkya decided to embrace another kind of life. [4.5.1]

Yajnavalkya said, "My dear Maitreyi, I am going to enter the monastic life and leave this householder's life now. Let me make a settlement between you and Katyayani." [4.5.2]

At this Maitreyi said, "Dear, if this whole earth is filled with wealth and becomes mine, will it make me immortal?"
"No," said Yajnavalkya, "your life will be exactly like that of wealthy people, but you cannot hope to achieve immortality through wealth." [4.5.3]

Maitreyi replied, "What shall I do with that which cannot give me immortality? Sir, please tell me about that only, which you know as the means of immortality." [4.5.4]

Yajnavalkya said, "Sweetheart, you have always been dear to me, and now you have increased what is dear to me. My dear, if you want I shall explain it to you. But while I am explaining, pay utmost attention to it." [4.5.5]

He said, "My dear, a husband is dear to a wife not for the sake of the husband, but for the sake of her own self. Also, a wife is dear to a husband not for the sake of the wife, but for the sake of his own self. Also, sons are dear to parents not for the sake of the sons, but for the sake of the parents themselves. Wealth is dear not for the sake of wealth, but for our own sake it is dear. A Brahmana is dear not for the sake of the Brahmana, but for our own sake he is dear. A Kshatriya is dear not for the sake of the Kshatriya, but for our own sake he is dear. The worlds are dear not for the sake of the worlds, but for our own sake they are dear. The gods are dear not for the sake of the gods, but for our own sake they are dear. Beings are dear not for the sake of beings, but for our own sake they are dear. Everything else is dear not for the sake of everything else, but for our own sake it is dear. My dear Maitreyi, Atman should be seen, heard of, reflected upon, and meditated upon. When Atman is seen, heard of, reflected upon and understood, all this is known. [4.5.6]

"The Brahmana rejects one who takes him to be different from Atman. The Kshatriya rejects one who takes him to be different from Atman. The worlds reject one who takes them to be different from Atman. The gods reject one who takes them to be different from Atman. Beings reject one who takes them to be different from Atman. Everything else rejects one who takes it to be different from Atman. This Brahmana, this Kshatriya, these worlds, these beings and everything else are only Atman. [4.5.7]

"As one is not able to grasp the particular notes by themselves of a drum that is beaten, but only by grasping the general note of the drum or the effect of particular strokes on it are those notes grasped; . . . [4.5.8]

"As one is not able to grasp the particular notes by themselves of a conch that is being blown, but only by grasping the general note of the conch or the effect of particular blowings on it are those notes grasped; . . . [4.5.9]

"As one is not able to grasp the particular notes by themselves of a vina (lute) that is being played on, but only by grasping the general note of the vina or the effect of particular playings on it are those notes grasped; . . . [4.5.10]

"As various forms of smoke arise from fire kindled with damp fuel, my dear, in the same way, the *Rigveda, Yajurveda, Samaveda, Atharvangiras*, history, mythology, arts, Upanishads, mantras, aphorisms, elucidations and commentaries came out of this great Being (Brahman). They indeed are the breath of It alone. [4.5.11]

"As the ocean is the merging place of all waters, as the skin is the merging place of all touches, as the nostrils are the merging place of all odors, as the tongue is the merging place of all tastes, as the eye is the merging place of all forms, as the ear is the merging place of all sounds, as the mind is the merging place of all intentions, as the intellect is the merging place of all knowledge, as the hands are the merging place of all actions, as the organ of generation is the merging place of all pleasures, as the anus is the merging place of all excretions, as the feet are the merging place of all walking, as speech is the merging place of all the Vedas, . . . [4.5.12]

"As a lump of salt thrown into water dissolves into water and cannot be taken out again, but from whichever part one takes the water, it has a salty taste, in the same way, my dear, this great, endless, infinite Being is a mass of consciousness. It emerges with these elements (the human body and its organs) and vanishes again with them. When it is gone there is no more individual consciousness. This is what I say, my dear." Thus spoke Yajnavalkya. [4.5.13]

Then Maitreyi replied, "Sir, just here you have thrown me into the midst of confusion."

Yajnavalkya said, "I do not understand. I am not saying anything confusing, my dear. This Atman is indeed unchangeable and indestructible. [4.5.14]

"When Atman appears with beings then there is duality. In duality one smells another, one sees another, one hears another, one speaks to another, one thinks of another, one knows another. But when everything has become Atman, then by what and whom should one see, by what and whom should one smell, by what and whom should one taste, by what and to whom should one speak, by what and whom should one hear, by what and of whom should one think, by what and whom should one touch, and by what and whom should one know? By what should one know That, through which all is known? This Atman is described as, 'not this, not this.' He is incomprehensible, because He can never be comprehended.

He is indestructible because He can never be destroyed. He is unattached because He does not attach Himself. He is unfettered, He does not suffer, He is not injured. My dear, indeed, by what should one know the knower? Thus you have been given the instruction, O Maitreyi. My dear, this indeed is the means of immortality." After saying this, Yajnavalkya left home. [4.5.15]

### Section 4.6

Now, here is the line of teachers:

Pautimashya received this knowledge of the *Shatapatha Brahmana* from Gaupavana, Gaupavana from another Pautimashya, this Pautimashya from another Gaupavana, this Gaupavana from Kaushika, Kaushika from Kaundinya, Kaundinya from Shandilya, Shandilya from Kaushika and Gautama, Gautama from Agniveshya, Agniveshya from Gargya, Gargya from another Gargya, this Gargya from Gautama, Gautama from Saitava, Saitava from Parasharyayana, Parasharyayana from Gargyayana, Gargyayana from Uddalakayana, Uddalakayana from Jabalayana, Jabalayana from Madhyandinayana, Madhyandinayana from Saukarayana, Saukarayana from Kashayana, Kashayana from Sayakayana, Sayakayana from Kaushikayani, Kaushikayani from Ghritakaushika, Ghritakaushika from Parasharyayana, Parasharyayana from Parasharya, Parasharya from Jatukarnya, Jatukarnya from Asurayana and Yaska, Asurayana from Traivani, Traivani from Aupajandhani, Aupajandhani from Asuri, Asuri from Bharadvaja, Bharadvaja from Atreya, Atreya from Manti, Manti from Gautama, Gautama from another Gautama, this Gautama from Vatsya, Vatsya from Shandilya, Shandilya from Kaishorya Kapya, Kaishorya Kapya from Kumaraharita, Kumaraharita from Galava, Galava from Vidarbhikaundinya, Vidarbhikaundinya from Vatsanapat Babhrava, Vatsanapat Babhrava from Pathin Saubhara, Pathin Saubhara from Ayasya Angirasa, Ayasya Angirasa from Abhuti Tvashtra, Abhuti Tvashtra from Vishvarupa Tvashtra, Vishvarupa Tvashtra from the two Ashvins, the Ashvins from Dadhyach Atharvana, Dadhyach Atharvana from Atharvana Daiva, Atharvana Daiva from Mrityu Pradhvamsana, Mrityu Pradhvamsana from Pradhvamsana, Pradhvamsana from Ekarshi, Ekarshi from Viprachitti, Viprachitti from Vyashti, Vyashti from Sanaru, Sanaru from Sanatana, Sanatana from Sanaga, Sanaga from

Parameshthin, and Parameshthin from Brahman. Brahman is eternal. Salutation to Brahman. [4.6.1-3]

## CHAPTER 5

### Section 5.1

The visible universe is full (infinite) and has come out of the invisible Brahman, which is also full (infinite). Even though the universe is of an infinite extension, it came out of Brahman, which still remains infinite.

Om is the ether-Brahman, the ether that is eternal. The son of Kauravyayani said that the ether containing air is "Kham." The seekers of Brahman have known that Om is the means of knowing It. Through Om only one knows It (Brahman), which should be known. [5.1.1]

### Section 5.2

The threefold offspring of Prajapati, namely, the gods, men and demons, lived with their father, Prajapati, as students practicing celibacy. After finishing their period of studentship the gods said to Prajapati, "Sir, please instruct us." He uttered the syllable "*Da*" to them and asked, "Did you understand?" They replied, "Yes, we did. You said to us, '*Damyata*,' which means, 'control yourselves.'" He said, "Yes, you have understood." [5.2.1]

Then the men said to him, "Sir, please instruct us." He uttered the syllable "*Da*" to them and asked, "Did you understand?" They replied, "Yes, we did. You said to us, '*Datta*,' which means, 'be charitable.'" He said, "Yes, you have understood." [5.2.2]

Then the demons said to Prajapati, "Sir, please instruct us." He uttered the syllable "*Da*" to them and asked, "Did you understand?" They replied, "Yes, we did. You said to us, '*Dayadhvam*,' which means, 'be merciful.'" He said, "Yes, you have understood."

This very instruction is repeated by the heavenly voice of thunder as "*Da, Da, Da*," which means, "control yourselves," "be charitable," and "be merciful." Therefore, one should learn these three—self-control, charity and mercy. [5.2.3]

## Section 5.3

Prajapati, mentioned above, is none other than this heart (*Hridaya*) in our body. It is also Brahman. It is all. This *Hridaya* consists of three syllables. One who knows "*Hri*" as the first syllable, receives gifts from his relatives and friends. "*Da*" is the second syllable. To him who knows thus, his relatives and others give power. One who knows "*Ya*" as the third syllable of *Hridaya* goes to the heavenly world. [5.3.1]

## Section 5.4

That Brahman was indeed this *Satya* ("Truth") only. He who knows this vast, adorable and firstborn Being as the Satya-Brahman, wins these worlds. Similarly, the enemy of him who knows this vast, adorable and firstborn Being as the Satya-Brahman, is vanquished. Satya is verily Brahman. [5.4.1]

## Section 5.5

In the beginning, after Prakriti (Nature) manifested itself, this universe was water only. That water created Satya (the manifested form of Brahman). Satya is Brahman. Brahman created Prajapati. Prajapati created the gods. The gods meditate upon Satya alone. This name "Satya" consists of three syllables. "Sa" is one syllable, "Ti" is another syllable, and "Ya" is the third syllable. The first and the last syllables are truth. The one in the middle is untruth. This untruth surrounded by truth on both sides is dominated by truth alone. Untruth does not hurt one who knows thus. [5.5.1]

That sun is Satya too. In the solar orb there is that Purusha, and in the right eye too, there is a Purusha. These two rest on each other. The Purusha in the sun rests on the Purusha in the eye through his rays. The Purusha in the eye rests on the Purusha in the sun through his Pranas. When a person is about to depart from his body he sees the solar orb clearly. The sun rays no longer come to him. [5.5.2]

Of that Purusha who is in the solar orb, "*Bhuh*" is the head. The head is one and the syllable "*Bhuh*" is one, too. "*Bhuvah*" is his arms. There are two arms, and "*Bhuvah*" has two syllables. "*Suvah*" is his two feet, and there are two syllables in "*Suvah*." His secret name is "*Ahah*," or the daylight. He who knows thus, destroys and shuns all sins. [5.5.3]

Of that Purusha (Person) who is in the right eye, "*Bhuh*" (earth) is the head. The head is one and the syllable "*Bhuh*" is one, too. "*Bhuvah*" (sky) is his arms. There are two arms, and "*Bhuvah*" has two syllables. "*Suvah*" (heaven) is his two feet, and there are two syllables in "*Suvah*." His secret name is "*Aham*," or I. He who knows thus, destroys and shuns all sins. [5.5.4]

## Section 5.6

That Purusha, radiant by nature, is reflected in the mind. He is in the interior of the heart and is of the size of a grain of rice or barley. Yet he is the Lord of all and the ruler of all. He rules whatever there is in the universe. [5.6.1]

## Section 5.7

It is said that lightning is Brahman. It is called lightning (*Vidyut*) from dispelling (*Vidanat*), because it dispels darkness. He who knows Brahman as lightning, dispels all his sins, because lightning is Brahman indeed. [5.7.1]

## Section 5.8

One should meditate upon speech (or the Vedas) as a cow. The speech-cow has four nipples which are the four sounds, "*Svaha*," "*Vashat*," "*Hanta*," and "*Svadha*," of the Vedas. The gods live on two of her nipples, the sounds "*Svaha*" and "*Vashat.*" Men live on the sound "*Hanta,*" and the Pitris on "*Svadha.*" Prana is her bull and mind her calf. [5.8.1]

(Offerings of food are made to the gods and fathers through the sacrificial fire by uttering the Vedic words *Svaha, Svadha,* etc.)

## Section 5.9

The fire which is within a person, and which digests the food in the stomach, is the *Vaishvanara* fire. When the ears are closed the sound that one hears is the sound produced by *Vaishvanara*. When one is about to pass away one does not hear this sound. [5.9.1]

## Section 5.10

When a man departs from this world, first he reaches air, which makes an opening for him in its body, like the hole in a chariot wheel. He goes upward through that and reaches the sun, which makes a hole for him in its body, like the hole (the dark part in the diaphragm) of a *tabla* drum. He goes upward through that and reaches the moon, who makes a hole for him in its body, like the hole of a drum. He goes through that and reaches a world where there is no grief and sorrow. He lives there for a long time. [5.10.1]

## Section 5.11

The suffering that a diseased person undergoes is a great penance. One who knows thus, wins a great world. Carrying a dead person to the forest is also a great penance. One who knows thus, wins a great world. Putting a dead man on the fire is a great penance too. One who knows thus, wins a great world. [5.11.1]

## Section 5.12

Some say that food is Brahman, but that is not correct, because food decomposes without Prana. Others say that Prana is

Brahman, but this is not correct either, because Prana cannot sustain itself without food. However, when food (materialism) and Prana (spiritualism) unite together they attain perfection. That is why, after understanding this principle, Pratrida said to his father, "I cannot honor or offend anybody by telling them this, because they must already know this principle."

His father disagreed with him. Raising his hand and trying to silence him, he said, "Pratrida, do not say so. There are people who believe either in food (materialism) or in Prana (spiritualism) only. They are unable to attain perfection by identifying with these two together."

Pratrida said, "Father, those people who are '*Vira*' (brave) can unite food and Prana together to achieve perfection. 'Vi' (of Vira) stands for food, and all beings indeed depend on food. 'Ra' (of Vira) stands for Prana. Prana is '*Ram*' (be happy), because all beings are happy if there is Prana. In one who knows this, all beings take refuge, and all beings take delight." [5.12.1]

## Section 5.13

(In this Section the Vedic terms *Uktha*, *Yajus*, *Saman* and *Kshatra* are equated with Prana. These terms occur in the *Karmakanda* portion of the Vedas.)

One should meditate upon Prana as the *Uktha* (a very potent laudatory hymn). Prana is indeed *Uktha* because it upholds this universe. To him who knows this is born a son who is a knower of Prana and who wins union with *Uktha* in the same world. [5.13.1]

One should meditate upon Prana as the *Yajus*. Prana is indeed *Yajus* because all beings are united (*Yuj*) if there is Prana. To him who knows this, all beings bring superiority by uniting, and he wins union with the *Yajus* in the same world. [5.13.2]

One should meditate upon Prana as the *Saman*. Prana is indeed *Saman* because all beings unite if there is Prana. To him who knows this, all beings bring superiority by uniting, and he wins union with the *Saman* in the same world. [5.13.3]

One should meditate upon Prana as the *Kshatra*. Prana is indeed *Kshatra* because it saves this body from getting wounds. He who knows this attains the *Kshatra* that needs no protector, and wins union with the *Kshatra* in the same world. [5.13.4]

## Section 5.14

(In this Section the importance of the Gayatri Mantra is described:)

*Bhumi* (the earth), *Antariksha* (the sky), and *Dyaus* (heaven) —these make eight syllables. The first foot of the *Gayatri* also has eight syllables (*Tat saviturvarenyam*). Therefore, the first foot of the Gayatri consists of those three worlds. He who knows the first foot of the Gayatri as above, wins whatever there is in those three worlds. [5.14.1]

*Richah*, *Yajumsi* and *Samani* (the plural forms of the three Vedas: *Rik*, *Yajus* and *Sama*) have eight syllables. The second foot of the Gayatri has eight syllables too (*Bhargo devasya dhimahi*). Therefore, this foot of the Gayatri consists of those three Vedas. He who knows this foot of the Gayatri as above, gains all the knowledge contained in the three Vedas. [5.14.2]

*Prana*, *Apana* and *Vyana* make eight syllables. The third foot of the Gayatri has eight syllables too (*Dhiyo yo nah prachodayat*). Therefore, the third foot of the Gayatri consists of the three Pranas. He who knows the third foot of the Gayatri as above, wins all creatures that exist in the universe.

Now the fourth, visible, supermundane foot of the Gayatri is this: "The sun that shines." That which is the fourth is called the "quarternary." It is the "visible" foot because the sun is visualized by Yogins. It is "supermundane" because he alone shines on the entire universe from above. He who knows this foot of the Gayatri as above, shines just like that with splendor and fame. [5.14.3]

That Gayatri (which represents three feet, three worlds, three Vedas and Prana) rests on this fourth, visible, supermundane foot, namely, the sun. That rests on truth. The eye is truth because it indeed is truth. If two persons came to us arguing that one saw and the other heard, we will believe him who saw. That truth rests on strength. Prana is strength, and therefore, truth rests on Prana. That is why they say that strength is more powerful than truth. Thus the Gayatri rests on Prana within the body. Gayatri is so called because it protects (*trayate*) the organs (*gayas*). The *Savitri Mantra* that the teacher imparts to the Brahmacharin during the *Upanayana* (sacred thread) ceremony is the same Gayatri. Gayatri saves the organs of the students to whom it is imparted. [5.14.4]

Some say that *Savitri* in the *Anushtubh* meter should be imparted to the pupil, because *Anushtubh* is the goddess of speech, and so they impart it. However, one should not do so. One should impart only that *Savitri Mantra* which is the Gayatri. If one knowing this secret of the three-footed Gayatri receives a large gift, even then it is worth it, because that gift is nothing compared to even one foot of the Gayatri. [5.14.5]

(*Savitri* in the *Anushtubh* meter has four feet and runs thus:
*Tatsaviturvrinimahe, vayam devasya bhojanam,*
*shreshtham sarvadhatam, turam bhagasya dhimahi.*)

The person who receives the three worlds full of wealth will receive treasure worth only the first foot of the Gayatri. The person who receives all the knowledge of the three Vedas will receive knowledge worth only the second foot of the Gayatri. The person who receives all creatures that exist in the world will receive something worth only the third foot of the Gayatri. While its fourth, visible and supermundane foot, which is the sun that shines, cannot be compared with anything materialistic. How could it be possible for someone to accept so many gifts? [5.14.6]

Praise of the Gayatri:
O Gayatri, the three worlds are your first foot, the three Vedas are your second foot, three Pranas are your third foot, and the shining sun is your fourth foot. Though you have these many feet, yet you are without feet, because you are not attainable. Salutation to you, the fourth, visible, supermundane foot! May the enemy (evil obstructions in the way of realization of the Gayatri) never gain his object! If a knower of Gayatri wishes that a certain person should not prosper, then that person does not prosper, and the

desired object of that person is also achieved by the knower of the Gayatri. [5.14.7]

On this there is a story:

Once Janaka, the Emperor of Videha, said to Budila Ashvatarashvi, "You call yourself a knower of the Gayatri, but then why do you carry loads like an elephant?"

He replied, "Because I do not know its mouth, O Emperor."

Janaka said, "Fire is its mouth. The fire burns a large amount of fuel that is put into its mouth. Even if one commits sins who knows thus, he burns them all up and becomes clean, pure, undecaying and immortal. [5.14.8]

### Section 5.15

Here mantra 1 of this Section is the reproduction of mantras 15 through 18 of the *Isha Upanishad*:

O Sun, like a shining golden lid you have, as it were, covered the entrance of the Truth (Brahman) within you. Please remove it so that I, a devotee of Brahman, may see Him.

O offspring of Prajapati, O lonely courser of the heavens, O supporter and controller of all, contract your rays, withdraw your brightness, so that I may see your most auspicious form.

That Person who dwells within you, I am indeed He. My breath is about to merge in the cosmic energy and my mortal body is about to be reduced to ashes. At this juncture, Om! O mind, remember my good deeds only.

O Agni, lead us by the good path so that we may enjoy the fruits of the good deeds we have done. Destroy all the deceitful sins in us. We salute you with words again and again. [5.15.1]

### CHAPTER 6

### Section 6.1

Om. He who knows the most superior and the best becomes the most superior and the best among his own people. Prana is indeed the most superior and the best among the organs. He who knows it thus, becomes the most superior and the best. [6.1.1]

He who knows the richest becomes the richest among his own people. Speech is the richest. He who knows it thus, becomes the richest among his own people. [6.1.2]

He who knows the stable basis becomes stabilized in this world and in the next. The eye indeed is the stable basis. He who knows it thus, becomes stabilized in this world and in the next. [6.1.3]

He who knows prosperity attains all desires, both divine and human. The ear indeed is prosperity. He who knows it thus, attains all desires, both divine and human. [6.1.4]

He who knows the abode becomes the abode of his people as well as of others. Mind is the abode (of all the organs). He who knows it thus, becomes the abode of his people. [6.1.5]

He who knows the procreant becomes endowed with offspring and animals. The organ of generation is indeed the procreant. He who knows it thus, becomes endowed with offspring and animals. [6.1.6]

The story in the rest of this Section, mantras 6.1.7 through 6.1.14, also occurs in Section 5.1 of the *Chhandogya Upanishad*:

Once the senses, disputing among themselves to claim superiority, went to Brahma and asked, "Who is superior among us?"
He replied, "He by whose departure the body looks the worst is the best of you." [6.1.7]

Speech then departed, and having stayed away for a year, returned. He then asked, "How have you been without me?"
They replied, "Like the mute without speaking, but breathing with the breath, seeing with the eye, hearing with the ear, thinking with the mind, and procreating with the organ of generation. Thus we lived." Then speech entered the body. [6.1.8]

The eye then departed, and having stayed away for a year, returned. He then asked, "How have you been able to live without me?"

They replied, "Like the blind without seeing, but breathing with the breath, speaking with the tongue, hearing with the ear, thinking with the mind, and procreating with the organ of generation. Thus we lived." Then the eye entered the body. [6.1.9]

The ear then departed, and having stayed away for a year, returned. He then asked, "How have you been able to live without me?"

They replied, "Like the deaf without hearing, but breathing with the breath, seeing with the eye, speaking with the tongue, thinking with the mind, and procreating with the organ of generation. Thus we lived." Then the ear entered the body. [6.1.10]

The mind then departed, and having stayed away for a year, returned. He then asked, "How have you been able to live without me?"

They replied, "Like idiots without knowing through the mind, but breathing with the breath, seeing with the eye, speaking with the tongue, hearing with the ear, and procreating with the organ of generation. Thus we lived." Then the mind entered the body. [6.1.11]

The organ of generation then departed, and having stayed away for a year, returned. He then asked, "How have you been able to live without me?"

They replied, "Like the impotents without procreating, but breathing with the breath, seeing with the eye, speaking with the tongue, hearing with the ear, and thinking with the mind. Thus we lived." Then the organ of generation entered the body. [6.1.12]

Now, when Prana was about to leave, tearing up the other senses, as a big Sindhu-born horse might uproot the peg to which he is tied, they gathered round him and said, "Sir, please do not depart. We shall never be able to live without you."

He said, "Then make me offerings."

"Very well," they said. [6.1.13]

Then speech said to him, "If I am the richest, that richness belongs to you." The eye said to him, "The stable basis which I have now belongs to you." Then the ear said to him, "The prosperity that belongs to me is yours now." The mind said to him, "If I am the abode, you are that now." The organ of generation said, "That procreant which I am, you are now."

Prana asked the other senses (organs), "What will be my food and clothing?"

They replied, "Whatever food there is, from the bird's food to the dog's food, is all yours too; and water is your clothing."

He who knows thus, never has to eat or accept anything that should not be eaten. For the above reason sages well versed in the Vedas sip a little water before and after taking food. Then they think that they are dressing this Prana. [6.1.14]

### Section 6.2

The following story of Shvetaketu also occurs in Sections 5.3 through 5.10 of the *Chhandogya Upanishad*:

Once, Shvetaketu Aruneya went to the assembly of the Panchalas. There he met king Pravahana Jaivali, whose servants attended on him. Seeing him the king asked, "My boy, have you been instructed by your father?"

"Yes, sir," he said. [6.2.1]

"Do you know how these beings take different paths after death?"

"No, sir."

"Do you know how they return here again?"

"No, sir."

"Do you know why the other world is never filled, even though so many people die repeatedly?"

"No, sir."

"Do you know, after offering how many libations does water rise up and speak in a human voice?"

"No, sir."

"Do you know the means to reach the path of the gods or the path of the Pitris, through which people gain access to the worlds of the gods or the Pitris? For we have heard these words of the mantra:

'I have heard of two paths for mortals, the path of the gods and the path of the Pitris. Going along these paths the universe is interconnected. The paths lie between heaven and earth.'"

"I do not know a single one of these questions." [6.2.2]

The king invited him to stay. Ignoring the invitation, the boy hurried back to his home. He went to his father and said, "You actually told me that you had fully instructed me."

"What happened, my brilliant son?"

Shvetaketu said, "That ordinary Kshatriya asked me five questions and I could not answer even one of them."

"What were those?"

"These," he said, and told him the questions. [6.2.3]

His father said, "Son, I taught you everything that I knew. Now let us go there and live with him as his students."

"Please go by yourself."

Then Gautama went to King Pravahana Jaivali's court. The king had him seated, had water served to him, and made reverential offerings. Then he said, "O revered Gautama, I would like to offer you a boon." [6.2.4]

Gautama replied, "O king, you have promised me a boon. Instead, please tell me what you spoke about to my boy." [6.2.5]

The king said, "Those are but divine boons, O Gautama. Please ask for a boon fit for humans." [6.2.6]

Gautama said, "Sir, you are aware that I could ask for gold, cattle, horses, maidservants, attendants and apparel. (But I do not want them.) Therefore, please do not hesitate to give me that plentiful, infinite and endless wealth."

"Then you must have it in a prescribed formal way."

"I come to you as a student."

In ancient times people approached a teacher only by verbal request. So Gautama lived with the king by merely announcing that he was his student. [6.2.7]

The king said to him, "O Gautama, please do not be offended, just as your grandfathers were not with mine. Before you, this knowledge was never imparted to the Brahmanas. But I shall impart it to you. Who can refuse you when you speak thus. [6.2.8]

"O Gautama, that heaven is a sacrificial fire, the sun is its fuel, the rays are the smoke, the day is the flame, the four directions its embers, and the intermediate directions its sparks. In this fire the gods offer the oblation of faith. Out of that oblation arises Soma, the king. [6.2.9]

"O Gautama, Parjanya (the god of rain) is the sacrificial fire. The year itself is its fuel, the cloud is its smoke, lightning is the flame, the thunderbolt is the ember, and the rumblings of the clouds are the sparks. In this fire the gods offer the oblation of Soma, the king. From that offering the rain is produced. [6.2.10]

"O Gautama, the world is the sacrificial fire, the earth is its fuel, the fire is its smoke, the night is the flame, the moon its embers, and the stars are the sparks. Into this fire the gods offer the libation of rain. From this offering food is produced. [6.2.11]

"Man, O Gautama, is the sacrificial fire, his open mouth is its fuel, Prana is the smoke, speech is the flame, the eye is the ember, and the ear is the spark. Into this fire the gods offer the oblation of food. From that oblation the seed is produced. [6.2.12]

"O Gautama, woman is the sacrificial fire. . . . In this fire the gods offer the libation of seed. From this offering a human is born. He lives as long as he is destined to live. When he dies— [6.2.13]

Then they carry him to be put on the funeral pyre. The fire itself becomes his fire, the fuel his fuel, the smoke his smoke, the flame his flame, the ember his ember, and the sparks his sparks. In this fire the gods offer the man. From that offering the man emerges with a glowing complexion. [6.2.14]

Those who know this meditation on fire as above, and the others living in the forest who meditate on the Satya-Brahman with faith, reach the deity of flame, from him to the deity of the day, from him to the deity of the bright fortnight, from him to the deity of the six months during which the sun travels northward, from there to the world of the gods, from there to the sun, and from there to lightning. Then a Purusha, created from the mind of Brahma, comes and leads them to the world of Brahma. Becoming perfect they stay in the world of Brahma for a long time. They do not return to this world any more. [6.2.15]

However, those who win various worlds through sacrifices, gifts and penances, reach smoke, from there to night, from there to the dark fortnight, from there to the six months when the sun travels southward, from there to the world of the Pitris, and then to the moon. Reaching the moon they become food (objects of use and abuse by the gods). There the gods eat (use) them, just as the priests drink the bright Soma juice saying, "more, more." When the fruits of their past work are exhausted they reach the very sky, from the sky to the air, from the air to rain, and from rain to the earth. Reaching the earth they become food. Then they are again offered in the fire of a male, and in the fire of a female. Then they are born to perform rites and to rise to other worlds. Thus they go on in a cycle of births and deaths. Those who do not know these two ways become insects, moths, and all the creatures that bite. [6.2.16]

## Section 6.3

A brief description of the process discussed in this Section occurs in mantra 5.2.4 of the *Chhandogya Upanishad*. Here it is in detail:

He who wishes to attain greatness should do as follows: On an auspicious day of a bright fortnight, under a constellation with a masculine name, during the northward journey of the sun, he should take a vow for twelve days relating to the *Upasads* (a rite connected with the Jyotishtoma yajna in which the sacrificer lives on milk only). He should gather all herbs and grains in a cup or bowl made of fig (*Gular*) wood, sweep and plaster the floor, add fuel to the household fire, spread the Kusha grass, purify the ghee according to the rules, insert the paste made of those herbs, and offer oblations saying these mantras:

"O fire, I offer their portion to all those gods under you who kill people's desires. May they be pleased and satisfy me with all objects of desire. Svaha. To that all-fulfilling goddess who, holding on to you remains unfavorable, thinking that she is the support of all, I offer this flow of ghee. Svaha." [6.3.1]

Offering libations in the fire, uttering the mantra, "This is to the eldest, Svaha," "This is to the best, Svaha," he should drop the remnant sticking to the ladle into the paste. Offering libations into the fire saying, "This is to Prana, Svaha," "This is to the richest, Svaha," he should drop the remnant sticking to the ladle into the paste. Offering libations into the fire saying, "This is to speech, Svaha," "This is to that which is stable, Svaha," he should drop the remnant sticking to the ladle into the paste. Offering libations into the fire saying, "This is to the eye, Svaha," "This is to that which has prosperity, Svaha," he should drop the remnant sticking to the ladle into the paste. Offering libations into the fire saying, "This is to the ear, Svaha," "This is to abode, Svaha," he should drop the remnant sticking to the ladle into the paste. Offering libations into the fire saying, "This is to the mind, Svaha," "This is to the procreant, Svaha," he should drop the remnant sticking to the ladle into the paste. Offering libations into the fire saying, "This is to the organ of generation, Svaha," he should drop the remnant sticking to the ladle into the paste. [6.3.2]

Offering libations into the fire saying, "This is to the fire, Svaha," he should drop the remnant sticking to the ladle into the paste. Offering libations into the fire saying, "This is to the moon, Svaha," he should drop the remnant sticking to the ladle into the paste. Offering libations into the fire saying, "This is to the earth, Svaha," he should drop the remnant sticking to the ladle into the paste. Offering libations into the fire saying, "This is to the sky, Svaha," he should drop the remnant sticking to the ladle into the paste. Offering libations into the fire saying, "This is to heaven, Svaha," he should drop the remnant sticking to the ladle into the paste. Offering libations into the fire saying, "This is to the earth, the sky, and heaven, Svaha," he should drop the remnant sticking to the ladle into the paste. Offering libations into the fire saying, "This is to the Brahmana, Svaha," he should drop the remnant sticking to the ladle into the paste. Offering libations into the fire saying, "This is to the Kshatriya, Svaha," he should drop the remnant sticking to the ladle into the paste. Offering libations into the fire saying, "This is to the past, Svaha," he should drop the remnant sticking to the ladle into the paste. Offering libations into the fire saying, "This is to the future, Svaha," he should drop the remnant sticking to the ladle into the paste. Offering libations into the fire saying, "This is to the universe, Svaha," he should drop the remnant sticking to the ladle into the paste. Offering libations into the fire saying, "This is to all, Svaha," he should drop the remnant sticking to the ladle into the paste. Offering libations into the fire saying, "This is to Prajapati, Svaha," he should drop the remnant sticking to the ladle into the paste. [6.3.3]

Then he touches the paste uttering the mantra: "You are moving in all bodies, you are blazing, you are complete, you are steadfast, you are where everything merges, you are Himkara (a portion of the *Samaveda*) and are chanted, you are the Udgitha and are sung, you are the call for recital as well as the response thereto, you are the brightness in the rain cloud, you are pervasive, you are commanding, you are food, you are light, you are death, and you are the absorber of all." [6.3.4]

Then he lifts the vessel of the paste saying, "You are all-knowing; we too are aware of your greatness. Prana is indeed the king, the lord and the ruler. May that king and lord make me the ruler." [6.3.5]

Then he drinks the paste uttering these mantras: "The sun is adorable, the wind blows sweetly, the rivers are pouring sweetness, may the herbs be sweet to us. This is to the earth, Svaha. We meditate upon the glory of the sun. May the days and the nights be sweet. May the dust of the earth be fragrant. May heaven, our father, be propitious. This is to the sky, Svaha. May he guide our intellect. May the Soma vine be sweet to us. May the sun be pleasant. May the directions be agreeable to us. This is to heaven, Svaha."
Then he repeats the whole Gayatri and all the *Madhumati* verses, and says at the end, "May I myself be all this. This is to the earth, sky and heaven, Svaha." Then he drinks the remnant of the paste, washes his hands, and lies behind the fire with head eastward. In the morning he salutes the sun with this mantra: "You are the one lotus of the directions. May I be the one lotus of men." Then he comes back by the same way that he went out, sits behind the fire, and repeats the line of teachers. [6.3.6]

Uddalaka Aruni, after imparting this to his pupil Vajasaneya Yajnavalkya, said that even if someone sprinkled the paste on a dry stump, branches would grow and leaves spring forth. [6.3.7]

Vajasaneya Yajnavalkya, after imparting this to his pupil Madhuka Paingya, said that even if someone sprinkled the paste on a dry stump, branches would grow and leaves spring forth. [6.3.8]

Madhuka Paingya, after imparting this to his pupil Chula Bhagavitti, said that even if someone sprinkled the paste on a dry stump, branches would grow and leaves spring forth. [6.3.9]

Chula Bhagavitti, after imparting this to his pupil Janaki Ayasthuna, said that even if someone sprinkled the paste on a dry stump, branches would grow and leaves spring forth. [6.3.10]

Janaki Ayasthuna, after imparting this to his pupil Satyakama Jabala, said that even if someone sprinkled the paste on a dry stump, branches would grow and leaves spring forth. [6.3.11]

Satyakama Jabala, after imparting this to his pupils said that even if someone sprinkled the paste on a dry stump, branches would grow and leaves spring forth. One should not teach this to anyone other than one's son or disciple. [6.3.12]

Four things should be of fig wood, namely, the ladle, the bowl, the fuel, and the two churning rods. The cultivated grains should be of ten kinds, namely, rice, barley, sesame, black beans, millet, panic seeds, wheat, lentils, pulse, and vetches. After grinding them he should soak them in yogurt, honey, and ghee, and offer them as a libation. [6.3.13]

## Section 6.4

The earth is the essence of all beings, water is the essence of the earth, herbs are the essence of water, flowers are the essence of the herbs, grains are the essence of the flowers, man is the essence of the grains, and the seed is the essence of man. [6.4.1]

Prajapati thought, "Let me make an abode for it (the seed of man)." He created woman. After creating her, he put her down on the earth and meditated on her. That is why a woman should be meditated upon. In creating woman, Prajapati applied all his skill of creativity. [6.4.2]

Woman is like a yajna. Her organ of generation is the place of yajna. Her hair is the *Kusha* grass. He who considers the whole process of procreation, from union with a woman to childbirth, as an auspicious yajna, and treats the woman as such, gets the fruits of good deeds of the woman. On the other hand, he who does not know this secret loses his fruits of good deeds to the woman. [6.4.3]

Knowing this, Uddalaka Aruni, Naka Maudgalya, and Kumaraharita said, "Many men, Brahmanas only in name, who have union with women without knowing the above secret, depart from this world impotent and devoid of merits. He who considers the woman as the means of satisfying his lust only—his seed (semen) is wasted." [6.4.4]

A person whose seed (semen) has been wasted should repent and think why it happened. He should touch water with his thumb and ring finger and then touch with them the area of the heart on his chest, and his forehead between the eyebrows, where the brain is (because what happened was caused by the misguided heart and mind). Then he should make this resolution: "This will not happen again. I shall regain my chastity, mental strength and fortune. May the fire god restore my lost position." [6.4.5]

If he happens to see his shadow in water, then he should utter this mantra, "May the gods give me luster, vigorous organs, reputation, wealth and merits."

The wife is graceful indeed, because she has put on clean clothes. Then he should approach that beautiful woman and talk to her. [6.4.6]

If she does not yield to him he should win her over by giving some desired gifts. If she does not yield still, he should persuade her by any means, and overpower her with this mantra: "I take away your virtue through mine consisting of manhood." Then she indeed becomes without virtue, as barren. [6.4.7]

If she yields to him, he should utter this mantra: "I impart virtue to you through mine consisting of manhood." Then both gain reputation (as parents). [6.4.8]

If a man wants his wife to be attracted to him he should please her by fulfilling all her desires. He should sit near her and caress her. He should utter this mantra in his mind: "O god of love, you are helping me bring out the essence of my organs and heart, as if you are the essence of my sense organs. Make my wife reciprocate my love. May she be in my control, like a doe is under a hunter's control when hit by a poison-dipped arrow." [6.4.9]

If a man wants his wife not to bear children, and instead wants her to lead a celibate life with him, then he should make her happy in all respects. The couple should practice *pranayama* (controlled breathing) and should unite their physical and mental strengths, not producing children, and leading a life of Brahmacharya. [6.4.10]

On the other hand, if the husband wants children from his wife, then he should try to get her cooperation in all matters. When both desire to have children the wife becomes pregnant. [6.4.11]

If a man's wife has a lover and he wishes to hurt him, he should feed the fire in an unbaked earthen pot, spread the tips of reeds upside down, smeared with ghee, in the fire, uttering the following mantras: "You have offered in my burning fire your Prana and Apana. I take away so and so." "You have offered in my burning fire your sons and cattle. I take away so and so." "You have offered in my burning fire your fruits of yajna and good deeds. I take away so and so." "You have offered in my burning fire your longings and hopes. I take away so and so."

The man whom a Brahmana versed in rites curses, departs from this world impotent and devoid of virtues. Therefore, one should not even joke with the wife of a Vedic scholar who is versed in this rite, because the Vedic scholar may become his enemy. [6.4.12]

If one's wife is going through her period of menstruation, she should drink from a vessel made of bell-metal, and no Shudra man or woman should touch her. At the end of three nights she should take a bath and put on clean clothes. Then she should thresh rice (do any hard work). [6.4.13]

If he wishes to beget a light-complexioned son, who would be versed in the Vedas and attain full longevity, he should have rice cooked in milk, mix ghee with it, and eat it with his wife. Then such a son would be born to them. [6.4.14]

If he wishes to beget a brown-complexioned son, who would be versed in the Vedas and attain full longevity, he should have rice cooked in yogurt, mix ghee with it, and eat it with his wife. Then such a son would be born to them. [6.4.15]

If he wishes to beget a son with dark complexion and red eyes, who would be a scholar and attain full longevity, he should have rice cooked, mix ghee with it, and eat it with his wife. Then such a son would be born to them. [6.4.16]

If he wishes to beget a daughter, who would be a scholar and attain full longevity, he should have rice and sesame seed cooked together, mix ghee with it, and eat it with his wife. Then such a daughter would be born to them. [6.4.17]

If he wishes to beget a son, who would be a reputed scholar, attend assemblies, speak words that one likes to hear, be versed in all the Vedas, and attain full longevity, he should have rice cooked with beef from a young or a mature bull, mix ghee with it, and eat it with his wife. Then such a son would be born to them. [6.4.18]

Early in the morning he purifies ghee according to the method in the Sthalipaka (a cookbook), and offers the food in an earthen pot, repeatedly taking a small quantity at a time, uttering the mantra: "This is to the fire, Svaha." "This is to Anumati, Svaha." "This is to the bright sun, the creator of the universe, Svaha."

After offering the oblations, he takes away the remaining food, eats a portion of it, and gives the rest to his wife. Then he washes his hands, fills the water vessel, and sprinkles her three times with the water, uttering this mantra: "O Vishvavasu, rise from here and seek another young wife who is with her husband. I shall join my wife." [6.4.19]

Afterwards he embraces her, uttering this mantra, "I am *Ama* (Prana), and you are *Sa* (Speech). You are speech and I am Prana. I am Saman and you are Rik. I am heaven and you are the earth. Come, let us try to have a son together." [6.4.20]

Then, separating from her he should say, "We united together, just as the earth and the sky meet, to produce offspring. Now we are separating."

He should think, talk and have desires similar to his wife's to make her happy. He should caress her hair from top to bottom thrice, and then should say, "May Lord Vishnu make your womb healthy, may the creator shape the fetus well in your womb, may the lord support the fetus firmly. O my praiseworthy sweetheart with beautiful hair, may you carry my child in your womb. May the divine Ashvin physicians, wearing garlands of lotus flowers, help the fetus grow. [6.4.21]

"The golden bright pair of husband and wife is like two wooden sticks that produce fire. When the two wooden sticks are rubbed, fire is produced. Similarly, with the union of the couple an offspring is produced. With the help of the divine Ashvin physicians we will welcome the birth of the child. Just as there is fire within the earth, Indra in heaven, and air in the directions, so do I establish this fetus in your womb." [6.4.22]

At the time of the birth of the child he should sprinkle water on the would-be mother and say this mantra: "As the wind makes movement on the surface of a lake, similarly may your fetus make movement in the womb to come out of it. This is the path of the Jivatman to come out in this world. O Jivatman, come out by breaking the diaphragm in the womb along with the umbilical cord." [6.4.23]

After the son is born, he should feed the fire, take the child in his lap, put a mixture of yogurt and ghee in a bell-metal vessel, and offer it in the fire, repeatedly taking little quantities, uttering this mantra: "May I, growing in this home of mine, support a thousand people. May the goddess of fortune with offspring and cattle never desert his line. Svaha. I offer to you with sound mind the Prana that is in me. Svaha. If I have performed any deed in excess or too little in this rite, may the all-knowing and highly benevolent fire make that deed of mine perfect." [6.4.24]

Then bringing his own mouth to the child's right ear, he should repeat this thrice, "Speech, speech, speech." Then, mixing yogurt, honey and ghee together, he should feed the child with a bare gold strip, saying these mantras: "I put the earth in you," "I put the sky in you," "I put heaven in you," "I put the earth, sky and heaven—all in you." [6.4.25]

Then he names the child, saying, "You are the Veda." That is indeed his secret name. [6.4.26]

Then handing over the child to his mother, he helps her feed him, uttering this mantra: "O Sarasvati, that breast of yours which is fruitful, the sustainer of all, full of milk, the bestower of deserts, generous, and by which you nourish all worthy beings, put that here so that my son can be fed." [6.4.27]

Then he addresses the mother thus, "You are the worthy Arundhati, the wife of Mitravaruna (Vasishtha), and with me as your partner you have borne a male child. You, who have blessed me with a son, be the mother of many sons."

To that son who is born to a Brahmana endowed with such knowledge, they say, "Oh, you have surpassed your father, and you have surpassed your grandfather. You have attained the highest limit through your fortune, fame and Brahmanical power." [6.4.28]

## Section 6.5

Because of the importance of the mother described as above, the line of the teachers of the Upanishad is enumerated here based on their mothers" names, unlike in Sections 2.6 and 4.6 of this Upanishad, where the names of the teachers are after their fathers' names. The teacher's name is after the disciple's name, going in an ascending order:

This is the line of teachers: Pautimashi's son received the
knowledge of the Upanishad from Katyayani's son, the latter from
Gautami's son, he from Bharadvaji's son, Bharadvaji's son from
Parashari's son, he from Aupasvasti's son, Aupasvati's son from another Parashari's son, that Parashari's son from Katyayani's son, the
latter from Kaushiki's son, Kaushiki's son from Alambi's son, he
from Vaiyaghrapadi's son, Vaiyaghrapadi's son from Kanvi's son
and Kapi's son, Kapi's son from Atreyi's son, Atreyi's son from
Gautami's son, Gautami's son from Bharadvaji's son, Bharadvaji's
son from (another) Parashari's son, Parashari's son from Vatsi's son,
Vatsi's son from (another) Parashari's son, he from Varkaruni's son,
this Varkaruni's son from another Varkaruni's son, he from
Artabhagi's son, Artabhagi's son from Shaungi's son, Shaungi's son
from Sankriti's son, Sankriti's son from Alambayani's son,
Alambayani's son from Alambi's son, Alambi's son from Jayanti's
son, Jayanti's son from Mandukayani's son, Mandukayani's son
from Manduki's son, Manduki's son from Shandili's son, Shandili's
son from Rathitari's son, he from Bhaluki's son, Bhaluki's son from
Kraunchiki's two sons, Kraunchiki's sons from Vaidabhriti's son,
Vaidabhriti's son from Karshakeyi's son, Karshakeyi's son from
Prachinayogi's son, Prachinayogi's son from Sanjivi's son, Sanjivi's
son from Prashni's son Asurivasin, Prashni's son from Asurayana,
and Asurayana from Asuri. [6.5.1-2]

Asuri learned it from Yajnavalkya, he from Uddalaka,
Uddalaka from Aruna, Aruna from Upaveshi, Upaveshi from Kushri,
Kushri from Vajashravas, Vajashravas from Badhyoga's son Jihvavat,
he from Asita Varshagana, he from Harita Kashyapa, Harita
Kashyapa from Shilpa Kashyapa, Shilpa Kashyapa from Kashyapa
Naidhruva, he from Vach, Vach from Ambhini, and he from Aditya.
These Shukla Yajurs (verses) received from the sun are explained
by Yajnavalkya Vajasaneya. The line of teachers is the same up to
Sanjivi's son. Beyond that, the son of Sanjivi received it from
Mandukayani's son, Mandukayani's son from Mandavya, he from
Kautsa, Kautsa from Mahitthi, Mahitthi from Vamakakshayana, he
from Shandilya, Shandilya from Vatsya, Vatsya from Kushri, Kushri
from Yajnavachas Rajastambayana, Yajnavachas Rajastambayana
from Tura Kavasheya, Tura Kavasheya from Prajapati, and Prajapati
from Brahman. Brahman is eternal. Salutation to Brahman. [6.5.3-4]

*****

# INDEX

do not sip or spit facing the fire - 114

all is water - 266, 175